Risk management in agriculture

Risk management in agriculture

EDITED BY **PETER J. BARRY**

IOWA STATE UNIVERSITY PRESS / AMES, IOWA

© 1984 The Iowa State University Press. All rights reserved

Composed and printed by The Iowa State University Press, Ames, Iowa 50010

First edition, 1984

Library of Congress Cataloging in Publication Data
Main entry under title:

Risk management in agriculture.

    Includes bibliographical references and index.
    1. Agriculture—Economic aspects. 2. Risk management. I. Barry, Peter J.
HD1434.R57   1984   630′.68   84–108782
ISBN 0–8138–1523–1

CONTENTS

PART 2.   Risk analysis in farm businesses

PART 3.   Financial dimensions of risk in agriculture

PART 4.   Policy issues and agricultural risk

PREFACE

THIS BOOK'S PURPOSE is to provide a comprehensive coverage of concepts, methods of analysis, and practical applications involving risk analysis in agriculture. The focus is on the farm production sector of agriculture in the United States, although the distribution of risks and risk bearing among input suppliers, primary producers, product handlers, and other stages of the food system is also considered. The risk consequences for farms with different structural characteristics are developed, as are the relationships between agricultural risks, financial markets, and public policy.

Within this context, the book's content addresses the following types of questions: What is risk? Why is it important? How are risks modeled and measured? Where do agricultural risks originate? What are farmers' attitudes toward risk? How can risks be effectively dealt with? and Who should deal with risks, including the public sector's role? Underlying all of these questions are concerns about the proper concepts and tools for studying risky behavior and improving risky decision making. Resolving these questions presents important and unique challenges to empirical analysis.

The book is intended for several types of users. It is well suited for students in agicultural economics programs, especially graduate and advanced undergraduate students with interests in the risk concepts of agricultural policy, finance, production economics, market analysis, and economic development. The book is also designed for professional agricultural economists in universities, industry, and government who have research and analysis responsibilities involving risk considerations in agriculture, and for extension specialists concerned with educational programs on risk management.

The book has resulted from the work of Western Regional Research Committee W-149 entitled "An Economic Evaluation of Managing Market Risks in Agriculture," which was active from 1976 to 1982. Cooperating agencies were the agricultural experiment stations of California, Colorado, Georgia, Illinois, Indiana, Michigan, Missouri, Nebraska, Ohio, Oklahoma, Oregon, Texas, Washington, Wyoming, and the Economic Research Service (ERS) of the U.S. Department of Agriculture (USDA), and the Board of Governors of the Federal Reserve System. The project's administrative advisors were B. Delworth Gardner, University of California, and Lloyd C. Halvorsen, formerly with the USDA. The Farm Foundation, under the direction of R. J. Hildreth, also contributed periodic support, both financial and inspirational, to the project's development and continuing activities.

While the authors of individual chapters carried the greatest weight in the book's development, it is important to acknowledge the inspiration, guidance, manuscript reviews, and even occasional prodding provided by Warren F. Lee, Rulon D. Pope, Lindon J. Robison, and Odell Walker who, together with the editor, formed the book's publication committee. Many other colleagues also provided critical reviews and suggestions. Finally, the editor expresses his grateful appreciation to Beatrice Harrell who worked tirelessly, cheerfully, and productively to help prepare the final copy.

Peter J. Barry

Organization of the book

THE BOOK IS ORGANIZED into four parts that consider the microfoundations of risk analysis, farm management applications, financial dimensions of risk, and public policy responses. Chapter 1 establishes the setting for risk management in agriculture. Chapter 2 then considers the risk attitudes of agricultural decision makers. The expected utility model is emphasized along with lexicographic utility and multiple-goal functions. Empirical studies of farmers' risk attitudes are reviewed based on different methodological approaches.

Chapters 3 and 4 focus on conceptualizing, modeling, and measuring risk in decision analysis. Objective and subjective concepts of probability are appraised for use in economic analysis. Chapter 3 considers alternative statistical estimation procedures using historic data to derive objective measures of risk. Chapter 4 reviews subjective probability concepts, evaluates alternative techniques of probability assessment, and considers their applicability in agricultural economics.

Chapters 5 and 6 present various decision rules and risk efficiency criteria for use in economic analysis. Chapter 5 emphasizes the relationships among alternative decision rules and the expected utility model. Chapter 6 introduces several efficiency criteria for ordering risky choices into efficient and inefficient sets. The traditional mean-variance criterion, along with recent developments in stochastic dominance, are evaluated in terms of trade-offs between their general applicability and their discriminatory power.

Chapter 7 establishes a noneconomic perspective, based on the psychology literature, for evaluating the traditional methods of measuring risk and risk attitudes. The elicitation procedures for utility functions and subjective probabilities are appraised in light of their predictive capacity. Cognitive biases, statistical sophistication, hypothetical gaming, multiple attitudes, and learning phenomena illustrate the forces influencing predictive accuracy.

Chapters in Part 2 address the risk analysis of farm businesses. Chapter 8 identifies the sources of agricultural risks (production, market, technological, legal, financial, human) and appraises farmers' various responses to risk in production, marketing, and finance. Modification of the decision process is another risk response. Several procedures for generating subjective probabilities are illustrated.

Chapter 9 focuses on alternative methods of risk analysis at the firm level. Included are quadratic risk programming, minimization of total absolute deviations, and simulation analysis. The models are introduced, appraised, and illustrated in research applications.

Chapters 10 and 11 focus on applications of risk programming and simulation at the farm level. Chapter 10 presents the application of quadratic programming, including the data needs, model development, and interpretation of results. Chapter 11 treats simulation analysis in a similar fashion. Several simulation studies of farm growth and survival are discussed and evaluated.

Chapter 12 focuses on educational programs to teach students, farmers, and others about risk management in agriculture. Payoff matrix and decision tree approaches are presented, and guidelines on developing educational programs for risk management are suggested.

Part 3 focuses on the financial dimensions of risk in agriculture. Chapter 13 establishes a portfolio approach to evaluating farmers' responses to business and financial risks, as well as to risks introduced by financial markets. The approach illustrates portfolio responses to changes in risk and is extended to risk pricing of farm assets in a market framework. Numerous empirical studies about financial responses to risk are reviewed.

Chapter 14 considers how financial intermediaries absorb, transmit, or increase agricultural risks, and the consequences for farm businesses. Financial innovations that modify a borrower's debt obligations under risk and inflation are suggested and evaluated for use by farmers and lenders.

Chapter 15 considers the risks associated with general inflation and financial market instability. Unanticipated changes in inflation are shown to influence price relationships for farm inputs and commodities, income tax obligations, and asset values and liquidity problems on farm investments. Inflation also influences the level and volatility of interest rates, thus bringing additional risks to leveraged farmers. The forces affecting credit availability from public and private sources are also reviewed.

In the final section Chapter 16 addresses agricultural policy and risk. The history of U.S. commodity programs is reviewed, including the shift from a focus on income support to stabilization of farm prices and incomes. The risk relationships between agricultural policy, commodity prices, output, farm income, and factor prices are qualitatively evaluated, as are the modeling applications of domestic and international policies under risk conditions. Developments in welfare analysis under risk are reviewed in a dynamic setting that accounts for commodity and monetary phenomena. Public assistance programs affecting farmers' risks are presented, and risks introduced by domestic and international policies are reconciled with various strategies for reducing policy risks.

Risk
management
in
agriculture

1

The setting

PETER J. BARRY

THIS CHAPTER ESTABLISHES a setting for the concepts, methods of analysis, and practical applications of risk management in agriculture. The importance of risks in agriculture is reviewed, emphasizing the close relationships between farm and nonfarm conditions. Implications for risk analysis are considered, along with the historical development of important concepts and analytical methods.

Risk and the farm sector

Risk management in agriculture has commanded substantial resources from farmers, agricultural lenders, agribusinesses, and the public sector. Most farms in the United States have a smaller scale, noncorporate structure with limited opportunities for enterprise diversification. Thus risk bearing is concentrated among individual farmers and farm families, rather than spread over numerous corporate shareholders. Low elasticities of prices and incomes for many commodities that are subject to weather and other uncontrollable events cause wide swings in commodity prices. Moreover, individual farmers have little capacity to influence resource or commodity prices. The effects of these factors combine to severely test farmers' risk bearing capacities and thus hamper their efficiency and welfare positions.

From the 1930s through the 1950s risk issues in agriculture were secondary to problems of low farm income and chronic misallocation of resources (Johnson 1947; Schultz 1949; Heady 1952). These decades witnessed substantial structural change as farms adjusted to income and resource problems. Farm numbers declined as many farmers left the industry. The remaining farms mechanized, modernized, and grew in size as farmers responded to the cost-size efficiencies of new technologies and

Peter J. Barry, University of Illinois.

sought greater incomes. Farmers also depended more on markets for acquiring farm resources. In turn, the per capita income for farm families has become comparable in the 1980s to the income of nonfarmers. Farmers have also earned more nonfarm income over time, especially in the small, part-time operations.

These structural changes occurring in an inflationary environment brought growing use of debt capital and continued reliance on leasing farmland. Financial leverage in the farm sector increased, especially for larger farms, thus obligating more of farmers' income to debt servicing (Brake and Melichar 1977). The longer term growth in returns to farm assets along with the dominance of real estate among these assets have brought much of farmers' total returns as unrealized capital gains (Melichar 1979a). When subject to financial analysis, these conditions indicate a highly solvent industry due mostly to unrealized capital gains on farm assets that are collateral for the growth in debt; however, farming also experiences chronic liquidity problems and cash flow pressures resulting from the continued low, but volatile current rates of return to production assets.

The improvement of farmers' income positions in past decades heightened the prominence of risk and instability issues in agriculture. Moreover, a richer, more complex risk environment has emerged reflecting the farm sector's growing sensitivity to forces in the general economy, international markets, government policy, and financial markets. Commodity price volatility increased sharply in the 1970s, due to modified government programs for many U.S. commodities, reduced crop inventories, variation in world production, devaluation of the U.S. dollar, and expanded, yet volatile foreign demand. By the early 1980s, sharp reversals in some of these conditions demonstrated that irregular or shock influences on farm units will likely continue in the future.

The later 1970s and early 1980s also brought unprecedented surges in rates of interest and inflation and anticipation of high variability in farm income, especially from uncertainties about export demands, factor costs, and national issues involving energy and transportation. Stronger relationships between farm and nonfarm sectors are transmitting instabilities in financial and resource markets to farmers more quickly and completely than before. Farmers' risks now come not only from their assets and income-generating activity, but also from unanticipated changes in their liabilities and debt servicing requirements. In sum, the combined effects of business and financial risks are high for most types of farms.

Public responses to agricultural risks also have experienced close scrutiny. More emphasis is on stabilization of commodity prices and farmers' income than on income support as in earlier decades. Government policy has mostly absorbed farm risks through programs that stabilize farm prices and incomes, control production, finance inventories for more orderly marketing, and provide credit, insurance, and other disaster assistance. But govenment also contributes to farm risks through unanticipated changes in policies, programs, and administrative procedures. One example is the sharp reduction in public risk bearing programs for farmers in the early 1970s when farm income was high, and their reinstatement through emergency loan programs and other instruments as farm adversities occurred later in the decade. Thus, stability in policy itself is important, along with policy's intended stabilizing role.

The financial outlook for farming in the 1980s is subject to much uncertainty about farm and nonfarm forces. The near-term prospects for farm income are weak due to the combination of widespread drought in 1980 and 1983, strong crop production in 1981 and 1982, diminished demand for farm products, mediocre livestock earnings, high debt in some farms, and high interest rates. Farm management under stress is highly visible in the early 1980s. The longer term prospects are brighter, however. Most long-term projections indicate stronger financial performance in farming and more moderate growth of farm debt (Hughes 1981). But these projections depend on the successful, permanent reduction in the nation's inflation rate; a stronger general economy; expanded international trade; and sounder government policies. Failure to achieve these national goals will likely yield a weak farm financial situation by 1990.

Most observers believe that the long period of pronounced change in sizes and numbers of U.S. farms has ended (*Structure Issues of American Agriculture* 1979; Hathaway 1981). The outlook for the year 2000 and beyond suggests a slower paced movement toward a bimodal distribution of farm sizes: many small farms, an increasing proportion of large farms, and fewer medium size farms (Lin et al. 1980). The more commercial of these future farms should have high quality personnel and strong skills in managing production, marketing, finances, and information. Dealing with risks will be an important part of these managerial activities.

Implications for risk management and analysis

The current risk environment is richer, more complex, and more demanding on managerial skills than in the past. Greater rewards should occur for superior risk management, but greater investment is needed to develop these skills in firms, government units, and policymaking. Innovations in risk management should be stimulated. Balancing private and public responses to risk without adding new risks will be important.

The current environment places greater demand on the concepts and methods used to study risks, understand their behavioral effects, and evaluate new and improved methods of risk response. Coming to the forefront in empirical analysis is more comprehensive treatment of sources of risk, measures of risk, attitudes toward risk, methods of managing risk, market effects, and the relationships to public policies. Combining empirical relevance with theoretical and analytical soundness in evaluating risk issues in agriculture is a challenging task. So is transmitting the findings to various clientele.

Past developments in risk analysis

The agricultural economics literature has a long, fruitful history in the study of risk attitudes and the methods for improving decision making under risk. It is paralleled by substantial developments in the general economics and business literature. In surveying the farm management and production economics literature Jensen (1977) cites Earl Heady's observations in 1949 that risk and the dynamics of the firm was a neglected area of farm management research. Jensen cites numerous studies during the subsequent years of such topics as the quality of farmers' expectations, measuring their risk attitudes and managerial characteristics, and responding to yield and income variability. The later developments in game theory, risk programming, utility measurement, and Bayesian analysis prompted his observation that

> whether these approaches will find their way into the actual planning of farms is difficult to know, but the existence of techniques for farm planning with probability distributions, strategies, and alternative decision criteria may serve to enhance the relevancy of farm planning to more farm families or other decision units.

Review articles by Brandow (1977) and by Brake and Melichar (1977) cite the early progress in understanding the origins of instability in agriculture, their relationships to farm income and resource allocation problems, and the policy choices for resolving instability problems. The suggested linkages between farming risks, credit rationing, and the consequences for resource adjustment and firm growth, as set forth by Johnson (1947) and Schultz (1949), provided testable hypotheses for numerous empirical applications. Heady's work on the principles of diversification is significant, and his 1952 book *Economics of Agricultural Production and Resource Use* contains several chapters on risk analysis.

The 1950s and 1960s stimulated much research on the growth processes of family-size farms and the consequences of greater financial leverage (*Economic Growth of the Agricultural Firm* 1977). Risk responses by many farmers were (and still are) strongly expressed through financial choices in managing liquidity where the linkages between farm risks and credit are important (Barry and Baker 1977). The 1970s also witnessed further developments in decision analysis under risk, as illustrated in the 1977 publica-

tion of *Agricultural Decision Analysis* by J. R. Anderson, J. L. Dillon, and
J. B. Hardaker. Their approach to decision analysis under risk "based on
the decision maker's personal strength of belief about the occurrence of
uncertain events and his personal evaluation of potential consequences
. . ." is a landmark in agricultural risk analysis.

Many risk concepts have deep-rooted historical origins. Bernoulli, for
example, postulated in the 1730s that investors maximize expected utilities
or in his terminology "moral expectation" rather than expected income.
Adam Smith in 1776 suggested the risk return trade-off:

> The wages of labor in different employments vary according to the probability
> or improbability of success
> [and]
> The ordinary rate of profit always rises more or less with the risk. It does not,
> however, seem to rise in proportion to it, or so as to compensate it completely.

Knight (1921) suggested a distinction between risk and uncertainty that
occupied the literature until the subjective concepts of probability in modern decision theory. In 1947 Von Neumann and Morgenstern revived and
extended the expected utility approach and demonstrated how to predict
the choices of individuals in risky situations. Savage (1954) in turn brought
focus to the subjective probability concepts and their relationship to expected utility. Markowitz (1959) and Tobin (1958) were leaders in developing portfolio theory. Markowitz (1959), Baumol (1963), Hanoch and Levy
(1969), and Hadar and Russell (1969) were pioneers in developing various
risk efficiency criteria that partially order risky choices for decision makers.

Arrow's (1974) work on risk bearing provided a rich framework for
empirically analyzing various market and social responses to risk. The refined measures of risk aversion developed by Arrow and by Pratt (1964)
provided for interpersonal comparisons of risk aversion and contributed
importantly to empirical analysis of risk attitudes. In capital market theory,
the capital asset pricing model developed by Sharpe (1964) and by Lintner
(1965) considered the risk pricing of various assets under different degrees
of market efficiency. In aggregative work, welfare analytic concepts developed and extended by Waugh (1966), Oi (1961), Massell (1969), and
Turnovsky (1976) could be applied to analyze the welfare effects for producers and consumers of market instability and various stabilization policies. Finally, modeling efforts by Brainard and Cooper (1968), Hueth and
Schmitz (1972), and Just et al. (1978) extended the analytical capacity to
account for the effects of risk on various aspects of international trade.

This brief literature review highlights some of the extensive literature
on risk analysis and also illustrates some of the analytical responses to the
changes in agriculture's risk environment. Many of these developments are
treated more fully in the following chapters.

1

Foundations of risk analysis

2

Risk attitudes: concepts and measurement approaches

LINDON J. ROBISON, PETER J. BARRY, JAMES B. KLIEBENSTEIN, AND GEORGE F. PATRICK

IN DEVELOPING A THEORY of risk averse behavior, Kenneth Arrow (1974) observed that "(a) individuals tend to display aversion to the taking of risks and (b) that risk aversion in turn is an explanation for many observed phenomena in the economic world." In agriculture, farmers express their risk attitudes in many forms: forward pricing, production practices, insurance, holding liquid reserves, diversification, liability management, and others. Moreover, the public sector expresses its attitude toward agricultural risks through various stabilization, credit, and assistance programs. Thus, information about the risk attitudes of farmers and other economic agents plays an important role in risk management.

Agricultural economists (and others) have invested considerable resources in conceptualizing, modeling, and measuring the risk attitudes of decision makers. Much progress has occurred, but much remains to be done. In this chapter, we review alternative approaches to modeling and measuring risk attitudes and present evidence from several empirical studies that apply these concepts. The expected utility model and lexicographic

Lindon J. Robison, Michigan State University; Peter J. Barry, University of Illinois; James B. Kliebenstein, University of Missouri; and George F. Patrick, Purdue University.

utility are emphasized. The final section of the chapter considers multiple-goal functions and evalutes the importance of risk for farmers relative to other goals.

Expected utility model

Modeling goals is a complex task. The goals can be single or multiple, and if multiple, may be valued simultaneously or as hierarchies. If, for example, profits (or wealth) were the goal and maximization the desired level of attainment, then the outcomes of actions would be expressed in monetary units, and the preferred action would have the highest expected monetary value. Monetary values are an effective common denominator when the action choices involve multiple comparisons among potentially dissimilar events. But maximizing the expected monetary value has proven highly abstract and ineffective in explaining many types of economic or financial behavior because it fails to distinguish between decision makers' attitudes toward additional wealth. Thus, a more general approach based on utility theory is sought to express attitudes under conditions of risk.

The expected utility model (EUM) is primarily a prescriptive tool. It infers that decision makers who obey certain axioms should choose actions that maximize their expected utility. But the EUM is also used to describe risk attitudes, and its predictive power is tested through experiments or inferences based on observed economic behavior (Robison 1982; Schoemaker 1982). Thus the EUM is a unique way to represent the goals of a decision maker.

DEFINING THE EXPECTED UTILITY MODEL. The EUM provides a single-valued index that orders action choices according to the preferences or attitudes of the decision maker. To summarize, the components of a decision problem include a set of action choices $A_1, A_2, \ldots, A_n$, a set of monetary outcomes X_{ij} associated with the jth action choice in the ith state of nature, and probability density functions $P(s_i)$ indicating the likelihood of outcomes in the respective states, for an action choice. To order these action choices, each monetary outcome, X_{ij}, is assigned a utility value according to a personalized, arbitrarily scaled utility function. The utility value for each possible outcome of an action choice is weighted by its probability and summed. The resulting expected utility is a preference index for the action choices. Action choices are ranked according to their level of expected utility with the highest value being most preferred.

Mathematically, the goal function is expressed as

$$\max_j \text{EU}(x) = \sum_i U(x_{ij}) P(s_i), \quad j = 1, 2, \ldots, n \qquad (2.1)$$

where the probability function is a discrete distribution and the notation is defined above.

The expected utility model clearly delineates between a decision maker's perception of the amount of uncertainty involved and his or her attitude toward additional income. The amount of uncertainty is reflected by the decision maker's expectations, which are expressed as probability density functions based on the subjective or objective concepts of probability (see Chaps. 3 and 4). The amount of uncertainty and other characteristics associated with the action choices are valued by the decision makers according to their unique attitudes, as they are encapsulated in the utility function.

The EUM is based on a theorem derived from a set of axioms about individual behavior. A complete development of the approach is found in the landmark works of Von Neumann and Morgenstern (1947) or Luce and Raiffa (1957). Only the highlights are presented here. The axioms are considered conditions or assumptions of how people behave; they amount to a general assumption that people are rational and consistent in choosing among risky alternatives. If the axioms hold, the theorem follows that an optimal risky choice is based on the maximization of expected utility.

The set of axioms is summarized as follows:

1. *Ordering of choices*

For any two actions choices, A_1 and A_2, the decision maker either prefers A_1 to A_2, prefers A_2 to A_1, or is indifferent between them.

2. *Transitivity among choices*

If A_1 is preferred to A_2, and A_2 is preferred to A_3, then A_1 must be preferred to A_3.

3. *Substitution among choices*

If A_1 is preferred to A_2, and A_3 is some other choice, then a risky choice $PA_1 + (1 - P)A_3$ is preferred to another risky choice $PA_2 + (1 - P)A_3$, where P is the probability of occurrence.

4. *Certainty equivalent among choices*

If A_1 is preferred to A_2, and A_2 is preferred to A_3, then some probability P exists that the decision maker is indifferent to having A_2 for certain or receiving A_1 with probability P and A_3 with probability $(1 - P)$. Thus A_2 is the certainty equivalent of $PA_1 + (1 - P)A_3$.

If a decision maker obeys these axioms (and several others that are more technical), a utility function can be formulated that reflects the decision maker's preferences (Hey 1979). Utility functions are typically estimated in a gaming situation involving repeated applications of the certainty equivalent axiom. The axiom requires four pieces of information: values for A_1, A_2, A_3, and P. If three of these items are prespecified, the decision maker provides an appropriate value for the fourth item. Then, changing one of the prespecified items brings a new value from the decision maker for the fourth item, and so on. As discussed below, the validity of this approach is based in part on the choice of prespecified values.

Suppose farmer A faces a risky alternative having a maximum possible gain of $1000 with probability P and a maximum possible loss of $1000 with probability $1 - P$. The scale of farmer A's utility function is fixed by arbitrarily defining a utility value of 1.0 for the gain, $U(1000) = 1.0$, and a utility value of 0.0 for the loss, $U(-1000) = 0.0$. Utility values for intermediate monetary values are found as farmer A indicates certainty equivalents for differing likelihoods of gain and loss. This procedure treats A_1, A_3, and P as the prespecificed values. It assumes that the utility of the certainty equivalent (CE) equals the expected utility of the risky alternative.

$$U(CE) = P(1.0) + (1 - P)(0.0) = P \qquad (2.2)$$

To illustrate, when $P = 0.5$, farmer A might indicate a sure loss of $250 as the certainty equivalent to gambling on a possible loss of $1000 at these odds. Thus the utility of $-$250$ is 0.5, $U(-250) = 0.5$. When $P = .8$, farmer A might indicate $400 as the certainty equivalent. Thus the utility of $400 for farmer A is .8, $U(400) = 0.8$. We now have four observations on utility and monetary values for farmer A. When enough utility values are available, a utility index or function can be fitted to these values perhaps using graphical or statistical procedures. This function will presumably yield a reliable ordering of farmer A's risky choices.

RISK ATTITUDES. A decision maker's attitude toward risk is inferred from the shape of his utility function. A linear utility function implies risk neutrality, a function concave to the origin implies risk aversion, and a convex function implies a risk preferring attitude. A decision maker may also have a utility function with both convex and concave segments indicating changes in risk attitude for different monetary outcomes.

To illustrate consider a decision maker with a linear utility function

$$U(X) = kX \quad \text{for } k > 0 \qquad (2.3)$$

who faces an action choice with mutually exclusive monetary outcomes X_1 and X_2 having probabilities $1 - P$ and P, respectively. The expected utility of this choice is

$$(1 - P)kX_1 + PkX_2 = k\bar{X} \qquad (2.4)$$

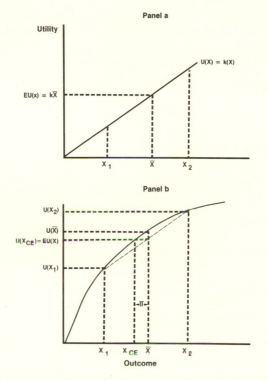

FIG. 2.1. Utility functions with constant and diminishing marginal utility.

where $\overline{X}$ is the action's expected value. In this case the expected utility is equal to the expected monetary value (see panel a, Fig. 2.1). Thus action choices are ordered by their expected monetary values for decision makers with linear utility functions. Because this ordering depends only on the expected value and not on other characteristics of the probability function, decision makers with linear utility functions are defined as risk neutral.

A concave utility function (panel b, Fig. 2.1) has a nonnegative first derivative [$U'(x) \geq 0$], and a negative second derivative [$U''(x) \leq 0$]; that is, utility always increases as wealth increases, but the marginal utility declines. Thus a risk averse decision maker, with a concave utility function, will prefer an action with a perfectly certain return to another action with an equal, but uncertain, expected return. This preference occurs because the loss of utility from a monetary loss exceeds the gain in utility from a monetary gain when the monetary loss and gain are of equal magnitude and likelihood.

For the risky action described above and the concave function in panel b of Fig. 2.1, the expected utility is a linear combination of $U(X_1)$ and $U(X_2)$.

$$EU(X) = (1 - P) \, U(X_1) + PU(X_2) \qquad (2.5)$$

As P changes, so does the expected utility. In general $EU(X)$ can be described by the straight line $EU(X) = P[U(X_2) - U(X_1)] + U(X_1) = \alpha_0 P + \alpha_1$, where α_0 and α_1 are parameters equal to $U(X_2) - U(X_1)$ and $U(X_1)$ respectively. Expected utility $EU(X)$ is represented on the vertical axis in panel b of Fig. 2.1. However, the utility of a certain $\bar{X}$ exceeds the expected utility of a risky action with $\bar{X}$ as the expected monetary value. Thus a risk averter would not purchase the risky action at a price equal to its expected monetary value, because the concave utility function would translate the zero monetary gain into a utility loss.

The risk averter would be willing, however, to pay a price for the risky action that would yield the same utility as the action's expected utility; that is, where $U(X_{CE}) = EU(X)$. This utility value is represented by $U(X_{CE})$ in panel b of Fig. 2.1, which translates into the certainty equivalent X_{CE} monetary value of the risky action. The term X_{CE} yields the same utility as owning an uncertain action choice consisting of outcomes X_1 and X_2 with mean $\bar{X}$.

For a risk averter, the certainty equivalent of a risky investment is always less than its expected monetary value. (Another reason why concave utility functions imply risk aversion is that any mean-preserving spread of probability density function reduces the certainty equivalent of the action choice.) The difference between the expected monetary value and the certainty equivalent is a risk premium, Π, which compensates the risk averter in utility terms for undertaking the risky action. (While not shown here, a similar approach is followed in showing the relationship between a risk preferring attitude and a convex utility function.)

The risk premium is determined by the concavity of the utility function, or its bending rate. The greater is the bending rate, the greater is the risk premium. To illustrate, the two utility functions in Fig. 2.2 are scaled to intersect at risky outcomes X_1, and X_2, with probabilities $1 - P$ and P, respectively. The risk premium is higher (and the X_{CE} lower) for $U^*(X)$, which has the greater bending rate.

These relationships between utility functions and risk attitudes imply that the sign of the function's second derivative indicates local risk aversion, risk neutrality, or risk preferring. However, the magnitude of the second derivative cannot be used for interpersonal comparisons of risk aversion, because an individual's utility function is only unique up to a positive linear transformation. Thus, the value of the second derivative can be arbitrarily varied by multiplying the utility function by a positive number.

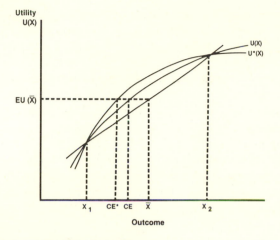

FIG. 2.2. Utility functions and risk premiums.

To facilitate interpersonal comparisons, Arrow and Pratt independently suggested measuring an individual's risk aversion by dividing the second derivative of the utility function by the first derivative. Two measures have resulted. One is a measure of absolute risk aversion:

$$R_a(x) \; = \; -U''(x)/U'(x) \tag{2.6}$$

The other is a measure of relative risk aversion:

$$R_r(x) \; = \; -xU''(x)/U'(x) \tag{2.7}$$

These measures are unaffected by arbitrary transformations of the utility function. They are larger for more risk averse people; and their signs signify the type of risk attitude. Moreover, these measures are considered functions of the object of utility. As such, they serve to test hypotheses about responses of risk aversion to changes in wealth or other objects of utility.

COMPARISON OF RISK AVERSION. The terms *risk aversion in the small* or *local measures of risk aversion* refer to evaluations of risk attitudes at specific monetary outcomes. Most comparisons of risk aversion among decision makers are valid only at these outcomes. One decision maker may be more risk averse than another at one monetary value, but not at another. This condition makes it difficult to generalize about differences in risk aversion among decision makers.

To illustrate, consider two individuals whose absolute risk aversion functions, $R_1(x)$ and $R_2(x)$, are shown in panel a, Fig. 2.3. Their shapes imply decreasing and increasing absolute risk aversion, respectively. Assume they are facing an action choice with possible outcomes X_1 and X_2, each having equal probabilities so that the mean outcome is $\bar{X}$. For this choice situation, individual 1 is the more risk averse since $R_1(\bar{X})$ exceeds $R_2(\bar{X})$. If, however, the action choice has outcomes X_3 and X_4 with equal probabaility and mean $\bar{X}^*$, then individual 2 is more risk averse since $R_2(\bar{X}^*)$ exceeds $R_1(\bar{X}^*)$.

Now suppose individuals 1 and 2 face an action choice with outcomes X_2 and X_3. In this case they cannot be ordered according to the local measures of risk aversion, because the result depends on the probabilities associated with the outcomes. But this is inconsistent with the condition that risk attitudes are independent of probability measures in determining expected utility.

Finally, if $R_1(X)$ were consistently greater than $R_2(X)$ as shown in panel b of Fig. 2.3, then individual 1 would be more risk averse in the large (globally) than individual 2. This condition would occur if the individuals

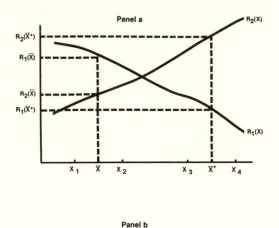

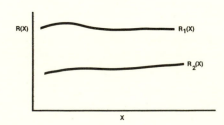

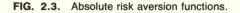

FIG. 2.3. Absolute risk aversion functions.

exhibit different, yet constant absolute risk aversion, or more generally, as long as their absolute risk functions do not intersect.

As this discussion shows, the degrees of risk aversion may differ among decision makers for different monetary outcomes. One person's degree of risk aversion dominates another person's only for the global case in panel b of Fig. 2.3; but this condition is very difficult, perhaps impossible, to measure empirically. Most studies of risk attitudes of farmers and other decision makers focus on local or small measures of risk attitudes.

Lexicographic utility: safety-first models

Lexicographic utility refers to sequential ordering of multiple goals. The highest priority goal must be achieved at a threshold level before considering the second goal, and so on. Thus, attaining a higher priority goal serves as a constraint on goals with successively lower priorities. Overachievement of goals has no effect on total utility, but an infinite disutility is associated with underachievement.

A lexicographic utility function is expressed as

$$U = f(Y_1, Y_2, \ldots, Y_n) \tag{2.8}$$

where the Ys represent the sequential goals. This approach is essentially an empirical one; no theoretical base or set of axioms guides the ordering of these goals. However, the sequential ordering concept has much intuitive appeal and appears consistent with the concept of a hierarchy of goals suggested by other behavioral disciplines (Maslow 1943). (Moreover, as shown in Chapter 5, several studies are exploring the relationship between expected utility maximization and decision rules having a threshold or target level of income.)

The safety-first rule is commonly used in risk analysis as a form of lexicographic utility. It specifices that a decision maker first satisfies a preference for safety in organizing a firm's activities, and then follows a profit-oriented course of action. Three types of safety-first rules have been suggested (Pyle and Turnovsky 1970). The first rule (SF1) put forth by Telser (1955–56) assumes that a decision maker maximizes expected returns ($\bar{E}$) subject to the constraint that the probability of a return less than or equal to a specified amount (E-min) does not exceed a stipulated probability (P).

The SF1 rule is expressed as

Maximize $\bar{E}$ $\tag{2.9}$
subject to $P(E \leq E\text{-min}) \leq P$

The decision maker first determines a threshold level of income and the probability with which incomes must exceed this level. These values are the key indicators of risk attitudes under the SF1 rule. The threshold income might, for example, cover a farm's future obligations for living expenses, debt repayments, and operating expenses. The decision maker then considers various actions that satisfy the constraint, and finally chooses among the actions based on the highest expected value.

This process is illustrated in Fig. 2.4 by curve *AF* that represents the lower confidence limits of income for a set of actions. Only plans above the *E*-min line have income levels at the lower confidence level for *P* that exceed *E*-min. Plans *A* and *F* do not qualify. Among the qualifying plans, *G* is preferred since it has the highest expected return.

The second safety-first rule (SF2) introduced by Kataoka (1963) chooses a plan that maximizes income at the lower confidence limit (*L*) subject to the constraint that the probability of income being less than or equal to the lower limit does not exceed a specified value *P*. In effect, this rule maximizes the return along a fixed lower confidence limit *P*.

Maximize L (2.10)
subject to $P(E < L) \leqq P$

In Fig. 2.4, the optimal choice according to SF2 is plan *C* since it yields the highest return for confidence limit *P*, while still exceeding *E*-min.

The third safety-first rule (SF3) developed by Roy (1952), chooses the plan with the smallest probability of yielding a return below some specified level. That is,

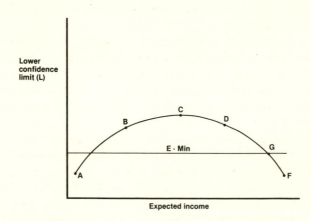

FIG. 2.4. Lower confidence limits and safety-first.

Minimize $P(E < E\text{-min})$ **(2.11)**

If, for example, the returns are normally distributed, then the optimum plan occurs where E-min is the greatest number of standard deviations away from the expected value. Plan C would meet this criterion in Fig. 2.4.

Measuring risk attitudes

Much empirical work has focused on measuring the risk attitudes of decision makers in agriculture. The approaches followed in these studies may differ considerably, depending on the research objectives; thus, the literature on risk attitudes is quite diverse. Normative studies may simply assume that decision makers have specific utility functions. Descriptive studies may focus on the type of risk attitude: averse, neutral, or preferring. Still other studies focus on predicting risky choices based on empirical measures of risk attitudes.

In this section, we consider several of the approaches to studying risk attitudes: (1) direct elicitation of utility functions (DEU); (2) interval measures of risk aversion; (3) experimental methods; and (4) observed economic behavior (OEB).

DIRECT ELICITATION OF UTILITY FUNCTIONS. The DEU method involves direct contact with decision makers to specify their risk attitudes. It can focus on a single-valued utility function, on lexicographic utility, or on a broader concept of multiple goals. Most DEU applications involve the expected utility approach. Several elicitation procedures exist, although they all use hypothetical gambles involving monetary gains and losses. Each procedure yields a series of points in utility-monetary outcome space that can be expressed as a utility function.

The best-known variations of the DEU approach are the Von Neumann-Morgenstern (VN) method, the modified VN method, and the Ramsey method. Each method implements the certainty equivalent axiom of the expected utility model in repeated applications of hypothetical gambles (Anderson 1977). The VN method requires the decision maker to identify the probability (P) in (2.2), for the favorable outcome that would yield indifference between the risky alternative and a sure thing whose value is the average of the favorable and unfavorable outcomes (Roumasset 1979). The modified VN method assigns equal probabilities to the favorable and unfavorable outcomes and elicits their certainty equivalent from the decision maker. The Ramsey method elicits certainty equivalents for a series of risky alternatives in order to overcome possible biases associated with gambling or selected probability levels.

The DEU method has been criticized as subject to bias from different interviewers, preferences for specific probabilities, confounding from extraneous variables, negative preferences toward gambling, absence of realism in the game setting, lack of time and experience of the participants to become familiar with the hypothetical choices, and compounding of errors in the elicitation process (Roumasset 1976; Binswanger 1980; Robison 1982). An inappropriate functional form for the utility function can also adversely influence implications about risk attitudes (Lin and Chang 1978).

While these criticisms are likely valid, they are often misdirected since few other approaches to studying the risky behavior of individual decision makers offer as rich an empirical setting. Moreover, these shortcomings have prompted considerable effort to refine, extend, and generalize the DEU methods so that their results will be more valid indicators of risk attitudes (Halter and Mason 1978). Much efficiency has also been gained in the elicitation techniques. Nonetheless, the DEU method is a costly technique to implement in economic analysis. It is likely best suited for microdecision situations and for basic research about farmers' risk attitudes.

THE RISK INTERVAL APPROACH. King and Robison (1981a, 1981b) have argued that the DEU method is not accurate enough to measure a uniquely defined utility function. They propose an *interval measure* of risk attitudes that explicitly accounts for possible errors in the measurement process. The method is based on identifying a confidence interval for the Arrow-Pratt measure of absolute risk aversion that is estimated by asking decision makers to order pair-wise comparisons of probability density functions.

The interval measurement procedure first recognizes that the constant risk aversion measure, λ, over a small range is a good approximation of the true absolute risk aversion function $R(X)$. Then, it calculates the constant absolute risk aversion measures, such that the expected utility for the two probability density functions, $f(X)$ and $g(X)$, are approximately equal. A decision maker is asked to choose between $f(X)$ and $g(X)$. If $f(X)$ is preferred, the average absolute risk aversion coefficient is greater than λ. If $g(X)$ is preferred, then the average absolute risk aversion is less than λ. Thus the response to one question bisects the absolute risk aversion space. By offering choices between other selected actions, the absolute risk aversion space that includes the decision maker's risk function is narrowed.

The analyst can specify a desired width for the confidence intervals of the risk aversion measure. At the extremes, the interval could have infinite width, or it could converge to a single line. The latter case is analogous to a single-valued utility function that would completely order the choices.

The interval approach gives the analyst flexibility in measuring risk attitudes and in risk efficiency analysis when error-free measures are not available. In risk efficiency analysis, using a large interval is not likely to exclude a preferred choice from the risk efficient set. However, a large interval has less ordering capacity and may not yield a manageable size of efficient set. Using a small interval would improve the ordering capacity but increase the likelihood of excluding a preferred choice. The best interval width for the analyst will depend on desired trade-offs between size of choice set and likelihood of excluding a preferred choice.

The interval method also allows greater generality in the relationship between a decision maker's absolute risk aversion and the level of monetary outcome. That is, an individual's absolute risk measure could increase, decrease, or remain constant over a range of monetary values. In contrast, algebraically specified utility functions have specific patterns of absolute risk aversion.

EXPERIMENTAL METHODS. Binswanger (1980) developed an experimental method for measuring the risk attitudes of about 350 peasants in rural India. The approach was based on gaming situations conducted in a series of visits over several weeks. Financial compensation added realism to the gaming situation by establishing incentives for the respondents to protect and increase their acquired wealth. Binswanger observed that before participating in games with significant outcomes, the participants believed they would act either more or less risk averse than should be the case. After participating in the game, their responses to hypothetical games did not differ significantly from their choices in games with significant outcomes.

Conducting the experiments over time permitted the respondents to reflect on each decision, discuss it with others, and benefit from the past experience. The researchers took extra care to teach the respondents about the game and to eliminate other sources of error.

Beyond these features, the experimental approach resembles the DEU method. Its use of financial compensation and the opportunity to learn from past experiences respond to some of the measurement flaws in the conventional DEU method.

OBSERVED ECONOMIC BEHAVIOR. The OEB method draws inferences about risk attitudes, based on the relationships between the actual behavior of decision makers and the behavior predicted from empirically specified models. Suppose, for example, that two decision makers are choosing between two investments, one having a lower expected return and risk than the other. If each decision maker makes a different choice, then the one preferring the lower risk investment is considered more risk averse. If these decision makers' choice set and criteria were modeled empirically, the amount of risk and the risk attitude could be measured.

Another example involves the effects of a farmer's risk attitude on fertilizer levels when crop yield is a random variable. Following the approach of Anderson et al. (1977) and Young et al. (1979), expected utility maximization leads to a first order condition

$$E(\text{MVP}_i) = \text{MFC}_i + R_a I_r \tag{2.12}$$

where $E(\text{MVP}_i)$ = expected marginal value product (MVP) of input i; MFC_i = nonstochastic marginal cost (MFC) of input i; and $R_a I_r$ = a risk adjustment based on the farmer's risk aversion coefficient (R_a), and the marginal contribution to risk of additional input use (I_r).

Assuming I_r is positive, risk aversion ($R_a > 0$) implies a positive *risk adjustment:* that is, a risk averse farmer will stop short of equating $E(\text{MVP})$ to MFC.

Equation (2.13) suggests a theoretical approach for measuring R_a empirically

$$R_a = [E(\text{MVP}_i) - \text{MFC}_i]/I_r \tag{2.13}$$

In practice, however, estimating I_r is difficult without making restrictive assumptions about the stochastic events.

The OEB method has several advantages. Like the DEU method, it can generate quantitative measures of risk aversion. It allows an analyst to handle large amounts of sample data, and is less costly than interviewing many subjects. Moreover, the OEB method avoids measuring risk attitudes from hypothetical gaming situations.

However, the OEB method is subject to several inference problems. By attributing risk attitudes to differences between actual firm performance (input use, output levels, enterprise combinations, credit use, and so on) and performance predicted by an assumed objective (e.g., maximizing expected profit), the OEB method attributes the entire difference to the decision maker's risk attitude. In reality, many other factors besides risk influence observed behavior. Goals other than profit and risk are important. So are differences among decision makers in the quality of decision information, expectations, resource endowments, capital constraints, and availability of methods for responding to risk.

Moscardi and de Janvry's (1977) work on the effects of farmers' risk attitudes on fertilizer application illustrates the OEB approach. To obtain their risk measures, they first assumed that decision makers maximized Kataoka's (1963) safety-first model:

maximize L

subject to $P(E < L) \leq P$, where L is the disaster income, E is the random return, and P is an arbitrary probability. They assumed that a generalized power production function captured the important input-output relationships with a multiplicative term. Finally, they assumed prices were known with certainty. From these (and other) assumptions, they obtained a unique risk measure that was treated as perfectly accurate, using it to infer risk attitudes about their sample of farmers.

Failure of any of these assumptions would bias the inferences about risk attitudes. Thus, the many assumptions needed to measure risk attitudes limits the applicability of the OEB method. Moscardi and de Janvry (1977) recommend careful screening of the data to eliminate influences other than risk attitudes, but this high degree of control is difficult to achieve in practice.

Another example of the OEB limitations is possible trade-offs among farmers' responses to risk. Consider the balance between business risk and financial risk that is shown in Chapter 13. A farmer might maintain relatively low business risk in his production and marketing plans to counter the financial risk from high leverage. Assessments of this farmer's risk attitudes would be misleading if they were based solely on the production and marketing activities., Thus, OEB approaches to measuring risk attitudes require a complete empirical specification of the OEB model and careful consideration of other goals besides profits and risk.

Empirical studies of risk attitudes

Several review articles provide excellent summaries of the extensive literature on farmers' risk attitudes (Dillon 1971; Anderson 1977; Young 1979; Young et al. 1979; Hazell 1982). This literature shows much diversity in the approaches to studying risk attitudes, including various ways of implementing the DEU and OEB methods. The purpose here is to highlight the major methods of analysis and findings about risk attitudes. This task is complicated because individual studies tend to build on previous ones and move from descriptive and experimental orientations toward more rigorous tests of alternative decision criteria. To illustrate, one can observe a transition from earlier attempts to elicit farmers' utility functions and draw inferences about risk attitudes, to testing their predictive accuracy, to evaluating the stability of utility measures over time, to studying how risk attitudes may change between different levels of monetary outcomes (including gains and losses), to analyzing the combined effects of risk attitudes and subjective probabilities, and finally to comparing single and multiple attribute utility functions.

Officer and Halter (1968) provide an early example of a predictive test of the EUM that compares different methods of eliciting utility functions. They derived mean-variance efficient sets of alternative feed reserves for a small panel of Australian farmers and found that utility functions estimated using the Ramsey model most accurately predicted the farmers' actual choices. At first, the expected cost model outperformed the EUM models, but it performed less favorably in subsequent tests, implying learning by the farmers during the elicitation process.

Lin et al. (1974) tested the predictive accuracy of the EUM, lexicographic utility, and expected profit maximization for a small panel of large-scale California farmers, using quadratic programming and the DEU method to predict the farmers' choices. Initially, the EUM predicted better than the other models in half the cases. In none of the cases did the EUM predict the farmers' actual plans, since those plans were not in the quadratic programming results. After reconstructing the choice sets, the EUM matched the actual choices for half the cases and was more accurate for the rest.

Herath et al. (1982) also compared expected profit maximization, single-attribute (profit) utility maximization, and multiple-attribute utility maximization in predicting crop variety selection by rice farmers in Sri Lanka. They report that the two utility criteria never performed worse than expected profit maximization, and that single-attribute utility outperformed the multiple-attribute approach. The farmers' risk attitides were judged important in their crop choice. The results also appeared sensitive to the farmers' expectations, thus indicating the combined importance of accurately eliciting risk attitudes and subjective probabilities in predictive analysis (Dillon 1971; Francisco and Anderson 1972).

Halter and Mason (1978) found a wide range of risk attitudes in their DEU study of 44 Oregon farmers. Nearly equal numbers of farmers were in the risk averse, neutral, and preferring categories. In addition, the farmers' age, education, and land tenure were significantly related, either separately or jointly, to their measures of absolute risk aversion. Consistent with the findings of Dillon and Scandizzo (1978) and Moscardi and de Janvry (1977), these authors cautioned that the risk attitudes of a population cannot be predicted from a single variable. A later study by Whittaker and Winter (1980) found changes over time in the risk attitudes of the same farmers studied by Halter and Mason, thus raising concern about the validity of the elicitation procedures and the stability of risk attitudes.

DEU results of Bond and Wonder (1980) indicated that risk aversion is a prevalent, yet mild, attitude of Australian farmers. Their study indicated that more than 25 percent of the 217 farmers were risk neutral or preferring, and nearly 40 percent changed their risk attitude at least once over different monetary outcomes. The authors were concerned that interview biases explained the changes in risk attitudes; however, their results are consistent with those of King and Robison (1981a), who observed different patterns of absolute risk measures over a range of monetary outcomes. These results are also consistent with Kahneman and Tversky's (1979) findings that risk preferring and averse behavior are associated with losses and gains, respectively, although neither study explicitly tested these phenomena. Finally, Binswanger's (1980) study of risk attitudes found a large concentration of Indian farmers with intermediate to moderate risk aversion, especially for situations with significant monetary outcomes.

A number of studies have used the OEB method to evaluate farmers' risk attitudes including both microstudies and aggregate analysis. The approach in the Moscardi and de Janvry study cited earlier involved solving farm models for different levels of risk aversion and selecting the level that gave the closest fit between the actual and predicted plans (Hazell 1982).

Brink and McCarl (1978) drew inferences about farmers' risk aversion based on differences between a farmer's actual cropping plan and the results of a linear programming model that minimized absolute deviations for different levels of returns (see Chaps, 6, 9). Their findings indicated relatively low risk aversion among the farmers, and thus little influence of risk attitudes on crop choices. However, Brink and McCarl cautioned that the results could differ in models that more completely specified the sources of risk, farmers' expectations, and the alternatives in marketing, investment, and finance.

Wolgin's (1975) study tested resource efficiency in crop production based on the anticipated equality of MVPs among different inputs and with input prices. He reasoned that ranking crops by their marginal increments to risk should correspond to the ranking of MVPs for crop inputs and to the ranking of intervals between MVPs and input prices. His empirical analysis of small farms in Kenya yielded MVPs consistent with these anticipations, implying that risk aversion and risk premiums are important in these farmers' crop decisions. However, Wolgin cautioned that limits on credit and other resources, the choice of production function, and other unaccounted forces could also be involved.

Wiens (1976) studied the risk attitudes of peasant farmers in a Chinese village by comparing the results of a quadratic risk program, solved for different levels of risk aversion, with the actual patterns of land use. His approach was to match the primal QP solution with the actual land patterns, and the shadow prices of the dual solutions with the market prices of the farm resources. He concluded that risk aversion appeared stronger than risk neutrality or credit constraints in explaining the farmers' behavior, although many other forces needed consideration.

Lins et al. (1981) studied the risk aversion characteristics of U.S. farmers in aggregate, based on differences in their holdings of risky and risk free assets. Their results suggested decreasing absolute risk aversion and constant relative risk aversion. However, the analysis was sensitive to the composition of risky and risk free assets. Moreover, no consideration was given to changes in farmers' portfolios, the farmers' leverage position, sources of risk, and other attitudinal characteristics.

Several other studies have considered the effects of risk and risk attitudes on aggregate farm production and on supply responses to risk (e.g., Behrman 1968; Just 1974; Hazell 1982). These studies are significant because they introduced risk into analyses of market equilibrium, policy issues, and welfare positions (see Chap. 16). However, these aggregative and sector analyses still experienced the inference problems of the OEB method, along with aggregation problems that hamper generalizations about farmers' risk attitudes. Nonetheless, some analysts (Young et al. 1979; Hazell, 1982) contend that the more cost-effective methods of measuring risk attitudes on a large-scale basis likely involve econometric procedures (e.g., Pope 1982); and that the predictive results may be more sensitive to risk measures and expectations, than to risk attitudes.

Multiple goals and risk analysis

Multiple-goal analysis has considered the importance of risk to farmers relative to other business and personal goals. Many of these multiple goals are hard to identify, order, and measure; thus, they are difficult to incorporate in economic and financial analysis. Nonetheless, information about other goals helps to understand the influence of risk attitudes on farmers' managerial behavior and on the economic organization of farm businesses. Thus, differences in the financial performance of farm firms (growth, profitability, leverage, liquidity) may be attributed to differences in the composition, ordering, and weights of the farmers' goals, rather than to shortcomings in management ability or to attitudes toward risk. Moreover, the effects of noneconomic goals may hamper the analysis of farmers' responses to public policies that are intended to affect their profit and risk position.

The setting for evaluating multiple goals is complex. It introduces a broader rage of concepts than is commonly used in economic analysis, many of which are not designed to yield optimal or equilibrium conditions. Multiple goals may be organized as hierarchies with a desired order of attainment, although the ordering and composition of the goals may differ greatly among decision makers. The attainment levels may reflect a satisfying rather than a maximizing approach to goal attainment (Simon 1959a). This distinction appears especially appropriate when the focus is on the process of decision making, rather than on the decision itself and its economic consequences. Distinctions among short-, intermediate-, and long-term goals become important, as does goal delineation for different types of decisions.

A common finding of multiple-goal research in agriculture is the relatively strong importance of risk to farmers and how they can protect against it. Several studies have evaluated farmers' goals in terms of their responses to a preselected set of goal statements. Attitudes toward risk are consistently among the higher ranked goals. A study by Patrick and Blake (1981) illustrates one approach to multiple-goal research. The study identified the goals of a sample of central Indiana farmers based on their responses to a selected set of goal statements. The goal statements were established in an investment situation as follows: (1) avoid being unable to make loan payments and/or foreclosure; (2) attain a desirable level of family living; (3) have net worth increase steadily; (4) select investment with the highest rate of return; (5) have a farm business which produces a stable income; (6) reduce physical effort and strain in farming; (7) have time away from immediate responsibilities for leisure or other activities; (8) and be recognized as a top farmer.

Paired comparisons, magnitude estimation, and multidimensional scaling procedures were used to analyze farmers' evaluations of these eight goals. Although the exact rankings differed, all three procedures indicated that these goals could be ordered into four clusters by importance: (1) goal 1, as the most important; (2) goals 2, 3, 4, and 5; (3) goals 6 and 7; and (4) goal 8, as the least important. Efforts to associate the goal ranking with various socioeconomic characteristics of the surveyed farms were largely inconclusive, although the farmers' ages, tenure positions, and credit use appeared important.

The importance of risk to this sample of farmers was confirmed by Fernandez (1982) using conjoint analysis. Farmers were asked to rank-order 27 combinations of annual income, probability of bankruptcy, and hours worked per day. Risk, defined as the probability of bankruptcy, was the most important factor for 56 percent of the farmers analyzed, while income and leisure were most important for 36 and 8 percent, respectively.

A study by Kliebenstein et al. (1980) focused on farmers' perceptions of benefits from farming. The benefits were measured against the base benefit of managerial freedom and were as follows: (1) doing something worthwhile; (2) provide good income; (3) sell in a free market; (4) sense of security; (5) work outdoors; (6) express myself; (7) meet fellow grain producers; (8) family tradition; (9) receive recognition; and (10) identified as a grain producer. The results indicated that profit (2) and security benefits (4) ranked second to managerial freedom, but considerably ahead of noneconomic benefits, such as 7 through 9. Discriminant analysis was then used in an attempt to classify farmers. In general, over 70 percent were classified correctly with benefit 4 (sense of security) being an important classification variable. This points out that farmers' threshold security levels differ substantially.

Studies by Harman et al. (1972), Smith and Capstick (1976), and Harper and Eastman (1980) also elicited farmers' responses to pair-wise comparisons of a number of specific goals ranging over profit, consumption, risk and security, credit use, leisure, esteem, and family accomplishments. Considerable differences occurred in the goal rankings by individual farmers in each study; however, the risk and security goals received consistently high rankings.

These empirical results about the importance of risk in farmers' goal functions are consistent with the empirical studies of risk attitudes cited earlier in the chapter. Risk attitudes appear to differ considerably among farmers, with most of the evidence indicating varying degrees of risk aversion. In addition, the multiple-goal research indicates that risk attitudes rank high relative to farmers' other goals and, therefore, may strongly influence farmers' behavior. Thus, risk attitudes and responses need careful consideration in economic analysis.

CHAPTER

Risk concepts and measures for decision analysis

DOUGLAS L. YOUNG

WHILE MOST ANALYSTS would probably claim a good feeling for the meaning of risk, one finds in the literature such fundamentally different risk concepts as *probability of loss, variance of profit,* and *size of the maximum possible loss.* Furthermore, risk can be based on the subjective expectations of individual decision makers, or on objective measures computed from historical or experimental data. Even analysts accepting the same risk concept frequently use different procedures for measuring risk or eliciting expectations.

The objectives of this chapter are (1) to identify risk concepts for different decision models, (2) to identify the role of subjective and objective probability measures in positive and normative decision models, and (3) to review and evaluate objective risk measures computed from time series data. Chapter 4 will focus on the subjective expectations and probability judgments of decision makers.

Risk concepts for alternative decision models

Risk concepts are identified for three classes of decision rules: (1) decision rules requiring no probability information, (2) safety-first rules, and (3) expected utility maximization.

Douglas L. Young, Washington State University.

DECISION RULES REQUIRING NO PROBABILITY INFORMATION. Halter and Dean (1971) discuss four decision rules requiring no probability information: (1) minimax loss or maximin gain, (2) minimax regret, (3) Hurwicz α index, and (4) LaPlace principle of insufficient reason. Criterion (1) focuses on an action's worst possible outcome (maximum loss or minimum gain) and then selects the action whose worst outcome is the least harmful. The minimax regret rule selects the action with the smallest maximum regret. The regret for each combination of actions and states is the difference between the respective outcomes and the highest possible outcomes for that state. The Hurwicz α index rule is:

$$\max \; [I_j \; = \; \alpha(M_j) \; + \; (1 \; - \; \alpha)(m_j)] \tag{3.1}$$

where α is supplied by the decision maker subject to $0 < \alpha < 1$, M_j equals the maximum gain of action j, and m_j equals the minimum gain of action j. The LaPlace principle of insufficient reason selects the action with the highest expected outcome, based on equal probabilities for all of the outcomes.

The theoretical weaknesses and practical naivete of these game theory decision rules are clearly established (Halter and Dean 1971, 82–92). Most modern decision theorists suggest that situations are rare in which (1) the decision maker has absolutely no subjective feelings or objective information about the probability distribution of outcomes or (2) the decision maker has subjective or objective probability information but ignores it. It might be argued these decision rules imply no direct concept of risk because they ignore probability information. A broader intepretation of risk, however, would consider the action with the largest possible loss or largest regret as most risky by minimax loss and minimax regret rules.

SAFETY-FIRST DECISION RULES. Safety-first rules, as summarized in Chapter 2, specify that a decision maker first satisfies a preference for safety, or a risk constraint, in selecting among action choices, and then follows a profit-oriented objective. The risk concept implied by a safety-first model is often described as chance of loss, which corresponds with the dictionary definition and popular usage of risk. Formally, the risk constraint in safety-first models is specified as

$$P(\Pi \; \leq \; d) \; \leq \; \alpha \tag{3.2}$$

where Π is stochastic income for an action and d is a threshold level of income to be met with probability α. Figures 3.1a and 3.1b show the important contrasts between chance of loss and variance as measures of risk. The chance of loss definition will unambiguously rank distribution 1*a* more

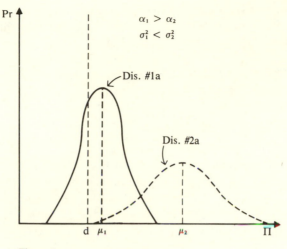

Figure 1a

where: Π = net farm income
       d = "disaster" level income

μ_i, σ_i^2, $(M_3)i$ = mean, variance, and skewness
                respectively, of distribution i

$\alpha_i = Pr(\Pi < d)$ for distribution i

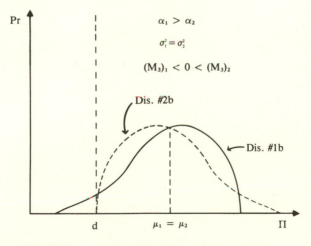

Figure 1b

FIG. 3.1. Chance of loss and variance measures of risk.

risky than 2*a*, and 1*b* more risky than 2*b*, because $\alpha_1 > \alpha_2$ in both figures. In contrast, the variance definition will rank 2*a* more risky than 1*a*, and 1*b* and 2*b* equally risky, because $\sigma_1^2 < \sigma_2^2$ in Fig. 3.1a and $\sigma_1^2 = \sigma_2^2$ in Fig. 3.1b.

EXPECTED UTILITY MAXIMIZATION. The expected utility (EU) for a risky action, a_j, can be evaluated as

$$(EU)_j = \sum_{i=1}^{n} [\Pi(\Theta_i, a_j)]P(\Theta_i) \tag{3.3}$$

where $\Pi(\Theta_i, a_j)$ represents the income level of the ith state of nature (Θ_i) and jth action (a_j); $U[\Pi(\Theta_i, a_j)]$ represents the utility equivalent of this income level; and $P(\Theta_i)$ denotes the probability of occurrence of the ith state of nature. By taking the expectation of the Taylor series expansion of the utility function about μ_j, the expected utility for action j is also represented as

$$(EU)_j = f(\mu_j, \sigma_j^2, M3_j, M4_j, \ldots) \tag{3.4}$$

where μ_j, σ_j^2, $M3_j$, $M4_j$, ... represent the mean, variance, skewness, kurtosis, and higher moments of the probability distribution of outcomes for action j (Anderson et al. 1977). The number of arguments required to accurately represent expected utility depends upon the characteristics of the probability distribution and of the decision maker's utility function. Assuming, for example, that the utility function is quadratic, or that profits are normally distributed, yields the simpler function of mean and variance

$$(EU)_j = f(\mu_j, \sigma_j^2) \tag{3.5}$$

As its names implies, the expected utility model (EUM) selects the action which maximizes (3.4) or (3.5).

Only for the restrictive assumptions generating (3.5) does the EUM identify variance (or standard deviation) as an unambiguous, single-dimensional index of risk. In general, risk under the EUM is represented by a vector of (potentially all) moments of the probability distribution. The potential relevance of higher moments is illustrated by Fig. 3.1b where distributions 1*b* and 2*b* have the same mean and variance but distribution 1*b* has negative skewness.

Subjective and objective probabilities for positive and normative uses

The probability distributions from which alternative risk concepts such as variance, chance of loss, or maximum loss are computed can originate from either objective or subjective sources. The terms *subjective* and *objective* refer to probability measures elicited from the decision maker or computed from historical observations, respectively. No necessary theoretical linkage exists between the specific risk concepts and sources; however, theoretical relationships may exist between some decision models and the probability sources. In particular, the EUM explicitly relies on subjective probabilities as well as subjective risk preferences (Dillon 1971; Anderson et al. 1977).

Subjective probabilities must be elicited from the decision maker; they cannot be computed directly from experimental or historical data. Thus subjective probabilities vary among persons and also over time for the same person in response to new experience and knowledge. However, decision makers may use experimental or historical probabilities as one input in formulating their expectations.

POSITIVE ANALYSES. Positive analyses attempt to explain or predict behavior. Use of subjective probabilities for such analyses is justified because people are considered to behave according to their personal perceptions of reality. Researchers interested in behavioral analyses or hypothesis testing should elicit and use subjective probabilities of the relevant decision makers whenever feasible. If objective probabilities are used in behavioral analyses, they essentially serve as proxies for subjective assessments. The following sections evaluate the use of subjective probabilties in several positive studies.

Firm-level behavioral studies. Lin et al. (1974) elicited subjective estimates of expected net returns and variances from farmers in comparing the predictive capability of the EUM, expected profit, and safety-first models. They relied on objective time series, however, for measuring the covariances of net returns of the farmer's income-generating activities. O'Mara (1971) and Roumasset (1976) elicited personal probabilities in studies of technology adoption by peasant farmers. Francisco and Anderson (1970) and Carlson (1970) also elicited subjective probabilities in studies of livestock stocking rates and crop disease control, respectively.

Other researchers, however, including Wolgin (1975), Moscardi and de Janvry (1977), Harris and Nehring (1976), Brink and McCarl (1978), and Conklin et al. (1977) have used risk indices computed exclusively from objective data in drawing inferences about or predicting farmer behavior. Studies that estimated stochastic production functions from experimental data also belong to this category (Anderson et al. 1977, Chap. 6). Little evidence is available to indicate that these objective probability measures were good proxies for the subjective beliefs of the relevant decision makers. As an exception, a recent methodological study by Bessler (1980) found rough similarity between objective risk indices derived from historic crop yield data detrended by autoregressive integrated moving average (ARIMA) processes and subjective probability assessments from a sample of California farmers.

Industry-level risk response studies. Industry models of supply response to risk are a fruitful application of risk theory. These studies generally rely on moving variance or moving standard deviation variables computed from past prices or returns (Just 1974; Lin 1977; Ryan 1977). Supply response analysts have generally acknowledged that their risk variables are proxies for subjective expectations of producers. Just's study, for example, attempted to ensure that the risk variables were consistent with processes believed to represent the producers' formulation of subjective expectations.

NORMATIVE ANALYSES. Some advocates of the EUM recommend use of subjective probabilities for both normative and positive analyses (Anderson 1977; Halter and Dean 1971). For normative analyses, they defend subjective probabilities on both theoretical and practical grounds. The fundamental theoretical justification is that personal satisfaction is maximized by selecting actions whose probability distributions, as perceived by the decision maker *ex ante,* are most compatible with the decision maker's risk preferences. The practical justification for use of subjective probabilities in normative problems is greater possible accuracy:

> If several or many historical observations on enterprise revenues are available and judged pertinent, they could be analyzed...to provide the desired statistics. However, because markets are usually changing and new varieties and new diseases are often emerging, the available historical data may be of dubious relevance—in which case assessment must rely heavily on judgment (Anderson et al. 1977, 33).

> In a problem like this one [a farm management problem constructed by the authors], the decision maker's subjective probability distribution probably reflects his local conditions better than a prior frequency distribution provided by an analyst (Halter and Dean 1971, 95).

On the other hand, using subjective probabilities in normative studies has several shortcomings:

1. Procedures for eliciting subjective probabilities are unreliable and subject to bias. Different procedures, interviewers, or both lead to different results (Hogarth 1975; Tversky and Kahneman 1975).
2. Even if accurate elicitation were possible, it would be costly and time consuming to obtain updated subjective probability assessments from each decision maker when managerial recommendations are made (Dillon 1971).
3. Strict adherence to subjective probabilities chains recommendations

to the manager's current knowledge. It provides no scope for the comparative advantage of economists and statisticians in assembling, processing, and using new information in prescribing managerial advice. This additional information could reduce long-term psychological pain from poor decision outcomes, even if the decision makers must modify their probability assessments. In view of these limitations for subjective probabilities the use of objective probabilities is often preferable in normative studies.

Objective risk measures

Objective probabilities are often defined by the relative frequency of an event's occurrence in a large set of observations. In practice, these observations are generated experimentally or based on historic events. Objective probabilities for many biological and physical processes, such as the inheritance of genetic characteristics, are usually estimated from repeated experiments. Most economic processes, however, cannot be replicated; thus objective probabilities for these phenomena are generally based on historical time series for prices, net returns, and other variables. In using such data, total variability should be distinguished from the random variability that constitutes risk. The latter concept represents the variability left after cyclical, seasonal, and other predictable or known trends have been removed. Statistical estimates of forecasting equations with explicit variance components is one technique for measuring random variability in time series data.

This section identifies and evaluates objective measures of risk for selected normative decision models.

MARKETING DECISION MODELS. Increased price volatility and greater crop storage by producers over the past decade make the timing of commodity sales a crucial challenge in risk management. Decision models that incorporate statistical forecasts of future prices have been developed to meet this challenge (Davis and Franzmann 1973; Dewbre and Blakeslee 1979; Purcell and Riffe 1980; Young et al. 1984). These decision models provide for the revision of selling plans as conditions change through time. As demonstrated below, these models suggest the use of statistical forecast variances as unambiguous measures of objective risk.

The model described here is based on the simple decision rule to hold a stored crop as long as the risk adjusted expected net gains from storage are positive (Young et al. 1984). Formally, if n discrete decision points are identified over the maximum storage horizon, the decision rule is:

For $i = 1, \ldots, n-1$: if $\hat{G}_{ij} \leq 0$ for all $j \geq i$, sell now
if $\hat{G}_{ij} > 0$ for at least one j, store one
more period and reevaluate

for $i = n$: sell

where $\hat{G}_{ij}$ = expected gains, net of risk and storage costs, of selling in future period j rather than at current decision point i.

$\hat{G}_{ij}$ is computed as follows:

$$\hat{G}_{ij} = \hat{P}_{ij} - (S_{ij} + I_{ij} + w\hat{\sigma}_{ij}) - P_i \qquad (3.6)$$

where $\hat{P}_{ij}$ = crop price forecasted for future period j at decision point i,
$\quad S_{ij}$ = accumulated costs of storing a unit of crop from decision point i to period j,
$\quad I_{ij}$ = foregone interest earnings of holding a unit of crop from decision point i to period j,
$\quad w$ = producer's safety-first risk aversion index. This index equals $t_{(\alpha,df)}$ in Fig. 3.2, where α denotes the producer's maximum acceptable probability of incurring a loss from storage.
$\quad \hat{\sigma}_{ij}$ = estimated standard error of forecast for $\hat{P}_{ij}$, and
$\quad P_i$ = known cash price of crop at decision point i.

Ordinarily, $i = 1$ represents the harvest date for the storable crop. If all $\hat{G}_{ij}$ are negative, the producer should sell at harvest. Crop quality considerations, storage space, or liquidity constraints will normally determine the maximum length of the storage horizon. The model ensures selling the commodity at period n, if not before.

As noted earlier, this decision rule identifies the standard error ($\hat{\sigma}_{ij}$) of the forecast as an objective risk measure associated with storing the crop for

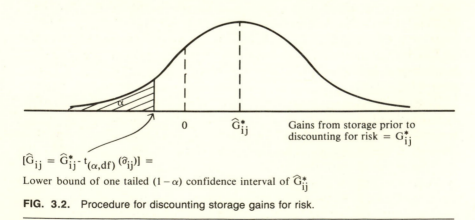

Gains from storage prior to discounting for risk = G^*_{ij}

$[\hat{G}_{ij} = \hat{G}^*_{ij} - t_{(\alpha,df)}(\hat{\sigma}_{ij})] =$

Lower bound of one tailed $(1-\alpha)$ confidence interval of $\hat{G}^*_{ij}$

FIG. 3.2. Procedure for discounting storage gains for risk.

sale at a later date. If, for example, $\hat{P}_{ij}$ is forecasted using ordinary least squares (OLS) regression, the standard error of a regression forecast beyond the data is appropriate (Johnston 1972):

$$\hat{\sigma}_{ij} = s[1 + c'(Z'Z)^{-1} c]^{1/2} \tag{3.7}$$

where s = standard error of regression; c = vector of regressors for the forecasted period, j; and Z = the information matrix used to estimate the forecast equation parameters.

Similarly, use of a Box-Jenkins autoregressive integrated moving average (ARIMA) process for an ℓ-step-ahead forecast implies use of the forecast standard error (Nelson 1973):

$$SE[e_t(\ell)] = [s_u^2(1 + \Psi_1^2 + \ldots + \Psi_{\ell-1}^2)^{1/2} \tag{3.8}$$

where s_u^2 = an estimate of the constant nonautocorrelated variance of the error term for the ARIMA process; and Ψ_i are weights determined by the structure of the process. The forecast variances of other statistical estimators could be inserted in similar fashion.

The forecast variance provides an objective measure of risk that is logically related to the decision rule. As illustrated in Fig. 3.2, use of the standard error of the forecast and the producer's maximum probability (α) of loss permits constructing a lower confidence limit on the forecasted gains from storage. This lower confidence limit forms the risk adjusted forecasted gains from storage, $\hat{G}_{ij}$. The grower should store as long as $\hat{G}_{ij}$ is positive for some future period. The proposed risk measure automatically accounts for variations in forecast precision as the forecasting horizon lengthens or as different statistical forecasting equations are used.

MEAN-VARIANCE MODELS. Mean-variance (EV) and mean-absolute deviation (EA or MOTAD) models as developed by Markowitz (1959) and Hazell (1971), respectively, are popular procedures for determining a risk efficient set. The EV criterion is based on the expected utility model in (3.5). The EV efficient frontier is found by minimizing the variance of net returns, $X'\Sigma X$, subject to successive fixed levels of an expected returns vector, $\mu'X$, where X is a vector of activity levels, μ is a vector of expected net returns per unit of activity, and Σ is the variance-covariance matrix of the activity set on a per unit basis. Nonnegativity and resource constraints are also commonly imposed in identifying the EV frontier (see Chaps. 6, 9).

The expected returns vector, μ, and the variance-covariance matrix, Σ, (or absolute deviations vector in the case of MOTAD) are commonly computed from time series data. The use of objective probability information is consistent with the normative nature of risk efficiency analyses. The EV or

EA frontiers contain alternatives from which managers can choose according to their personal risk attitudes.

No general agreement on appropriate concepts and procedures for estimating parameters of probability distributions from historical data for EV analysis has emerged in the literature. Early agricultural applications of EV analysis by Freund (1956), Scott and Baker (1972), and Thomas et al. (1972), computed income variances about the mean of an arbitrary historical period and used means of the entire period, or a recent subset of years, as income expectations. Other studies derived variances from a time series of detrended historical data and based income expectations on average values from recent periods (Halter and Dean 1971; Adams et al. 1980; Bravo-Ureta and Helmers 1980a). Several researchers observed marked sensitivity of the efficient EV sets to alternative methods of estimating expectations and variances. Frankfurter et al. (1971), Dickenson (1974), Klien and Bawa (1976), and Jobson and Korkie (1980), among others, have examined the imprecision of EV efficient solutions caused by the sampling error of E and V estimates. Persaud and Mapp (1979) showed that the composition of risk efficient EA sets for Oklahoma farms was strongly sensitive to whether deviations were computed about: (1) the overall mean of the historical data period, (2) a simple moving average of the past three years, or (3) a fixed, descending, weighted moving average of the past three years. Adams et al. (1980), and Bravo-Ureta and Helmers (1980a), showed that EV frontiers are sensitive to detrending procedures and to the functional form used to specify income expectations.

Thus, a clear criterion is needed for estimating parameters of probability distributions in risk efficiency studies. If the practical value of EV sets to decision makers rests on the normative information they provide about future outcomes of current decisions, then the vector μ should represent *forecasted* expected returns for the future decision period. Similarly, Σ is the variance-covariance matrix of these forecasts. Fried (1970) has proposed a forecasting framework based on OLS regression that specifies the square of (3.7) as the appropriate risk measure in EV analysis. Although appearing in 1970, Fried's procedure has had little use in agricultural applications. However, Berck (1981) recently applied this procedure in estimating EV risk efficient combinations of crop activities and hedging in commodity futures for California cotton farmers. He used Theil's (1971) seemingly unrelated regression technique to forecast Es for both gross margins on crops and returns from futures positions.

Even simple forecasting models, such as weighted average net returns for the past few years, as in Adams et al. (1980), and Mapp et al. (1979), will generally represent a better forecast of next period's expected returns than using, say, the average of returns over the past twenty years. However, researchers should also consider more sophisticated procedures, such as Box and Jenkins (1970) (ARIMA) procedures or fundamental econometric equations as used by Berck (1981), in forecasting expected returns for EV analyses. More accurate forecasts will improve the credibility of EV sets as normative guides. Comparison of the mean square forecast errors of ARIMA, econometric, and other predictions could aid in evaluating these forecasting procedures.

In past EV studies, the estimation of variances and expected returns often occurred independently. The forecasting criterion advanced here, however, suggests these parameters should be jointly estimated. The variances and covariances of the series of residuals of the expected returns models over the historical data series should be used to construct the forecast variance-covariance matrix (Fried 1970). This permits interpreting the variances as measures of precision of the expected returns forecasts.

Variability indices as general purpose extension information. Agricultural economists in several states have published measures of variability for prices, yields, gross and net returns for single enterprises, and occasionally for cropping systems (Carter and Dean 1960; Wildermuth et al. 1971; Mathia 1975; Yahya and Adams 1977; Patrick 1979b). These objective risk measures are often justified as a source of supplemental information to help farmers and extension specialists improve decisions about enterprise selection and diversification. Musser et al. (1981b), for example, suggested that estimates of the standard deviation and expected value of net returns could be used to compute lower confidence limits on net returns as in (3.9).

$$L_i = E_i - Z_{(\alpha)}s_i \qquad \textbf{(3.9)}$$

where L_i is a $(1 - \alpha)$ lower confidence limit for crop i; α is a specified probability level; E_i is expected net returns for crop i; $Z_{(\alpha)}$ is a one-tailed normal Z statistic; and s_i is estimated standard deviation of net returns for crop i. Extension outlook reports could present both point estimates of expected returns and lower confidence limits for crops grown in a particular farming area. Farmers can use measures of variability of agricultural prices, yields, and returns to make decisions about enterprise selection and diversification for future production. This forward-looking orientation implies that such indices should be constructed as forecast standard errors about the point forecasts of expected returns, prices, or yields.

Past studies, however, generally have not used variance about an explicit forecast as the theoretical basis for computing agricultural variability indices. Carter and Dean (1960), Wildermuth et al. (1971), Mathia (1975), and Yahya and Adams (1977) each used the variate difference method to measure random variability. The method, as described by Tintner (1940), assumes that a time series has two parts: (1) a mathematical expectation with consecutive items being highly correlated, and (2) a random element with zero mean, zero correlation between random elements, and zero correlation between the random element and its associated expected component.

The variate difference method does not explicitly identify a functional form of the forecast equation for the expected component (E) of the data series. However, an explicit equation is needed in order to make forecasts. The variate difference method also implies a restrictive functional structure of the expected component of the time series. Differencing of the nth order can totally remove an expected component that is a simple nth order polynomial of a time index as in (3.10).

$$E_t = a + b_1 t + b_2 t^2 + \ldots + b_n t^n \tag{3.10}$$

However, the method is not applicable to the zig-zag configuration of many economic time series (Tintner 1940).

If the time series data are generated by a stable time-dependent process, then formal identification of the complete ARIMA Box-Jenkins process with an explicit forecasting equation and forecast variance is appropriate (Ibrahim and Williams 1978; Bessler 1980; Landon 1982). Alternatively, an econometric approach incorporating exogenous variables for supply and demand could be used. In other cases, simple forecasting models such as a short-span moving average or a linear time trend may be adequate. However, the statistical forecast variance could be reported regardless of the model's simplicity or complexity. These procedures for generating probabilistic outlook information provide a sound statistical basis for constructing confidence limits about point forecasts as in (3.9) or to operationalize dynamic decision rules as in (3.6).

Summary and conclusions

The appropriate risk concept is specified by the decision rule used to predict or prescribe behavior. For example, a simple EUM rule as in (3.5) focuses on variance of outcomes, whereas a safety-first rule as in (3.2) focuses on the probability of loss. Once the appropriate risk concept is identified, subjective probabilities elicited from decision makers are appropriate risk measures when predicting their choices. Objective probabilities are appropriate when the analyst is identifying normative strategies for a stated decision rule.

Normative decision models require information on the expected returns and risk of future actions; consequently the expected returns parameter is viewed as a statistical forecast. Similarly, the statistical variance of the forecast is an appropriate measure of risk for normative decision models. This interpretation provides a sound statistical basis for constructing confidence intervals and other probability statements about the expected returns variable.

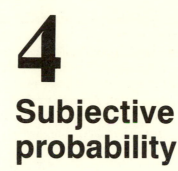

C H A P T E R 4

Subjective probability

DAVID A. BESSLER

SUBJECTIVE PROBABILITY is well accepted in the theory of individual choice. Almost nobody today argues for its nonexistence or its inappropriateness for describing rational choice under uncertainty. Among theorists of individual decision making, the heated debates about types of probability are essential reading only for historical purposes. The modern view presumes that a decision maker's subjective probabilities are conditioned on any set of information that is relevant to the question at hand—including but not necessarily limited to historical frequencies (de-Finetti 1974). Sims (1981) has recently distinguished between a subjective probability, which he requires for a theory of individual decision making, and an objective probability, which is required to reflect scientific consensus. This distinction (which seems consistent with Russell 1948, Chap. 1) attributes to science a quasi-supernatural role, whereby science can know more than the aggregate of the individuals. As this superhuman probability is not required for individual decision making, we do not pursue its description here.

Despite its widespread acceptance in the theoretical literature, the formal use of subjective probability in applied problems is not extensive, with the two possible exceptions of weather forecasting and sports wagering. For example, at a recent conference on commodity price forecasting, no attention was given to the assessment of subjective probabilities by forecasters and other analysts (Hayenga 1981). Other works (Anderson 1979) are similarly void in their treatment of subjective probability, despite some convinc-

David A. Bessler, Texas A. & M. University.

ing arguments in the professional literature urging the use of probabilistic forecasts (see Barnard 1979 for a view counter to that suggested here).

Another argument is that economic agents do not formally use subjective probabilities. Experiments by numerous researchers demonstrate that probability assessors often do not meet basic rationality conditions (Tversky and Kahneman 1974). Assessors can complete experimental tasks yielding results that are similar to subjective probabilities. That is, they can give quantitative weights to beliefs that are between zero and one. However, these responses oftentimes do not meet the more subtle coherence conditions; e.g., probabilities assigned to mutually exclusive and exhaustive events should sum to one and prior information ought to be used in accordance with Bayes's theorem.

This lack of use and the poor experimental results related to the assessment of formal probabilities in applied decision problems may stem more from a lack of familiarity with the method and less from a basic or inherent difficulty associated with formulating coherent assessments.

Most people become skilled at deductive rules of argument before grasping inferential methods that involve uncertainty. Moreover, most people prefer a deductive argument to one based on inductive inference (the former is neater). Yet, where evidence is available on the extensive use of subjective probability by real world assessors, the results are quite good. Murphy and Winkler (1977), for example, present results that show very reliable assessments on precipitation and temperature by professional weather forecasters. These assessors have many years of experience issuing short-term, probabilistic forecasts; thus they likely differ from the less experienced assessors studied by Tversky and Kahneman (1974), and others. In addition, the weather forecasters are probably more highly motivated to give accurate forecasts because the event they are forecasting is their professional activity.

In this chapter my purpose is to expand on the role of experience and motivation in probability assessment. I direct these discussions to the assessment of subjective probabilities in agricultural markets. Much of the technical material is found elsewhere in one form or another. Thus, the chapter is cast as a review of the subjective probability concept; it is not intended to make new contributions to the literature. For more details on probability elicitation, the reader may see Savage (1971) or Hogarth (1975).

The remainder of the chapter has three sections. First, subjective probability is defined. In doing this, a priori restrictions on, and *ex post* analysis of, probabilistic assessments are evaluated. Next, a few methods for obtaining probability statements are discussed within the context of assessor motivation. The final section considers possible areas of application in agricultural economics.

Subjective probabilities: definition and restrictions

Subjective probability refers to beliefs held by individual agents (people) that reflect their degree of uncertainty about some idea, event, or proposition. These beliefs are essential concepts that make decision making under certainty different from decision making under uncertainty. By a *subjective probability distribution,* we mean a set of subjective beliefs defined over a set of mutually exclusive and exhaustive ideas, events, or propositions.

The sole normative criterion applied to these beliefs is that they meet a condition of coherence. This condition puts restrictions on the admissible probabilistic beliefs that an individual can hold without involving a fundamental contradiction. *Coherence* can be defined as a condition on a set of probabilities for which a particular system of bets guarantees a priori no winner or loser. For example, once an individual has evaluated probabilities on a set of events, the following two cases are possible: either a bet can be arranged with him that assures a gain no matter what outcome occurs, or else this possibility does not exist. In the first case, the assessment is labeled incoherent—the stated probabilities involve an inconsistency. In the second case, the assessment is labeled coherent.

The coherence restriction is illustrated as follows. Consider an individual's assessment of the probabilities of rain, $P(r)$, and no rain, $P(\bar{r})$. The following system of bets can be arranged. If we fix the stakes as $s(r) = \$100$ and $s(\bar{r}) = \$100$, and require the assessor pay an amount $P(r)s(r) + P(\bar{r})s(\bar{r})$ to participate in the gamble, we have two equations that represent gains to the assessor

$$G(r) = \$100 - \$100P(r) - \$100P(\bar{r})$$
$$G(\bar{r}) = \$100 - \$100P(\bar{r}) - \$100P(r)$$

If it actually rains the net payoff to the assessor is given as $G(r)$, his winnings less his outlays. A similar payoff calculation is made if it does not rain, $G(\bar{r})$. If the individual evaluates the probabilities as $P(r) = .5$ and $P(\bar{r}) = .8$, we have an obvious incoherency. With this particular bet the assessment results in a guaranteed loss of $30. On the other hand, if the individual evaluates the probabilities as $P(r) = .2$ and $P(\bar{r}) = .5$, we again have an incoherency; however this evaluation results in a guaranteed gain of $30.

The set of coherent points (for fixed stakes) is described by the hyperplane that separates the set of preferred bets by the assessor (guaranteed gains) from the set of preferred bets by the person offering the bet. In Fig. 4.1 we have plotted assessments $P(r)$ and $P(\bar{r})$ on each axis and isogain lines associated with alternative assessments for the rainfall example. All assess-

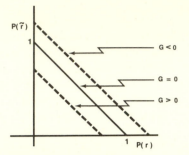

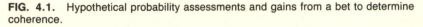

FIG. 4.1. Hypothetical probability assessments and gains from a bet to determine coherence.

---

ments lying to the northeast of the line labeled $G = 0$ represent a guaranteed loss for the assessor. These assessments will not be preferred to points lying on or below line $G = 0$. The assessor will prefer assessment points southwest of the $G = 0$ line — toward the origin. However, these points that lie below line $G = 0$ represent guaranteed losses to the person proposing the bet. He wants to move outward in a northeast direction. The set of points which is acceptable to both parties is on line $G = 0$. These points have coordinates that sum to one. These are the coherent assessments for mutually exclusive and exhaustive events. The conditions of coherence described here assume a linear utility function for money. Where such an assumption is not valid, the entire argument can be reconstructed with the assessor's utility function (deFinetti 1974, 79).

The condition of coherence can be used to derived the entire calculus of probability. That is, from the coherence definition we can derive the usual restrictions applying to disjunction (addition), conjunction (multiplication), and equivalence.

The coherence condition is given much attention in the literature because of its fundamental role in subjective probability. Since probabilities are subjective, only the coherence condition obliges an assessor to follow any particular rules, laws, or restrictions. Failure to admit the condition would ultimately compel the analyst and assessor to accept an "anything goes" position. Detailed treatments of the coherence restrictions are given in deFinetti (1937, 1974) and Bessler (1981). A recent derivation of the restrictions in a linear programming framework is given by Nau (1981). He shows that the coherence restriction for conditional probabilities can be derived from a standard linear programming problem. These restrictions are not obvious to most assessors when complex conditional statements are required. Assessments can be checked (using Nau's work) and changed (if suggested) as a regular course of the assessment task.

The coherence restrictions apply to a priori analysis of subjective probabilities. Only assessments that fail to meet these restrictions can be rejected out of hand. Recently, considerable interest has occurred in the calibration of probability assessments (De Groot and Fienberg 1981; Dawid 1982). Calibration applies to *ex post* analysis of probabilities. An assessor is said to be well calibrated if, for those trials on which he forecasts the probability *x*, the long-run frequency is *x*. De Groot and Fienberg and others demonstrate that a well-calibrated forecaster need not be informative; they introduce the concept of a *more refined* and *less refined* probability assessor. An assessor is considered more refined than another if the latter's probability can be obtained as stochastic transformation of the former's probability. In a sense calibration is a test of an assessor's performance over many trials. As such, it is not particularly useful in obtaining or motivating an assessor in providing his beliefs (as is the case for scoring rules discussed below); however, it is suggested that calibration can be useful as a feedback mechanism to make future assessments better.

As is obvious from the definition, to calibrate an assessor one must have his probabilistic assessments and actual outcomes on the event of interest over many trials. This requirement may prove too rich for reliable calibration of many forecasters. Indeed, where the event of interest (outcome) occurs infrequently (relative to the life of the assessor) one may not expect much in the way of *ex post* evaluations. As an extreme example, the observations for calibration calculations on assessors making statements on the probability of a nuclear reactor accident of a specified magnitude sometime in the next 20 years are long in coming. Yet, subjective probability statements on such events are an essential element in making rational choices about the construction of nuclear power plants.

A less extreme example, involving assessments on yearly crop prices and yields, offers greater potential for calibration; but still, the potential for obtaining numerous actual outcomes for the calibration calculation is meager—clearly not approaching what Murphy and Winkler (1977) found for weather forecasting.

Where the event occurs infrequently, some type of artificial or analogous assessment task and subsequent calibration may provide useful information. That is, we might tentatively accept that a well-calibrated assessor on weekly or monthly price changes may be well calibrated on yearly price changes too. Or, that an assessor who is well calibrated in assessing Monte Carlo generated crop yields (without knowledge of the underlying model) may be well calibrated in assessing actual crop yields. Of course such may not be the case.

Assessment and assessor motivation

The coherence and calibration restrictions (either *ex ante* or *ex post*) aid in analysis of a particular assessment or set of assessments. They are not designed to actually obtain probability assessments. Various approaches have been discussed in the literature for eliciting the assessments. These can be classified by whether or not an explicit motivation is built into the task. That is, some elicitation procedures involve an explicit payoff or reward given to the assessor depending on the outcome of the uncertain event studied. Other procedures (nonmotivating procedures) do not build such a reward into the elicitation procedure. While nonmotivating methods are generally easier to use, they probably are less accurate and at best ad hoc. A brief review of a few of these follows. As they are generally easier to use, they may provide a rough indication of probabilistic beliefs in difficult assessment tasks.

We suggest that if more than a rough indication of probabilities is required, the motivation methods be used. These may involve actual monetary payoffs. This suggestion is made by various authors including the following of Good (1965): "Probability judgments can be sharpened by laying bets at suitable odds. If people always felt obliged to back their opinions when challenged, we would be spared a few of the 'certain' predictions that are so frequently made." Of course, not all motivation methods involve such an explicit confrontation as Good suggests.

Among nonmotivating methods, probably the simplest is mere ranking of discrete outcomes. Suppose an assessor is asked to rank the n intervals defined on the real line (possible price outcomes) given in Fig. 4.2. We ask for the assessor to rank the n intervals, giving the most probable interval a rank of 1, the second most probable interval a rank of 2, ..., and the least most probable interval a rank of n. Here n is a positive integer and δ a positive number determining the interval bounds on outcome x. The construction of interval bounds can be troublesome when the random variable is continuous. Judgment and perhaps interactive adjustments in the initial testing of an assessment questionnaire can be used to specify these bounds.

The rank-order method provides very little information about the probability of each interval. All we know is that the probability of the first interval is greater than or equal to $1/n$; the second ranked interval may have

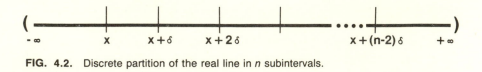

FIG. 4.2.   Discrete partition of the real line in n subintervals.

probability between zero and one-half. In general, the probability associated with the hth ranked interval ($h \geq 2$) may vary from zero to $1/h$.

An alternative nonmotivating assessment method, which is sometimes suggested for use, is the triangular probability distribution (Anderson et al. 1977). Here, assessment is on a continuous outcome space (not discrete outcomes). The assessor is asked to provide his subjective beliefs on the minimum value (defined here as A), the most likely value (B), and maximum value (C) that the random variable (X) will likely take. Density and distribution functions can be written as approximate indications of the assessor's subjective beliefs using these three parameters (see Chap. 8 for illustration).

The assignment of the range of possibility by the assessor, (A, C) can present problems, especially if he is providing an assessment on an unbounded random variable (price). Where the tails of the distribution are likely to present problems, the assessor could be asked to present upper and lower bounds such that the range includes, say, approximately 99 percent of the probability density.

Another approach to eliciting subjective probabilities that does not use an explicit motivation is the *judgmental fractile* method (Raiffa 1970). Here the assessor is asked to determine the P fractile, which is defined as the number X_o such that the probability that the random variable is less than or equal to X_o is P. To capture X_o a series of questions using reference gambles can be constructed. The .5 fractile can be determined by asking the subject to choose between two gambles. The subject is asked to choose between one gamble that pays G if $X_n > X_{no}$ and another which pays G for $X_n < X_{no}$. The choice will indicate whether the value X_{no} is at the .5 fractile or not. If the subject were to choose the gamble involving $X_n > X_{no}$, then the value for X_{no} can be increased and information on a new reference gamble obtained. After a number of iterations, the process should converge to the .5 fractile, X_{no}^*.

A similar line of questioning will establish the .75 fractile. Taking the median (.5 fractile) as a reference point, structure a second set of gambles in which the subject is paid a value G for X_n between the median point X_{no}^* and a reference point X_{no} or G for $X_n > X_{no}$. By continuing to question until the subject is indifferent between the two gambles, the .75 fractile is established. This questioning process can be continued until a sufficiently detailed description of the subject's probability distribution is obtained (see Johnson and Rausser 1982).

Nonmotivating methods assume that the assessor can easily translate his true beliefs to his stated beliefs. Since these beliefs exist solely in his mind, there is no way to determine the accuracy of this translation. Motivational assessment methods offer the assessor a reward or penalty to improve the accuracy (or correlation) between true and stated beliefs. In effect, the motivational methods establish a bet with the assessor such that an explicit outcome can be determined (*ex post*) and a payoff given relative to that outcome.

The reward or penalty can be determined according to optimality conditions. If the assessor seeks to maximize his expected payoff, he should equate his stated probabilities (*P*) and his true probabilities (*r*). A rule which satisfies this requirement is called a proper scoring rule.

Two proper scoring rules are the quadratic (deFinetti 1962) and the logarithmic (Good 1952). To illustrate these, consider an individual who must make a probability assessment for an event E that consists of n mutually exclusive and collectively exhaustive outcomes $E_1, E_2, \ldots, E_n$. Let the vector $P = (P_1, \ldots, P_n)$ denote the individual's assessment, where P_i is the assessor's stated probability that E_i will occur. Suppose the vector $r' = (r_1, \ldots, r_n)$ represents the assessor's true judgment, where r_i is his subjective probability that E_i will occur. Further, let the vector $d = (d_1, \ldots, d_n)$ represent the observation, where $d_i = 1$ if E_i occurs and zero otherwise.

The quadratic scoring rule, $Q(P, d)$ is defined as

$$Q(P, d) = 1 - \sum_{i=1}^{n}(P_i - d_i)^2$$

If outcome E_j occurs, $d_j = 1$ and $d_i = 0$ for all $i \neq j$. Thus,

$$Q_j(P, d) = \left(2P_j - \sum_{i=1}^{n} P_i^2\right)$$

The range of this rule is given as $-1 \leq Q_j \leq 1$. The assessor's expected score is given as

$$E(Q) = \sum_{j}^{n} r_j \left(2P_j - \sum_{i=1}^{n} P_i^2\right)$$

If the assessor seeks to maximize his expected payoff from $Q(P, d)$, he must set his stated beliefs equal to his true beliefs (Bessler 1981).

The logarithmic rule, $L(P, d)$, is defined as

$$L(P, d) = \ln\left(\sum_{i=1}^{n} d_i P_i\right)$$

When outcome j occurs $d_j = 1$ and $d_i = 0$, $i \neq j$, so that $L_j(P, d) = \ln P_j$. The range of the logarithmic rule is $-\infty < L_j \leq 0$. Here too, maximization of the expected score requires the assessor choose the vector $P = r$.

The quadratic rule is called a total measure of validity because it involves all of the probabilities in an assessment; while the logarithmic rule is a partial measure because its payoff is in terms of a single probability. Generally, we prefer a rule that encompasses all probabilities, but often expediency requires we use the simpler logarithmic rule. (Clearly, analysts will not want to use the logarithmic rule without modification in many assessment studies. Bessler and Moore [1979] discuss a truncated logarithmic rule which may be useful in applied assessment tasks.) The logarithmic rule is important because of its simplicity, especially when used in field work involving untrained subjects in a time-constrained environment. Shuford et al. (1966) show that the only proper scoring rule involving just the probability of the event that occurs is logarithmic. This is an important point that research workers should consider in designing an assessment study. A need to keep the assessment task simple may well preclude use of all but the logarithmic rule.

Applications in agricultural economics

The ideas discussed in the preceding sections of this chapter have direct application in research and extension efforts in agricultural economics. Both normative and positive applications are involved. The rules of coherence should be studied and adhered to in any assessment; they will be useful in educational efforts on decision making under risk. Lindley (1974b), for example, argues that we should divert our efforts away from the description of how people actually perceive uncertainty to the more important task of teaching people to properly assess probability. The coherence conditions are essential to this task.

Analysts in government agencies, universities, private research firms, and other institutions often make predictions about random variables that interest large groups of users. Examples include: aggregate forecasts of agricultural yield and production levels, forecasts of aggregate price and employment levels for the general economy, and forecasts of price levels for particular commodities. These predictions are often given as point forecasts; they are elicited with little or no explicit motivation and often with no explicit feedback or systematic evaluation. The proper scoring rules and calibration calculations can aid assessors in providing these predictions.

While simple assessment tasks may not actually require formal recognition of coherence, more complex assessments (e.g. joint and/or conditional probabilities) will require such recognition. Even the best trained assessors make mistakes. Accordingly, they should check to be sure that their assessments satisfy these conditions. The recent work of Nau (1981) may help to check for coherency (be useful in setting out coherence restrictions) in the more complex assessment tasks.

Calibration of assessments can be useful in providing feedback on past efforts and may provide evidence on possible adjustments. However, as pointed out above, the infrequent nature of many events, especially agricultural phenomena, seriously diminishes the applicability of calibration — at least directly.

While the normative field of application is wide, an equally wide field exists for describing how agents actually form their subjective beliefs, despite the argument of Lindley given above. This knowledge will improve our efforts to model economic agents' behavior. Much econometric work, for instance, requires modeling of agents' expectations on future variables. Unfortunately, it is not always clear how (or if) this modeling can be done. Muth (1961) and others argue that economic agents are rational; they form their expectations according to the relevant economic theory. Alternatively, H. A. Simon (1959b) argues that agents do not necessarily use all relevant information and in particular are not (in some senses) rational. Nerlove (1979) takes a middle ground by arguing for a quasi-rational expectation mechanism.

The consequences of these different approaches to expectations modeling are profound; they go to the very heart of what we can and cannot do in modeling agricultural markets. For instance, under Muth's rational expectations approach, the researcher will experience an argument in which the very parameters being estimated are in some sense assumed known by the economic agent. While some very simple rational expectations models can be handled, in most cases the economic structure will be too complex to model with standard econometric methods (Sims 1980).

If we do not assume economic agents are fully rational, then a relevant question is: How much information do they use in forming their expectations? Nerlove (1979) suggests using a univariate (or perhaps a multivariate) autoregressive integrated moving average (ARIMA) mechanism for modeling agents' expectations. While our earlier work (Bessler 1980) supports this suggestion for crop yields, we are still uncertain about its applicability to prices and revenues.

While these comments refer to econometric modeling of economic agents' expectations, similar uneasiness applies to models of agents' beliefs on variance. The early work of Just (1974), for instance, could be replicated under varying degrees of rationality, each resulting in a different measure of subjective variance and perhaps differing degrees of risk response. It is not clear that updating prior distributions by Bayes's theorem will necessarily generate subjective measures of risk that resemble those of real world agents (Tversky and Kahneman 1974).

In agriculture, we have not made serious extended efforts at studying the formation of expectations over time. Perhaps we should.

5

Decision rules in risk analysis

ROGER SELLEY

THE PRECEDING CHAPTERS have presented some foundations for risk analysis in agriculture. Alternative ways to model and measure risk and risk attitudes were considered, emphasizing expected utility and objective and subjective probabilities. This chapter introduces the concept of a decision rule and demonstrates its use in decision analysis under risk. Several commonly used decision rules are presented and evaluated relative to the expected utility model. Identifying the relationships among these rules should contribute to a richer, more general framework for implementing decision analysis and evaluating empirical studies, as well as for developing the various efficiency criteria in the following chapter.

Decision rule concepts

A decision rule consists of an orderly framework for evaluating alternative courses of action. Under conditions of risk a decision rule would include a selection criterion reflecting the decision maker's risk attitudes, instructions for describing the alternatives, and computational procedures for evaluating the alternatives. A logically consistent decision rule should accurately reflect the goals of the decision maker and the decision choices, while being easy to apply and understand. In practice, these attributes are difficult to attain. Moreover, the actual specification of the components of a decision problem may vary with the type of analysis: behavioral, prescriptive, or predictive. Nonetheless, well-formulated decision rules will provide an orderly, efficient approach to decision analysis under risk.

Roger Selley, University of Arizona.

A decision problem under risk can typically be described as follows: (1) mutually exclusive actions, A_j ($j = 1,\ldots, m$); (2) mutually exclusive states of nature, S_i ($i = 1,\ldots, n$); (3) probability functions, $P(S_i)$, associated with the possible states of nature; (4) a consequence, C_{ij}, associated with each of the j actions and i states of nature; and (5) a decision criterion for ordering the actions. These components are illustrated in the payoff matrix of Table 5.1 where C_{23}, ($n = 2$, $m = 3$), for example, is the consequence of state S_2 occurring with action A_3. (The payoff matrix in Table 5.1 is not the most general formulation. The uncertainty associated with unknown states of nature or unknown probabilities would require an alternative concept.)

Specifying the optimal choice as the action yielding the highest expected value provides one type of criterion for solving the decision problem. Here the expected value is the weighted average of an action's consequences over the respective states of nature using the probabilities as weights. If the consequences are measured as profits, then the decision rule is called expected profit maximization. If, however, the consequences are measured as utilities, the decision rule is called expected utility maximization.

The properties of the expected utility model (EUM) were developed in Chapter 2, with emphasis on the EUM's use in measuring risk attitudes. The axioms underlying the EUM were presented, relationships between utility functions and risk attitudes were demonstrated, and various ways to empirically measure risk attitudes were considered. However, other decision rules have also been used in risk analysis. Some were derived from the EUM, while others have been or could be derived from particular utility functions. The rest of the chapter discusses alternative decision rules and their relationship to the EUM. Included are expected profit maximization, mean-variance analysis, mean-absolute deviation analysis, mean-semivariance analysis, and safety-first analysis.

Expected profit maximization

The theory of profit maximization is extended to incorporate risk by assuming that decision makers maximize *expected* profit. Expected profit is

Table 5.1. Components of a decision problem under risk

State, S_i	P_iS_i	Consequences, C_{ij}		
		Action $A1$	Action $A2$	Action $A3$
S_1	$P(S_1)$	C_{11}	C_{12}	C_{13}
S_2	$P(S_2)$	C_{21}	C_{22}	C_{23}
S_3	$P(S_3)$	C_{31}	C_{32}	C_{33}

defined as the summation of the possible levels of profit multiplied by their respective probabilities. (Discrete distributions will be used to illustrate these concepts. The i events are assumed mutually exclusive and exhaustive so that the probabilities sum to one.) Where M_k is the kth level of profit and $P(M_k)$ is the probability of the kth level of profit, expected profit, $E(M)$, is defined as

$$E(M) = \sum_k M_k P(M_k) \tag{5.1}$$

Consider the outcome distribution given in Table 5.2. Its expected profit (column c) is \$231.25. Expected profit maximization selects the action with the largest expected profit. Alternatively, if revenue and cost functions are specified, expected profit maximization can be expressed by first-order conditions similar to those derived from the theory of the firm under conditions of certainty. (Just (1975a) has shown that where the expected marginal cost of planned production is nonlinear, the maximization of expected profit involves the variance and other higher moments of prices and output. Thus empirical evidence linking behavior with higher moments of output and prices can be consistent with expected profit maximization.)

Expected profit maximization assumes that a decision maker's satisfaction is measured by the level of profit. However, this assumption is inappropriate if the decision maker's marginal utility for profits diminishes, for example, as profits increase. Expected profit maximization is in fact a special linear case of the more general EUM. To show this relationship, let expected utility be specified as

$$E(U[M]) = \sum_i U[M_i]P(M_i) \tag{5.2}$$

For a linear utility function (Fig. 5.1a) $U[M_i] = a + bM_i$ and

$$
\begin{aligned}
E(U[M]) &= \sum_i U[M_i]P(M_i) \\
&= \sum_i (a + bM_i)P(M_i) \\
&= a \sum_i P(M_i) + b\sum_i M_i P(M_i) \\
&= a + bE(M)
\end{aligned}
$$

Maximizing $a + bE(M)$ for $b > 0$ is equivalent to maximizing $E(M)$; thus maximizing expected profit is a special case of maximizing expected utility.

Table 5.2. Expected profit and variance of profit for ABC stock

Profit ($)	Probability	Probability times profit	Deviation from E(Profit) ($)	Squared deviations ($)	Probability	Probability times squared deviations
(a)	(b)	(c)	(d)	(e)	(f)	(g)
−200	0.05	−10.00	−431.25	185,977	0.05	9,299
−50	0.10	−5.00	−281.25	79,102	0.10	7,910
25	0.25	6.25	−206.25	42,539	0.25	10,635
300	0.45	135.00	68.75	4,727	0.45	2,127
700	0.15	105.00	468.75	219,727	0.15	32,959
Sum 1.00		Expected profit $231.25			Sum 1.00	62,930
					Variance	62,930

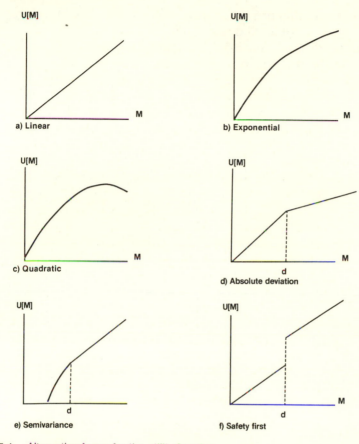

FIG. 5.1. Alternative forms for the utility function.

The mean-variance model

Expected profit was defined as the weighted average of all possible outcomes. The variance of profit is the weighted average of the squared deviations of profit from expected profit. Therefore variance of profit, $V(M)$, is defined as

$$V(M) = \sum_i [M_i - E(M)]^2 P(M_i) \tag{5.3}$$

Variance measures the dispersion of profit about its expected value. Using squared distance (deviation) as the measure of closeness gives larger deviations more importance. For the ABC stock in Table 5.2, a profit of

$700 has a deviation of $468.75 from the expected value. Profits of $-$50 and $25 show a combined deviation of $-$281.25 $-$ 206.25 $=$ $-$487.50. Even though the deviation of $700 is smaller than the combined deviation of $-$50 and $25, the squared deviation for $700 is much larger, 219,727 versus 79,102 $+$ 42,539 $=$ 121,641. The property of penalizing alternatives with wide deviations from the expected value can make the variance an attractive measure of risk depending upon the individual's risk preferences (utility function). However, penalizing alternatives equally for deviations above and below the expected value can be a shortcoming of the variance, as discussed below.

Markowitz (1959) proposed that decision makers select a portfolio based on a decision rule that minimizes the variance of profit for a given level of expected profit. When the level of expected profit is varied, this approach yields an efficiency frontier where variance is the measure of risk.

To show the relationship of the mean-variance model to expected utility, consider the exponential utility function (Fig. 5.1b).

$$U[M] = a - be^{-\lambda M} \tag{5.4}$$

where b and λ exceed zero.

If profit M is normally distributed (either by assumption, empirical verification, or application of the control limit theorem for the sum of several random variables (Goldberger 1964), then it can be shown that

$$E(U[M]) = a - be^{-\lambda E(M) + (\lambda^2/2)V(M)} \tag{5.5}$$

Maximizing (5.5) is equivalent to maximizing (Freund 1956)

$$E(U[M]) = E(M) - (\lambda/2)V(M) \tag{5.6}$$

Hence mean-variance analysis applies when maximizing the exponential function in (5.4), and normality is assumed. The magnitude of λ represents the degree of risk aversion under exponential utility. The larger is λ the more penalty is placed on large variances and the more risk averse is the individual. Maximizing (5.6) for a given λ is the mean-variance decision rule. It provides an ordering of alternatives consistent with the EUM. Where λ is unknown, (5.6) can be used as an efficiency criterion to order risky choices into efficient and inefficient sets (see Chaps. 6, 9).

The mean-variance efficient set is also consistent with a quadratic utility function (Fig. 5.1c). To illustrate, consider the quadratic function

$$U[M] = M - \lambda M^2 \tag{5.7}$$

where $\lambda > 0$.

Expected utility is

$$E(U[M]) = E(M) - \lambda E(M^2) \tag{5.8}$$

and since $V(M) = E[M - E(M)]^2 = E(M^2) - (E[M])^2$, solving for $E(M^2)$ and substituting into (5.8) results in expected utility as a function of expected profit and variance,

$$E(U[M]) = E(M) - \lambda V(M) - \lambda[E(M)]^2 \tag{5.9}$$

Note that the quadratic utility function does not increase monotonically. It reaches a maximum at $U' = 1 - 2\lambda M = 0$, where U' is the first derivative of utility with respect to profits M. For a given λ, the maximum monetary value consistent with nonnegative marginal utility is $M = 1/2\lambda$. In contrast, the exponential utility function is monotone increasing; however it requires normally distributed returns for mean-variance analysis.

Mean-absolute deviation analysis

Mean-absolute deviation analysis is a decision rule in which the measure of risk is based on the absolute deviation of profit from the mean. The absolute deviation is equal to $M - d$ for $M \geq d$ and $-(M-d)$ for $M < d$ where $d = E(M)$. The absolute deviation is represented by $|M-d|$ and the expected absolute deviation, A, is

$$A = E|M-d| \tag{5.10}$$

For $d = E(M)$, mean-absolute deviation analysis measures risk as deviations from expected profit; however, it does not penalize the larger deviations as does mean-variance analysis. Johnson and Boehlje (1981) have argued that for symmetric distributions, mean-expected absolute deviation analysis will in theory provide the same ordinal ranking of alternatives as mean-variance analysis.

To consider the relationship between expected utility and mean-absolute deviation analysis, let utility be specified as (see Fig. 5.1d)

$$U = a + bM - \lambda|M-d|, \quad b \text{ and } \lambda > 0 \tag{5.11}$$

which results in expected utility of the form

$$E(U) = a + bE(M) - \lambda E|M-d| \tag{5.12}$$

Maximizing expected utility based upon (5.12) for a fixed d is equivalent to determining the optimal trade-off between expected profit and the expected absolute deviation about d, that is, mean-absolute deviation analysis about a fixed point. Mean-absolute deviation analysis about the mean is not consistent with expected utility maximization, however. Comparing alternative actions with different means would result in different values for d in (5.11). Hence the utility function would not give the same utility for the same income for all alternatives as is required under the expected utility model.

Mean-semivariance analysis

The probability distribution for XYZ stock in Table 5.3 has the same mean and variance as the ABC stock distribution in Table 5.2. According to mean-variance analysis, these two distributions are equivalent. However, differences in their probabilities of negative returns—16 percent for ABC and 6 percent for XYZ—may be important to decision makers who are concerned with other performance characteristics besides means and variances. In this case, the nonsymmetry of the XYZ distribution may not be suitably evaluated by the mean-variance criterion alone.

Another decision rule that focuses on the downside of a distribution is mean-semivariance analysis. The semivariance of profit about the target d, SV_d, is the expected value of the squared deviations of profit below d, $E(M-d \mid M<d)^2$. Therefore semivariance of profit about the target d is

$$SV_d(M) = \sum_i \min(M_i - d, 0)^2 \, P(M_i) \tag{5.13}$$

The calculation of semivariance is illustrated in Table 5.4 for the ABC and XYZ distributions. Letting $d = -\$50$ results in a semivariance of 1125 and 1350, for ABC and XYZ stocks, respectively. Recall that the expected value of each investment is $231.25. Hence, a decision maker would prefer the ABC stock if concerned in particular about losses of $50 or more. However, a more conservative investor seeking to avoid returns below $100 ($d = 100$) would select the XYZ stock since it has the lower semivariance. Thus, mean-semivariance analysis is preferred to mean-variance analysis when the outcome distributions are asymmetric.

Porter (1974) has investigated the mean-semivariance approach when the utility function is specified as (see Fig. 5.1e)

$$
\begin{aligned}
U[M] &= a + bM - \lambda(M - d)^2 \quad \text{for } M < d \\
&= a + bM \qquad\qquad\qquad \text{for } M \geq d
\end{aligned}
\tag{5.14}
$$

where b and $\lambda > 0$. This specification avoids the negative marginal utility

Table 5.3. Distribution of profit for XYZ stock

Profit ($)	Probability	Probability times profit ($)	Deviation from E(Profit) ($)	Squared deviations	Probability times squared deviations
−200.00	0.06	−12.00	−431.25	$185,977	11,159
0	0.20	0	−231.25	53,477	10,695
190.38	0.15	28.56	40.87	1,670	251
231.25	0.44	101.75	0	0	0
752.95	0.15	112.94	521.70	272,171	40,825
Sum	1.00	231.25			62,930

Table 5.4. Semivariance of ABC and XYZ stocks

Distribution 1: ABC stock

Profit ($)	Probability	Min (M − d, 0) ($)		Squared deviations ($)		Probability times squared deviations ($)	
		d = −50	d = 100	d = −50	d = 100	d = −50	d = 100
−200	0.05	−150	−300	22,500	90,000	1125	4500
−50	0.10	0	−150	0	22,500	0	2250
25	0.25	0	−75	0	5,625	0	1406
300	0.45	0	0	0	0	0	0
700	0.15	0	0	0	0	0	0
Sum	1.00					1125	8156

Distribution 2: XYZ stock

Profit ($)	Probability	Min (M − d, 0) ($)		Squared deviations ($)		Probability times squared deviations ($)	
		d = −50	d = 100	d = −50	d = 100	d = −50	d = 100
−200.00	0.06	−150	−300	22,500	90,000	1350	5400
0	0.20	0	−100	0	10,000	0	2000
190.38	0.15	0	0	0	0	0	0
231.25	0.44	0	0	0	0	0	0
752.95	0.15	0	0	0	0	0	0
Sum	1.00					$1350	$7400

problem of the quadratic function as long as the expression $a + bM - \lambda (M - d)^2$ reaches its maximum at $M > d$. Expected utility for (5.14) is

$$E(U[M]) = a + bM - \lambda E(M - d \mid M < d)^2 \qquad (5.15)$$

Mean-semivariance analysis can be computed about the mean or a fixed point. As with mean-absolute deviation analysis about the mean, mean-semivariance analysis about the mean is not consistent with expected utility maximization, while mean-semivariance about a fixed point can be (when (5.15) is maximized, for example).

When the distributions are symmetrical, the mean-variance model has the advantage of requiring only one parameter to represent the level of risk aversion. In contrast, the mean-semivariance model requires information on both λ and d to represent risk aversion. This point is further illustrated when these models are used as efficiency criteria. The semivariance model requires derivations of separate efficient frontiers for each value of d, based on parametric variations in λ (Hogan and Warren 1972).

Safety first

The safety-first rules have focused on the probability of achieving the target return d (Pyle and Turnovsky 1970). These rules were presented in Chapter 2 and are summarized as follows. Telser's formulation, (2.9), assumes that a decision maker maximizes expected profits subject to the constraint that the probability of a return less than d does not exceed a given probability. Kataoka's formulation, (2.10), involves maximizing the target d that can be achieved at a given probability level. Roy, (2.11), considered minimizing the probability of returns falling below target d.

To evaluate the relationship between expected utility and the safety-first model, consider the following utility function:

$$\begin{aligned} U[M] &= a + bM - \lambda \text{ for } M < d \\ &= a + bM \quad\quad \text{ for } M \geq d \end{aligned} \qquad (5.16)$$

where b and $\lambda > 0$. Finding expected utility results in

$$E(U[M]) = a + bE(M) - \lambda\alpha \qquad (5.17)$$

where $\alpha = P(M < d)$, which for given α and d corresponds to Telser's safety-first formulation where λ represents the preference weight for returns above target d. In contrast to the utility function for mean-semivariance analysis, (5.16) is linear in income for all M with a discontinuity at $M = d$ (Fig. 5.1d). Thus, the safety-first model does not penalize large deviations below the mean as do the mean-variance and mean-semivariance models. Safety first can also be used to rank action choices, as illustrated by the ABC and XYZ stock investments. For $d = -\$50$ the safety-first model ranks ABC over XYZ since $1 - \alpha = 0.95$ and 0.94, respectively. For $d = \$100$, XYZ is preferred over ABC since $1 - \alpha = .74$ and $.60$, respectively.

The safety-first rules are frequently characterized as ad hoc because they cannot be derived from the maximization of expected utility (Anderson 1977). As illustrated above, however, maximizing expected utility based on (5.16) and (5.17) is equivalent to a safety-first problem.

Moreover, Fishburn (1977) has shown that utility functions of the form

$$
\begin{aligned}
U[M] &= a + bM - \lambda_0(M - d)^{\lambda_1} \quad \text{for } M < d \\
&= a + bM \qquad\qquad\qquad\quad \text{for } M > d
\end{aligned}
\tag{5.18}
$$

where b and $\lambda_0 > 0$, $\lambda_1 > 0$, are consistent with the axioms of the expected utility model. Equation (5.16) is a special case of (5.18) where $\lambda_1 = 0$. The reader can verify that any of the functional forms in Fig. 5.1 will satisfy the axioms of the expected utility model. Consider for example, $A_1 = W + M$, $A_2 = W$, and $A_3 = W - M$. Then for any W, any positive M, and positive marginal utility, $A_1 > A_2$, and $A_2 > A_3$ for all utility functions (ordering). Also for positive marginal utility, $A_1 > A_2$, $A_2 > A_3$, and $A_1 > A_3$ (transitivity). For $P = .5$ or for any other positive P, $.5A_1 + .5A_3 > .5A_2 + .5A_3$ (substitution). Also a value of P exists such that $PA_1 + (1 - P)A_3 = A_2$ (certainty equivalent).

Specification of outcomes in risk models

In the discussion above, initial wealth, W, was assumed certain (deterministic) while M represented the outcome from a risky prospect. Expected final wealth then is

$$
E(W + M) = W + E(M)
\tag{5.19}
$$

and the variance of final wealth is

$$
V(W + M) = V(M)
\tag{5.20}
$$

Therefore risk (mean-variance) analysis in terms of final wealth provides the same result as risk analysis in terms of M, the outcome of the risky prospect.

Where initial wealth is stochastic, expected final wealth becomes

$$E(W + M) = E(W) + E(M) \qquad (5.21)$$

However, the variance of final wealth becomes

$$
\begin{aligned}
V(W + M) &= E[W + M - E(W + M)]^2 \\
&= E[W - E(W)]^2 + E[M - E(M)]^2 \\
&\quad + 2E[W - E(W)] [M - E(M)] \\
&= V(W) + V(M) + 2\,\text{Cov}(W, M) \qquad (5.22)
\end{aligned}
$$

where the covariance between W and M is by definition

$$\text{Cov}(W, M) = E[W - E(W)] [M - E(M)] \qquad (5.23)$$

Because of the difficulty in measuring the covariance between initial wealth and individual investment alternatives, empirical measures generally represent gains and losses from utility functions for alternative actions without considering current portfolios. This approach implies that initial wealth is nonstochastic. As Hildreth (1974) pointed out, however, an assumption of nonstochastic initial wealth ignores important components of risky decision making. In a normative framework initial wealth should be specified as stochastic where possible.

The psychology literature on utility theory and elicitation procedures has typically worked with gains and losses, implying that the utility function does not respond to changes in wealth over time. Whether actual behavior is more consistent with the formulation of utility in final wealth or gains and losses is an important empirical question.

Concluding comments

The decision rules reviewed in this chapter are summarized in Table 5.5, in terms of their solution algorithms, relationships to utility functions, and behavioral implications. Each decision rule can be applied in a mathematical programming algorithm where profit is linear in the activities and constraints. The use of linear programming (LP) to maximize expected profit is straightforward under these conditions as is the use of quadratic programming (QP) in mean-variance analysis. LP is also used for absolute deviation analysis about the mean as shown in later chapters. Hogan and Warren (1972) have developed a modified QP for solving mean-semivariance analysis about a fixed point. And Selley (1980) has reported a procedure requiring multiple LP solutions for use in safety-first analysis.

Each decision rule in Table 5.5 has an equivalent under the expected utility model. Mean-variance analysis follows from exponential utility and

Table 5.5. Some characteristics of selected decision rules

Decision rule	Solution algorithm	Utility function	Prefer more to less	Diminishing marginal utility	Penalize skewness to left
Expected profit max	LP	$a + bM$	Yes for $b > 0$	No	No
Mean-variance analysis	QP	$a - be^{-\lambda M}$ for M normal	Yes for b and $\lambda > 0$	Yes	No
Mean-variance analysis	QP	$a + bM - cM^2$	Not for $M > b/2C$	Yes	No
Mean-absolute deviation analysis	LP	$a + bM - \lambda|M - d|$ for fixed d	Yes for $b > 0$	Only in steps	Yes for $d < E(M)$
Mean-semivariance analysis	Modified QP	$a + bM - \lambda(M - d)^2$ for $M < d$, $a + bM$ for $M \geq d$; for fixed d	Yes for $b > 0$	Yes for $M \geq d$	Yes
Safety-first analysis	LP	$a + bM$ for $M < d$, $a + bM$ for $M \geq d$; for fixed d	Yes for $b > 0$	No	Yes for $d < E(M)$

normality, or from quadratic utility; mean-absolute deviation analysis about a fixed point, mean-semivariance analysis about a fixed point, and safety-first analysis all follow from particular specifications of the utility functions.

Each decision rule can be further characterized in relationship to expected utility. For example, more income should generally be preferred to less, which holds for all the utility functions except the quadratic. Diminishing marginal utility is also a common characteristic of individuals that is violated for expected profit maximization and safety-first analysis, and for some levels of income when using mean-absolute deviation and mean-semivariance analysis around a fixed point. A risk averter should also prefer a positively skewed distribution to a negatively skewed one if both distributions have the same mean and variance. Of the utility functions in Table 5.5, only those with a target income penalize negative skewness.

Future developments in theory and methods of analysis should continue to bring decision rules with greater generality and wider applicability. Broadening the concept of expected utility and its axiomatic base has received attention too. Machina (1979), for example, recently explored conditions in which expected utility is a specific case of a more general model that does not require the substitution axiom. He shows that most of the results derived from expected utility maximization based on a concave utility function are still valid in the more general case.

The axioms of expected utility are not the only possible set of axioms for decision making under risk. The psychology literature treats the formation of personal probabilities as an expression of probability preferences. Kahneman and Tversky (1979) use the idea of a probability preference function to develop an axiomatic theory of behavior that allows the decision maker to be less than fully consistent with the expected utility model. They demonstrate that much of the behavior that appears inconsistent with expected utility is consistent with their prospect theory. It is an empirical question whether prospect theory or perhaps an alternative such as expected utility without the substitution axiom will better serve the researcher in predicting behavior and specifying decision rules.

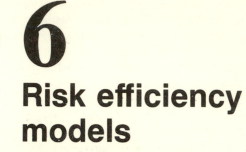

Risk efficiency models

ROBERT P. KING AND LINDON J. ROBISON

THIS CHAPTER INTRODUCES the concept of an efficiency criterion and presents five widely used criteria: (1) first degree stochastic dominance, (2) second degree stochastic dominance, (3) mean-variance efficiency, (4) mean-absolute deviation efficiency, and (5) stochastic dominance with respect to a function. (This list is not exhaustive. Other efficiency criteria, such as Baumol's [1963] expected gain confidence limit and Whitmore's [1970] third degree stochastic dominance are not discussed. Similarly, recent advances in multiattribute efficiency criteria [Kihlstrom and Mirman 1974; Levy and Paroush 1974] and in convex stochastic criteria [Fishburn 1974] are not reviewed.) The strengths and weaknesses of each criterion are evaluated and an empirical application shows the differences in their structure, generality, and ease of application.

Concept of an efficiency criterion

The expected utility model (EUM) is the basis for much of decision theory under uncertainty. The model provides a choice criterion — expected utility maximization — that integrates information about a decision maker's preferences and expectations in order to identify preferred choices under uncertainty. Despite the EUM's wide acceptance in decision theory, operational problems often occur in its practical application. Particularly serious are difficulties in accurately measuring a decision maker's preferences.

The most direct way to measure preferences is to estimate a decision maker's utility function. A utility function relates the possible outcomes of

Robert P. King, University of Minnesota, and Lindon J. Robison, Michigan State University.

a choice to a single-valued index of desirability. As such, it is an exact representation of preferences. For several reasons, however, an estimated utility function may not be completely accurate. Shortcomings in interview procedures (Officer and Halter 1968; Binswanger 1980), problems in statistical estimation (Knowles 1980), and individuals' lack of knowledge about their preferences (Zadeh 1973) may all hamper the estimation process.

Some of the problems with single-valued utility functions are overcome by using an efficiency criterion to order choices. Given specified restrictions on the decision maker's preferences and, in some cases, on the probability distributions of feasible alternatives, an efficiency criterion provides a *partial* ordering of choices. As Levy and Sarnat (1972) note, an efficiency criterion divides the decision alternatives into two mutually exclusive sets: an efficient set and inefficient set. The efficient set contains the preferred choice of every individual whose preferences conform to the restrictions associated with the criterion. No element in the inefficient set is preferred by any of these decision makers. Thus, the inefficient alternatives are no longer considered.

An efficiency criterion applies for a particular class of decision makers, as defined by a set of restrictions on their utility functions. If these restrictions are rather general in nature, the criterion can order alternatives, while requiring only minimal information about preferences. If enough alternatives are eliminated, decision makers can make a final choice from the efficient alternatives. A major problem with efficiency criteria, however, is the possible trade-off between their discriminatory power and general applicability. Efficiency criteria that place few restrictions on preferences, and so apply for most decision makers, may not eliminate many choices from consideration. Conversely, criteria that identify small efficient sets usually require more specific information about preferences. Thus efficiency criteria help resolve some of the problems of single-valued utility functions but have shortcomings of their own.

Efficiency criteria are useful in situations involving a single decision maker whose preferences are not known, in situations involving several decision makers whose preferences differ yet conform to a specific set of restrictions, and in analyzing policy alternatives or extension recommendations that affect many diverse individuals. They are also useful in deriving widely applicable theoretical results. As such, efficiency criteria are valuable tools in risk analysis.

First degree stochastic dominance

First degree stochastic dominance (Quirk and Saposnik 1962; Hadar and Russell 1969; Hanoch and Levy 1969) is the simplest and most universally applicable efficiency criterion. First degree stochastic dominance

(FSD) holds for all decision makers who have positive marginal utility for the performance measure being considered. Under FSD an alternative with an outcome distribution defined by cumulative distribution function $F(y)$ is preferred to a second alternative with cumulative distribution function $G(y)$ if

$$F(y) \leq G(y) \tag{6.1}$$

for all possible values of y and if the inequality is strict for some value of y. (For any value y^* of the random variable Y, the corresponding value of the cumulative distribution function, $F(y^*)$, is the probability that a sample observation of Y will have a value less than or equal to y^*.) Graphically, this condition means that the cumulative of the dominant distribution must never lie above the cumulative of the dominated distribution. In Fig. 6.1, for example, $F(y)$ dominates $G(y)$ by FSD, but neither $F(y)$ nor $G(y)$ can be ordered with respect to $H(y)$.

The FSD criterion holds for all decision makers who prefer more to less. This wide generality limits the usefulness of FSD, however, since this criterion often eliminates few choices from consideration. Consider, for example, the three outcome distributions in Table 6.1 and their cumulative distributions in Fig. 6.2. Though most individuals would prefer B, none of these distributions is eliminated from the FSD efficient set. For most outcome levels, the cumulative of B lies below the cumulative of both A and C. Between outcome levels of $-4,000$ and $-5,000$, however, the cumulative of distribution A lies below that of B; thus B cannot dominate A. Similarly, the cumulative of C lies below that of B between outcome levels 35,000 and 36,000, so B cannot dominate C. Finally, since the cumulative functions of A and C also intersect, neither A nor C can dominate the other.

These three distributions can be easily ordered by inspection. However,

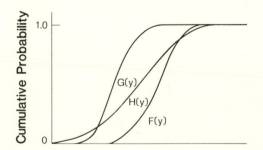

FIG. 6.1.   First and second degree stochastic dominance.

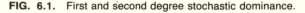

Table 6.1. Three sample outcome distributions

	Distribution		
	A	B	C
	−4,000	−5,000	−5,000
	−4,000	5,000	5,000
	−4,000	15,000	5,000
	25,000	25,000	5,000
	25,000	35,000	36,000
Mean	7,600	15,000	9,200
Standard deviation	14,207	14,142	13,948
Mean-absolute deviation	13,920	12,000	10,720

Note: Each element of each distribution has an equal probability, .2, of occurring.

when many alternatives must be evaluated, FSD may not effectively reduce the choice set.

Second degree stochastic dominance

Second degree stochastic dominance (Hadar and Russell 1969; Hanoch and Levy 1969) is more discriminating than FSD. Second degree stochastic dominance (SSD) holds for all decision makers whose utility functions have positive, nonincreasing slopes at all outcome levels. These individuals are risk averse. Under SSD, an alternative with the cumulative distribution function $F(y)$ is preferred to a second alternative with cumulative distribution function $G(y)$ if

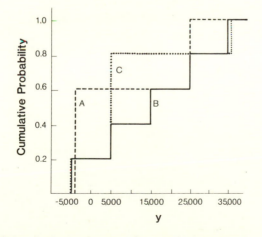

FIG. 6.2. Cumulative distribution functions for sample distributions.

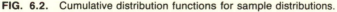

$$\int_{-\infty}^{y} F(y)\, dy \leq \int_{-\infty}^{y} G(y)\, dy \qquad\qquad (6.2)$$

for all possible values of y, and if the inequality is strict for some value of y. Under SSD distributions are compared based on the accumulated area under these cumulative distributions. Graphically, because the accumulated area under $F(y)$ in Fig. 6.1 is always less than or equal to that under either $G(y)$ or $H(y)$, only $F(y)$ is in the SSD efficient set for these three alternatives. When only $G(y)$ and $H(y)$ are considered, neither dominates the other by SSD, since the accumulated area under $G(y)$ is less than the area under $H(y)$ for low values of y, while the opposite condition occurs at high values of y.

SSD is a widely used efficiency criterion. It has more discriminatory power than FSD, and the risk averse assumption seems reasonable for many situations. However, the assumption of risk aversion does not always hold. Empirical evidence indicates that decision makers do, at times, exhibit preferences for risk (Officer and Halter 1968; Conklin et al. 1977). Recent theoretical work by Kahneman and Tversky (1979) also indicates that risk preferring behavior may be more prevalent than was earlier believed. Furthermore, although SSD is more discriminating than FSD, it still may not effectively reduce the number of alternatives. In an application by Anderson (1975), for example, 20 of 48 randomly generated farm plans were in the SSD efficient set.

This lack of discriminatory power is also illustrated in Table 6.1. Distribution C is dominated by B under SSD. As Fig. 6.2 shows, the accumulated area under B is always less than or equal to the area under C. Distributions A and B cannot be ordered under this criterion, however, since the accumulated area under the cumulative of A is less than that for B at low levels of y while the opposite condition occurs at high levels of y. In this example, then, SSD still fails to eliminate one alternative that few individuals would prefer.

Mean-variance efficiency

Mean-variance efficiency (Markowitz 1959) is the most familiar and most widely used efficiency criterion. Like SSD, mean-variance (EV) efficiency requires that the decision maker be risk averse. In addition, EV efficiency requires that the outcome distributions be normal or that the decision maker's utility function be quadratic. When these restrictions are met, the EV efficient set is identical to the SSD efficient set.

When outcome distributions are normal, or when the decision maker's utility function is quadratic, all relevant information concerning the probability distributions of alternative choices is conveyed by means and variances. Therefore, the EV efficiency criterion is stated in terms of these two moments. Outcome distribution F, with mean E_F and variance V_F, dominates distribution G, with mean E_G and variance V_G, if $E_F \geq E_G$ and $V_F \leq V_G$ and if one of these two inequalities is strict. Consider, for example, the three normal distributions defined in Table 6.2. Distribution X dominates Z, since X has a higher mean and a lower variance. Distributions X and Y cannot be ordered, however, since X has a higher mean and variance than Y.

EV efficiency is widely used for several reasons. The means and variances of probability distributions are easy to work with and familiar to most analysts. In addition, much theoretical work on decision making under uncertainty has used the EV criterion for analytical convenience. The extensive literature on portfolio analysis is an example. Perhaps the greatest strength of the EV efficiency criterion is its use in mathematical (quadratic) programming. In the most widely used formulation, the variance of the outcome distribution is minimized subject to the constraint that the distribution's expected value is greater than or equal to some specified value. By varying the expected-value constraint parametrically, an EV efficient set can be identified. In contrast, both FSD and SSD require pair-wise comparisons between alternatives. Therefore, they are not well suited for use in mathematical programming models. (Markowitz [1977] has developed a linear programming algorithm designed to identify strategies that are undominated under the criterion of SSD. The algorithm requires a special computer code and is not generally available.) This limitation becomes severe as the number of feasible alternatives in a decision situation increases.

Several problems are also associated with EV efficiency. As with SSD, the decision maker is assumed to be everywhere risk averse. When this assumption does not hold, the preferred choice may be excluded from the EV efficient set. Furthermore, like SSD, EV efficiency often does not effectively reduce the number of decision alternatives. In addition, when the EV criterion is used to order nonnormal distributions, which are common in agricultural situations, the resulting efficient set may differ from the SSD efficient set. In Table 6.1, for example, distribution B dominates C under SSD, yet the two are not ordered by the EV criterion. (The standard devia-

Table 6.2. Three normal outcome distributions

	Distributions		
	X	Y	Z
Mean	20,000	10,000	18,000
Variance	100,000	80,000	105,000

tion is simply the square root of the variance. Since this is a positive, monotonic transformation, if the variance of one distribution is larger [smaller] than that of another, its standard deviation will also be larger [smaller].) Conversely A and B are not ordered by SSD, yet B dominates A under the EV criterion. Nonetheless, Tsiang (1972) and Levy and Markowitz (1979) have shown that the EV criterion often serves as a reasonable approximation of SSD.

Mean-absolute deviation efficiency

The mean-absolute deviation (MOTAD) criterion is an approximation to EV efficiency that can be modeled with linear programming (Hazell 1971). Linear programming algorithms are more widely available and less difficult to use than are the quadratic programming algorithms required for EV analysis. Direct links between the MOTAD criterion and the form of the decision maker's utility function cannot be made analytically. It is generally assumed, though, that MOTAD efficiency holds for risk averse decision makers. When the distributions being ordered are approximately normal, the MOTAD efficient set closely resembles the EV efficient set.

Under the MOTAD criterion, the mean and the mean-absolute deviation of outcome distributions are used to order alternatives. The mean-absolute deviation, $A,$ is defined as

$$A = \frac{1}{n} \sum_{i=1}^{n} \left| y_i - \mu_y \right| \tag{6.3}$$

where n is the number of observed outcome levels, y_i is the ith observed outcome level, and μ_y is the expected value of the outcome variable. Outcome distribution $F,$ with mean E_F and mean-absolute deviation $A_F,$ dominates distribution $G,$ with mean E_G and mean-absolute deviation $A_G,$ if $E_F \geq E_G$ and $A_F \leq A_G$ and if one of the two inequalities is strict.

Consider again the three distributions in Table 6.1. Distribution A is dominated under MOTAD by B and C since it has both a lower mean and a higher mean-absolute deviation. Distributions B and C cannot be ordered under MOTAD, since B has a greater mean and mean-absolute deviation than C. The MOTAD efficient set is comprised of B and $C,$ as is the EV efficient set. Again, this result does not coincide with the SSD efficient set comprised of distributions A and B. When distributions are not normal, the ordering by MOTAD efficiency may poorly approximate the ordering by SSD. Furthermore, like SSD and EV efficiency, MOTAD efficiency is sometimes limited by its requirement of risk aversion and its low discriminatory power.

Despite these shortcomings, the MOTAD criterion is frequently used in risk programming. In Hazell's (1971) formulation, the sum of negative absolute deviations is minimized subject to an income constraint. The sum of negative absolute deviations can be shown to equal $(n/2)A$, where n is the number of observed outcome levels and A is mean-absolute deviation. Since this is a positive, monotonic transformation, orderings based on negative absolute deviations will be identical to those based on mean-absolute deviations. An efficient set of strategies is identified by varying the income constraint.

Stochastic dominance with respect to a function

Each criterion described above has relatively low discriminatory power. None will reliably reduce a large number of choices to an efficient set that can be ordered directly by the decision maker. Furthermore, SSD, EV, and MOTAD efficiency may be unrealistic if risk aversion does not always hold.

Stochastic dominance with respect to a function (SDRF) is a more discriminating efficiency criterion that allows for greater flexibility in representing preferences (Meyer 1977b). It also requires more detailed information on preferences, however. The SDRF orders uncertain choices for decision makers whose absolute risk aversion functions lie within specified lower and upper bounds. The absolute risk aversion function is defined as (see Chap. 2)

$$R_a(y) = -U''(y)/U'(y) \tag{6.4}$$

More formally stated, SDRF establishes necessary and sufficient conditions under which the cumulative distribution function $F(y)$ is preferred to the cumulative distribution function $G(y)$ by all individuals whose absolute risk aversion functions lie everywhere between lower and upper bounds $r_1(y)$ and $r_2(y)$. As developed by Meyer, the solution procedure requires the identification of a utility function $u_o(y)$, which minimizes

$$\int_{-\infty}^{\infty} [G(y) - F(y)] u'(y) \, dy \tag{6.5}$$

subject to the constraint

$$r_1(y) \leq -u''(y)/u'(y) \leq r_2(y) \quad \text{for all values of } y \tag{6.6}$$

Expression (6.5) accounts for the difference between the expected utilities of outcome distributions $F(y)$ and $G(y)$. If, for a given class of decision makers, the minimum of this difference is positive, then $F(y)$ is unanimously preferred to $G(y)$. This condition implies that the expected utility of $F(y)$ is always greater than that of $G(y)$. If the minimum is zero, an individual in the relevant class of decision makers may be indifferent between the two alternatives. Thus they cannot be ordered. Should the minimum of (6.5) be negative, $F(y)$ is not unanimously preferred to $G(y)$. In this case the expression

$$\int_{-\infty}^{\infty} [F(y) - G(y)]u'(y)\, dy \qquad\qquad (6.7)$$

must be minimized subject to (6.6) to determine whether $G(y)$ is unanimously preferred to $F(y)$. As with other efficiency criteria, a complete ordering is not ensured by SDRF. The minimum of both (6.5) and (6.7) can be negative, which implies that neither distribution is unanimously preferred by the relevant class of decision makers. (Meyer uses optimal control techniques to derive a rule for determining the absolute risk aversion function of the utility function that minimizes (6.5). This rule can be applied if the relatively unrestrictive assumption is met that $[G(y) - F(y)]$ changes sign a finite number of times. Details of the solution technique are given in Meyer [1977b] and an example is given in King and Robison [1981a].)

SDRF imposes no restrictions on the width or shape of the relevant risk aversion interval. The absolute risk aversion functions that define the relevant class of decision makers need not be constants; they can be placed anywhere in risk aversion space. Moreover, FSD and SSD are special cases of the more general SDRF criterion. The requirement for positive marginal utility under FSD places no restrictions on the decision maker's absolute risk aversion function, so that $r_1(y) = -\infty$ and $r_2(y) = \infty$ for all possible values of y. The requirement under SSD that marginal utility be decreasing as well as positive implies that $r_1(y) = 0$ and $r_2(y) = \infty$ for all values of y.

The greater discriminatory power of SDRF is illustrated in Table 6.1. Let the lower and upper bounds for the absolute risk aversion functions be constants, equal to $-.0001$ and $.0007$, respectively. Under these conditions distribution B dominates both A and C. Unlike the other efficiency criteria, SDRF can identify a single distribution that is preferred by most individuals. Had the relevant range of absolute risk aversion levels been set higher, however, A and B or A alone would be in the efficient set. Similarly, had the relevant range of absolute risk aversion been set lower, the efficient set could include B and C or C alone. Thus, the ordering of choices based on SDRF depends on the specified lower and upper bounds.

SDRF is a powerful analytical tool. However, it requires specific information on the lower and upper bounds for a decision maker's absolute risk aversion function. A procedure developed by King and Robison (1981b) uses information revealed through a series of choices between carefully selected distributions to establish these lower and upper bounds. The degree of precision in measuring preferences can be specified in accordance with the problem under consideration. At the extremes, the interval can have infinite width, or it can converge to a single line.

Interval preference measurements for two decision makers are shown in Fig. 6.3. The form of the risk functions for the upper and lower bounds is not restricted. For decision maker *A,* the bounded interval slopes downward, while for decision maker *B* it slopes upward, then downward. The interval measurements for both decision makers contain negative as well as positive values at some income levels. In contrast, the relevant range of absolute risk aversion levels for the other efficiency criteria is infinitely wide and fixed by assumption. Similarly, the properties of absolute risk aversion functions derived from estimated utility functions are determined by the functional form (Lin and Chang 1978).

Like FSD and SSD, SDRF cannot be incorporated into a standard mathematical programming model. However, a generalized risk efficient Monte Carlo programming model that uses SDRF as an evaluative criterion was developed by King (1979). In this model, the outcome distributions of randomly generated strategies are determined by Monte Carlo simulation techniques. The tabulations are evaluated sequentially using interval preference measurements and SDRF. Because generalized risk efficient Monte Carlo programming employs a user-supplied simulation model, it is more flexible in problem formulation and modeling of complex stochastic processes than are linear and quadratic risk programming models. It can be used in problems involving integer variables, flexible strategies, nonlinear constraints, and nonlinear interactions between stochastic factors (King and Robison 1980). Generalized risk efficient Monte Carlo programming is,

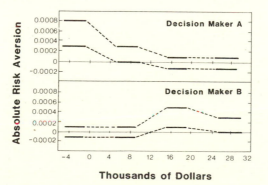

FIG. 6.3.   Interval measurements of absolute risk aversion.

however, more difficult to use and less efficient computationally than are linear and quadratic programming algorithms.

An empirical comparison of efficiency criteria

In this section, distributions for ten marketing strategies are constructed and ordered with the five efficiency criteria. The commodity to be marketed is pinto beans. For simplicity, sales in only three months are considered: October (the first month of the marketing year), March, and June. The performance measure is return to storage, R, which is defined as:

$$R = RS_{OCT} * M_{OCT} + RS_{MAR} * M_{MAR} + RS_{JUN} * M_{JUN} \qquad (6.8)$$

where RS_{OCT}, RS_{MAR}, and RS_{JUN} are returns to storage for each marketing month, and M_{OCT}, M_{MAR}, and M_{JUN} are amounts marketed in each month. The term RS_{OCT} is nonstochastic and equal to zero, since no storage occurs if the crop is sold at harvest. Terms RS_{MAR} and RS_{JUN} are equal to the difference between the market price in the indicated month and the harvest price less storage costs. These variables are stochastic, since market prices for March and June are not known at harvest when a marketing strategy is selected. The joint distribution for these two variables is defined by the returns to storage for the 1975–1980 marketing years. These distributions are given in Table 6.3.

In any month 0, 300, 600, or 900 cwt of beans can be sold, and all 900 cwt must be sold by the end of June. Given these restrictions, ten marketing strategies are defined in Table 6.4, along with their outcome distributions.

FSD eliminates none of these distributions from the efficient set. SSD eliminates only strategy 1 from the efficient set. In this case, SSD is not much more discriminating than FSD. The EV and MOTAD efficient sets are identical to the SSD efficient set, even though these outcome distributions are not normal. Thus EV and MOTAD reliably approximate the SSD results, even though their underlying assumptions do not hold.

Table 6.3.   Distributions of returns to storage until March and June

	Month of Sale	
Year	March	June
74–75	33.03	24.41
75–76	−4.54	−4.93
76–77	−7.66	−10.25
77–78	−2.98	−3.65
78–79	−2.59	2.03
79–80	6.28	4.93

Note: Each element of each distribution has an equal probability, .167, of occurring.

Table 6.4. Marketing strategies and their associated outcome distributions

	Strategy									
	1	2	3	4	5	6	7	8	9	10
M_{Oct}	0	0	0	0	300	300	300	600	600	900
M_{Mar}	0	300	600	900	0	300	600	0	300	0
M_{June}	900	600	300	0	600	300	0	300	0	0
Outcome Distribution[a]										
	21,969	24,555	27,141	29,727	14,646	17,232	19,818	7323	9909	0
	−4,437	−4,320	−4,203	−4,086	−2,950	−2,841	−2,724	−1479	−1362	0
	−9,225	−8,448	−7,671	−6,894	−6,150	−5,373	−4,596	−3075	−2298	0
	−3,285	−3,084	−2,883	−2,682	−2,190	−1,989	−1,788	−1095	894	0
	1,827	441	−945	−2,331	1,218	−168	−1,554	609	−777	0
	4,437	4,842	5,247	5,652	2,958	3,363	3,768	1479	1884	0
Mean	1,881	2,331	2,781	3,231	1,254	1,704	2,154	627	1077	0
Standard deviation	10,000	10,751	11,572	12,449	6,667	7,436	8,299	3333	4150	0
Mean absolute deviation	7,548	8,245	8,942	9,639	5,032	5,729	6,426	2516	3213	0

[a]Each element of each distribution has an equal probability, .167, of occurring.

The ten strategies were also ordered using SDRF and the interval measurements in Fig. 6.3. For decision maker *A,* whose absolute risk aversion interval slopes downward as returns increase, only strategies 9 and 10, which have the lowest losses, are in the efficient set. Given this decision maker's high risk aversion for negative returns, it is not surprising that these safer strategies are preferred. The risk aversion interval for decision maker *B* slopes upward, then downward. Only strategies 8 and 10 are eliminated from his efficient set.

Several aspects of these results are noteworthy. First, strategy 1 was dominated under SSD, EV, and MOTAD efficiency; however, it is an efficient strategy for decision maker *B* whose absolute risk aversion interval includes negative values at low return levels. Second, the efficient sets for decision makers *A* and *B* differ greatly, demonstrating that any preference pattern can be represented with interval measurements. Finally, the SDRF efficient set for decision maker *B* contains eight of the nine strategies in the SSD efficient set. Despite the increased informational requirements of SDRF, this criterion does not always reduce the efficient set to a minimal number of strategies. In this case, the rankings of strategies appear quite sensitive to small changes in absolute risk aversion.

Concluding comments

Stochastic efficiency criteria can partially order uncertain choices without requiring an exact representation of a decision maker's preferences. Efficiency criteria can be judged by how well their inherent assumptions about preferences conform with the empirical characteristics of the problem, by their discriminatory power, and by their ease of use in problems with numerous alternatives. The relative importance of these factors depends on the decision situation.

The generality of an efficiency criterion and its discriminatory power are closely linked. Restrictions on utility functions are typically used to define the class of decision makers for whom a particular efficiency criterion applies. In general, as the amount of information implied by these restrictions increases, the discriminatory power of the criterion also increases. At the same time, however, the number of decision makers for whom the criterion applies tends to decrease. This trade-off between discriminatory power and generality must be considered in selecting an efficiency criterion for a given decision situation. At one extreme FSD places essentially no restrictions on preferences, yet it has low discriminatory power. In contrast, SDRF can be quite discriminating, but it requires more specific information about the decision maker's preference.

SSD, EV, and MOTAD efficiency are similar in their restrictions on preferences and discriminatory power. However, an important question about their validity is the assumption that decision makers are everywhere risk averse. EV and MOTAD efficiency are easier to use when the decision situation can be modeled by quadratic or linear programming. However, mathematical programming is less applicable for problems with nonlinear interactions among stochastic factors, nonlinear constraints, integer choice variables, and adaptive strategies. Simulation models based on search procedures are typically used to solve such problems.

7

Psychological perspectives on risk analysis

WESLEY N. MUSSER AND **LYNN MATHER MUSSER**

THE DEVELOPMENT of expected utility and subjective probability theories by mathematicians, statisticians, and economists has stimulated considerable psychological research on risky decision making. Comprehensive survey articles are provided by Edwards (1954, 1961), Kogan and Wallach (1967), and Slovic et al. (1977). The interdisciplinary nature of this research is illustrated in articles authored or coauthored by psychologists in statistics and economics journals. Moreover, psychological literature has influenced the risk analyses of some agricultural economists as illustrated by the textbook of Anderson et al. (1977) and papers presented at a 1976 conference on risk in agriculture (Roumasset 1979).

Psychological literature is relevant to risk analysis because it focuses on measuring peoples' preferences (or attitudes), probabilities, intelligence, learning, and other components of decision making under risk, many of which are unobservable aspects of human behavior falling outside the traditional focus of empirical economics research. Economists' growing concern with risk management in agriculture has brought greater attention to the effects of these behavioral characteristics, as indicated by the numerous studies using expected utility or similar decision rules as the analytical framework. Thus the psychological literature should be beneficial in studying the risk behavior of farmers and other agricultural decision makers.

This chapter considers the implications of psychological literature for

Wesley N. Musser and Lynn Mather Musser, University of Georgia.

risk analysis in agricultural economics. A complete survey of relevant psychological literature is beyond our scope; therefore, several general issues are emphasized. The first issue is the applicability of expected utility theory to individual decisions under risk. General psychological principles and specific risk research are utilized to critique the major components of expected utility theory—risk preferences and probability distributions. Next is a review of the application of psychological measurement principles to empirical studies of expected utility in agricultural economics. The final section considers the implications for future research.

Critique of expected utility theory

Agricultural economics research on farm income risk has been concerned with the behavior of individual farm firms and with their aggregate effects. At both micro- and macrolevels, some research has sought to specify optimal behavior and some has sought to predict behavior. In positive aggregate research and in some of the positive firm research, utility functions and individual probability distributions serve as theoretical constructs, which are used for hypotheses or conceptual frameworks for analysis, without empirical measurement. In normative research and in some positive firm research, empirical measurement of these theoretical constructs is essential. This latter utilization of expected utility theory is the major concern in this chapter. This section utilizes selected psychological literature to critique these empirical applications of expected utility theory. One research issue is the relationship between risk preferences (or attitudes) and behavior. A second research issue involves the methods of eliciting individual judgments of probabilities.

ATTITUDE AND BEHAVIOR. Attitudes refer to relatively long-lasting clusters of feelings, beliefs, and behavioral tendencies directed toward specific people, objects, or ideas (Baron and Byrne 1981). Although theoretical constructs are often difficult to reconcile among disciplines, we will assume that the economic construct of preferences is similar if not equivalent to attitudes (Ajzen and Fishbein 1972). Scales for precisely measuring attitudes have been available for more than fifty years (Thurstone 1931; Likert 1932; Guttman 1944). The relationship between attitudes and actual behavior has been studied for almost as long (e.g., LaPiere 1934). As recently as 1969, Wicker proposed that attitudes are not likely to predict behavior because too many other variables, including other attitudes, intervene to influence behavior. A less pessimistic view of the attitude-behavior relationship is offered by Fishbein and Ajzen (1975). To understand their view, some theoretical background is helpful.

An attitude has an evaluative component, a belief or knowledge component, and a behavioral component. The evaluative component consists of a general positive or negative feeling about a person, object, or issue. For example, "I *hate* Datsun trucks," or "Chevy trucks *are great.*" The belief component refers to the information people possess. The information may be factual, or it may be an opinion. For example, "Chevy trucks are made in America," or "Datsun trucks have poor repair records." The behavioral component refers to an overt action, for example, buying a Chevy truck. According to Fishbein and Ajzen (1975), one problem with attitude measurement is that these three components are often measured at different levels of specificity for such dimensions as time, product, or other persons involved. Fishbein and Ajzen point out that attitudes are good predictors of behavior if the attitude and behavior are measured at the same level. Using the above example, a person might be asked about his or her general evaluation of Chevy trucks ("How do you feel about Chevy trucks?"). This general evaluation would not be a good predictor of the specific behavior of buying a small Chevy truck from Firm X next December. However, the general evaluation might be a good predictor of buying a Chevy truck sometime in the future, if indeed a truck is purchased.

Weigel and Newman (1976) illustrate the importance of measuring attitudes and behavior at the same level of specificity. These investigators studied the relationship between attitudes toward the environment and willingness to engage in proenvironmental behavior. Ninety people in a community were surveyed on a variety of issues. Embedded in the survey were 16 questions assessing concern for the environment. Scores on these 16 items were summed to form a single index of each person's general attitude toward the environment. Three months later each survey participant was contacted by a second investigator who presented several pro-environment petitions. Participants were asked to circulate and return the petitions. Several weeks later, the same people were contacted by a third investigator to solicit their participation in an antilitter campaign. Lastly, participants were contacted by a fourth investigator to ask for their participation in a recycling campaign.

Several specific behavioral measures were obtained from these 90 people: petition signing, volunteering to pick up litter, and recycling over a two-month period of time. Each specific behavior yielded only modest correlations with the general attitude measure (.12–.57, with most in the .20–.35 range). However, when the specific behaviors were combined to form a more general behavioral index (i.e., several behaviors measured at different times rather than only one time), the correlation between attitudes and behavior rose to .62. These results are consistent with Ajzen and Fishbein's theory (1972). A general attitude measure will not predict specific behaviors with much precision. However, if behavior is also measured at a general level, a general attitude measure will do a satisfactory job of predicting behavior.

These findings have several important implications for the elicitation of utility functions. In most cases, utility functions of farmers and other decision makers are elicited with generalized games (see Chap. 2; Anderson et al. 1977). The attitude literature suggests that such utility functions will not be useful for predicting behavior in a specific managerial decision but may be more useful in specifying a comprehensive set of risk management strategies. For example, a generalized utility function would not be expected to predict a farm's acreage of corn and soybeans but may be useful in predicting the set of production, marketing, and finance strategies used by the firm. Several agricultural economists have recently emphasized this issue from slightly different perspectives: Hildreth (1977) notes that current prospects must be considered in evaluating a risky venture, and Gabriel and Baker (1980) argue that both business and financial risk must be considered in analyzing risk management strategies. In contrast to standard procedure, the attitude literature suggests that utility functions for analysis of specific management decisions should be elicited in the context of the particular decision. The high predictive accuracy achieved by Officer and Halter (1968) from their elected utility functions is an example of this methodological view.

COGNITIVE BIASES IN PROBABILISTIC JUDGMENTS. Probabilistic judgments are required in elicitation of both utility functions and subjective probability distributions. In order to make a probabilistic judgment, one must first observe the relevant events over time, make inferences about relationships among events, and then judge the probability of future events. Recent work by psychologists shows that cognitive biases may affect the processing and use of information in these judgments. These biases, or heuristics, systematically affect how people perceive events, store them in memory, and retrieve them for future use (Nisbett and Ross 1980). This section reviews three heuristics that may affect probabilistic judgments—representativeness, availability, and anchoring (Tversky and Kahneman 1974)—and considers their implications for eliciting utility functions and subjective probabilities. We also briefly review prospect theory, developed by Kahneman and Tversky (1979) as an extension of expected utility theory.

Representativeness. Representativeness refers to the resemblance between an event and its population. When using this heuristic, a person judges the probability of an event by (1) its similarity to essential features of the parent population, and (2) the process by which it is generated. Similarity to the parent population is explained with an example from Kahneman and Tversky. People are first given this description: "All families of six children in a city were surveyed. In 72 families the exact order of births of boys and girls was GBGBBG" (Kahneman and Tversky 1972, 432). Then they must estimate the families with the birth order of BGBBBB. The two birth sequences are not equally *representative:* the first contains three girls and three boys while the second contains one girl and five boys. Since the latter sequence does not reflect the proportion of boys and girls in the parent population, most people judge the latter sequence, BGBBBB, as less likely, even though both sequences have the same probability of occurrence.

Besides reflecting the parent population, uncertain events are considered random. Two features of randomness are irregularity and local representativeness. In a series of fair coin tosses, for example, the regular outcome HTHTHT is judged less likely than the irregular outcome of HTTHTH, which appears more random. Local representativeness is a belief that the law of large numbers applies to small numbers as well; people believe that the essential characteristics of a parent population should be present both in a large sample and in each component of the sample (Kahneman and Tversky 1972). Thus, one might expect five heads and five tails in a sample of ten coin tosses. This proportion would occur in a large sample, but not necessarily in a small sample. Thus, the use of representativeness can lead to errors in probability judgments if probability and representativeness are not influenced by the same factors.

Availability. Availability is the ease with which relevant instances come to mind. A farmer may easily recall several past dry years and base his judgment about their frequency on the remembered years. In some cases, this process may reflect reality since frequent events are usually easier to recall. However, other factors influence availability and may lead to erroneous conclusions about the frequency of events (Tversky and Kahneman 1973).

Bias associated with availability may occur in the initial sampling of events, in storage, or in recall. Characteristics of events that may influence initial sampling include the event's emotional or personal relevance; its imaginability or concreteness; the ordering of occurrence; and the event's salience, extremity, and severity. In addition, actual events are more noticeable than nonoccurrences. Events are more easily stored in memory and recalled if they are linked to information already stored, and if the information can be coded verbally and as a "mental picture" (Nisbett and Ross 1980). For example, a farmer may overestimate the frequency of dry years because of their emotional and financial impact, especially if a dry year recently occurred.

The frequency of occurrence of pairs of items can also be overestimated. A high association between two events may influence expectations about their joint occurrence. This bias, termed illusory correlation (Chapman and Chapman 1969), is explained by the availability heuristic. Two highly related items may be jointly stored in memory and retrieved. However, illusory correlation may imply a relationship when none exists. A farmer who sees advertisements that link fertilizer *A* with a high yield, may begin to associate fertilizer A with high yields. The farmer may thus overestimate the actual frequency of high yields derived from fertilizer A.

Anchoring. Anchoring may also affect probability judgments. An initial value, either given or computed, becomes the starting point and thus the basis for additional judgments. Estimates are then biased toward the starting point. Although some adjustment may occur, it is typically insufficient (Tversky and Kahneman 1974). Generally, different reference points will yield different estimates. For example, a farmer may base his yield distribution on likely adjustments around a reference yield. The distribution will differ depending on whether maximum or minimum yield is the reference point. The anchoring heuristic is less complex than the others but is as important in biasing judgments.

Implications for elicitation. These cognitive biases suggest that the typical methods of elicitation may not yield accurate utility functions and subjective probability distributions. Subjective probability distributions will usually reflect all three heuristics. Since elicitation of utility functions requires probability judgments, heuristics also likely bias these data. While not directly related to the heuristics, the preference reversal phenomenon illustrates biases in the elicitation of utility functions. The preference reversal phenomenon was reported by Lichtenstein and Slovic (1971) and has been replicated several times, most recently by economists (Grether and Plott 1979).

The paradigm differs from that used in utility functions, but it illustrates potential weaknesses in relationships between certainty equivalents and risk preferences. The phenomenon relates to choices between two lotteries, A and B. These lotteries have a zero payoff and a positive payoff ($\$_i$) with probability P_i. The payoffs and probabilities for the lotteries are specified as $\$_A < \$_B$ and $P_A > P_B$. The experiments which yield preference reversals involve two steps. One step determines the subject's preference between the lotteries; the second step determines the subject's reservation price to sell the lotteries, $\overline{\$}_A$ and $\overline{\$}_B$. Grether and Plott (1979) note that expected utility theory implies $\overline{\$}_A > \overline{\$}_B$, if A is preferred to B. This prediction follows from noting that the $\$_i$ are certainty equivalents so that individuals are indifferent between $\overline{\$}_i$ and ($\$_i$, P_i). By transitivity, $\overline{\$}_A > \overline{\$}_B$ if A is preferred to B. However, a large proportion of people violated this prediction in all the experiments. Thus certainty equivalents need not have any relationship to preferences for a lottery.

Persistence of biases. Advocates of statistical decision theory will likely suggest that biases in probability judgments can be overcome. For example, Anderson et al. (1977, 19–21) recommend more research to design elicitation methodologies that minimize the biases of heuristics. D. V. Lindley (1974a) took a stronger position in discussing a paper by Tversky: "Why do you spend your time studying how people make decisions, when we know how they *should* make decisions? Would it not be better to devote your energies to teaching them the principles of maximum expected utility?" (Emphasis in the original, 181.)

Considerable research evidence on overcoming biases is becoming available. Tversky and Kahneman (1974) note that individuals with considerable statistical training are less likely to commit some statistical fallacies but still tend to use some of the heuristics. Winkler (1967) explicitly considered the effect of statistical training in the assessment of personal probability distributions. The experiments involved three sets of subjects at the University of Chicago: (1) graduate business students with only an introductory course in statistics, (2) graduate business students with at least a course in business statistics that emphasized Bayesian methods, and (3) Ph.D. candidates and a professor in statistics. Not surprisingly, Winkler concluded that the performance of the third group was much superior. However, little difference existed between the first and second groups. Hogarth (1975) reviews several studies that compare the judgments of statisticians on particular subjects with those of individuals experienced in the subject areas. For example, weather forecasters demonstrated as much statistical expertise as statisticians in forecasting the weather. Hogarth attributed this result to the frequent feedback on prediction that weather forecasters receive. As Tversky and Kahneman (1974) note, most people experience slower rates of feedback that preclude learning the appropriate statistical rules.

These findings suggest that farmers may not be able to use statistical concepts for elicitation processes. Few farmers have advanced graduate study in statistics. In addition, farm management is not likely to provide the feedback or training to overcome the heuristics cited above. Farmers must make many probabilistic decisions due to the risks inherent in agriculture; however, sequential production processes do not provide the frequent feedback that weather forecasters experience. Observations on yields typically occur once a year, at harvest, while yield forecasts are formed before planting. In contrast, the more frequent flow of outlook information on commodity prices may contribute to more accurate estimates of price distributions (Nelson 1980).

Prospect theory. Kahneman and Tversky (1979) developed prospect theory as an alternative to expected utility theory for explaining and predicting the outcomes of individual decisions under uncertainty. Their analysis indicates that prospect theory may be more consistent with empirical research on risky decisions than is expected utility theory. This theory postulates two sequential stages in a decision process—editing and evauation. Editing reduces the number of options to be evaluated and/or organizes them for ease of evaluation. Some forms of editing apply to each option separately while others jointly apply to sets of options.

The evaluation stage of the decision process determines the value (or payoffs) of the edited options, as expressed by the following equation:

$$V = \sum_{i=1}^{n} \Pi(P_i) v(x_i) \qquad\qquad (7.1)$$

where V = value of option, $\Pi(P_i)$ = decision weight placed on outcome i, P_i = probability of outcome i being obtained, $v(x_i)$ = value of outcome i, and x_i = measure of gain from outcome i, such as dollars. The option with the highest V is the desired choice. The evaluation equation is similar to the definition of expected utility in that a weighted sum of the value of alternative outcomes is calculated. However, the components in V differ from the components in expected utility. The value function is similar to a utility function for gains and losses except that Kahneman and Tversky (1979) postulate a particular form for the function. Individuals are risk averse for gains and risk seekers for losses, $v''(x) < 0$ for $x > 0$ and $v''(x) > 0$ for $x < 0$. In addition, a discontinuity exists at zero, so that $v'(x)$ is greater for $x < 0$ than $x > 0$. The decision weights are related to subjective probabilities but do not follow the probability axioms. The weights are assumed to be a function of "objective" probabilities with $\Pi(0) = 0$ and $\Pi(1) = 1$. Outcomes with low P_i are overweighted, $\Pi(P_i) > P_i$. However, subcertainty is hypothesized for the distribution of all outcomes,

$$\sum_{i=1}^{n} \Pi(P_i) < 1.$$

Thus, outcomes with P_i that are not small have $\Pi(P_i) < P_i$.

Prospect theory responds to some of the weaknesses of expected utility as a postive theory of individual behavior; however, Kahneman and Tversky do not expect that (7.1) would be empirically estimated due to problems in elicitation procedures discussed above (1979, 284). Rather, hypotheses about different options can be derived from this equation and tested empirically. An example is the hypothesis that the overweighting of losses with small probabilities explains the purchase of insurance even though people are risk seekers for losses. Based on the heuristics discussed above, individuals with recent losses would place a higher subjective probability on the possibility of future losses. Thus, the loss outcomes would be less overweighted and the purchase of insurance would be less likely. Testing such hypotheses may yield new insights about risky behavior of farmers.

Principles of measurement

The preceding review of psychological literature suggests that expected utility theory is subject to several shortcomings and limitations that may hamper its application to individual decisions under risk. Many of the proposed limitations need further study. Adequacy of the elicitation procedures is particularly important and has had limited attention in economics. This section discusses the importance of reliability and validity in the construction of any scale, test, index, instrument, or questionnaire used to gain information about an individual. Economists generally use elicitation procedures (EP) to measure risk preferences. This term is used here although the psychometric and psychology literature use the terms identified above (scale, test, etc.).

Reliability is concerned with the consistency and accuracy in a measurement procedure. Validity is concerned with whether the procedure measures the desired phenomena. The statistical relationship between these concepts and the principles of measurement is shown as follows: Following Allen and Yen (1979), EP would yield a measure X, which is the sum of the true measure, T, and E, an error in measurement. Assuming that E and T are independent, $\sigma_x^2 = \sigma_T^2 + \sigma_E^2$, where $\sigma_i^2 =$ variance of variable i. Reliability is concerned with minimizing the value of σ_E^2. Validity is concerned with the relationship between T and unobservable variables such as risk preferences.

RELIABILITY. Although many types of reliability exist in the literature, reliability over time and consistency within a procedure are of most interest to economists. Reliability over time, or test-retest reliability, assesses the degree to which a procedure yields the same results for the same examinee at two different times. The same procedure, administered at one time, should yield similar results two weeks, two months, or two years later, although the relationship between the two measures may decrease as the interval between administrations increases. Correlation coefficients or related statistics between the intertemporal measures are utilized to measure test-retest reliability (Allen and Yen 1979). A few studies in agricultural economics have considered reliability over time (Officer and Halter 1968; Binswanger 1980).

Reliability based on internal consistency considers the correlation between each item in a measurement procedure. Different methods can be used for determining internal consistency; examples are comparing two halves of the test or comparing every item to every other item or each item to the total score. The internal consistency of a procedure indicates whether or not the items are measuring the same thing. Problems of internal consistency often arise in eliciting utility functions. For example, a risk preferring response might occur in a set of risk averse responses (Anderson et al. 1977, 70–76).

A fully reliable procedure should minimize the error variance. Zero error variance is not possible because of normal human errors. However, vague instructions, unfamiliar activities or processes, and lack of standard administration can increase the measurement error. All these characteristics exist in elicitation procedures. The monetary games involved in eliciting utility functions may be unfamiliar to the respondent. Explaining the games can be tedious and complex. Many individuals also lack experience with the laws of probability. In addition, standard administration of the procedures may not be possible. Anderson et al. (1977) suggest a series of check questions to overcome internal consistency problems in utility elicitations; however, this solution can introduce administrator bias into the responses. Roumasset (1979) illustrated this administrative bias when he, Dillon, and Anderson obtained different utility functions from the same individual.

Another reliability issue is the length of the measurement procedure. In general, the more questions asked, the more reliable is the procedure (Allen and Yen 1979, 85–88). The overall error approaches an expected value of zero as the number of questions increases. Thus, eliciting risk aversion coefficients with one question should be less reliable than using a utility function elicited with a number of games.

VALIDITY. Validation considers whether a measurement procedure really measures the desired phenomena. Validity is more complex than reliability and this chapter only summarizes the issue; interested readers should consult other sources on psychometrics or psychological methodology (e.g., Allen and Yen 1979; Cook and Campbell 1979). Unlike reliability no simple statistical tests can be utilized to measure validity. Assessing the validity of a measure is a continuous process aimed at answering the following questions: (1) Does the measurement procedure predict the intended behavior? (2) Does it correlate with other measures that predict the same behavior? (3) Is it uncorrelated with other theoretically unrelated measures? (Betz and Weiss 1976).

These questions should be considered in the validation process. For example, a study of the impact of risk preferences on adoption of an agricultural practice might elicit risk preferences and obtain behavioral measures related to the practice. If the risk preferences are valid, they should be related to the behavior. At the same time, scales designed to measure risk attitudes could be administered. These also should correlate with the elicited risk preferences and the behavior. Other tests that measure theoretically unrelated phenomena could also be administered. Political attitudes might be measured if no theoretical relationship between political opinions and risk preferences is suspected. The correlation between these measures should be low. Such a research plan would provide information on all three of the validation questions.

More attention to validation is warranted in order to appraise potential problems with the elicitation procedures. Of particular relevance is research on alternative measures of willingness to assume risk. Such research may demonstrate that other scales to measure risk preferences not subject to elicitation problems may be valid predictors of economic behavior.

Implications for further research

The psychological literature suggests that elicited risk preferences and subjective probability distributions are subject to severe limitations in empirical research. As recently suggested by Young (1979), Sonka (1979), and Roumasset (1979), use of alternative procedures warrants consideration. For measuring risk preferences or subjective probabilities of farmers, indirect measures may experience less bias than the direct measures involved in elicitation. King and Robison (1981a) have recently proposed an interval approach to measuring risk attitudes (Chap. 2). This approach may require less statistical sophistication than traditional elicitation methods, but cognitive biases may still occur. As with other measures, research on *reliability* and *validity* of this procedure would be helpful.

In some research, psychological measurement scales that have extensive data on their reliability and validity may be useful. Examples are Kogan and Wallach's (1967) scale of willingness to assume risk and Azjen and Fishbein's (1972) use of Likert scales to measure risk preferences. These alternatives appear suitable for measuring the influence of risk preferences on economic behavior. They have desirable psychometric properties and are easier and less time consuming to administer than the elicitation procedures.

It must be stressed that psychology is largely concerned with individual behavior. The issues addressed here do not imply that expected utility theory is invalid as a positive theory to predict aggregate behavior. Following Friedman (1953), a positive theory must abstract from various nuances of individual behavior. In a summary of psychological research on expected utility theory, Coombs (1975, 65) supports the view that expected utility theory fulfills this methodological position: "In the work reported in this section, (expected utility) theory is found unacceptable as a descriptive theory of individual risky decision making, but it does provide a good approximation to data, which perhaps accounts for its viability in the face of persistent criticism." Exploration of new developments such as prospect theory (Kahneman and Tversky 1979) as a source of aggregate hypotheses is warranted, but it is doubtful that prospect theory will aggregate as successfully as expected utility theory.

PART 2

Risk analysis in farm businesses

8

Risk management and decision making in agricultural firms

STEVEN T. SONKA AND GEORGE F. PATRICK

RISK AND UNCERTAINTY influence the efficiency of resource use in agriculture and the decision-making processes of farmers. Risk management is important whenever decision outcomes are uncertain, as occurs for most farming situations. More precisely, Dillon (1971, 4) indicates that, "Risky choice prevails when a decision maker has to choose between alternatives, some or all of which have consequences that are not certain. . . ."

The importance of risk management is illustrated by its impacts on a static decision process. The components of this process are: (1) define the problem and goals; (2) get ideas, make observations, and list major alternatives; (3) analyze the alternatives and determine the outcomes; (4) decide which alternative to select; (5) act on the decision; and (6) bear responsibility for the outcome (Herbst 1976). Risk influences this decision process in several ways. One way is by disguising the problem. A cash flow shortfall, for example, may be a symptom of several diverse problems that are difficult to distinguish. In addition, variations in prices and yields may further obscure problem identification.

Steven T. Sonka, University of Illinois, and George F. Patrick, Purdue University.

Risk management is especially important in steps 3 and 4 of this decision process. Typically, decision processes focus on the most probable outcome. However, the most probable outcome generally differs from the actual outcome. Hence, considering a range of possible events and outcomes as a part of risk management can help farmers make better decisions.

In this chapter, several aspects of risk management in the farm firm are considered. The first section contrasts alternative views of risk and evaluates their adequacy for decision making. The typical sources of risk in agriculture are identified, as are risk responses available to and utilized by farm operators. Two methods of eliciting subjective probabilities are then identified as a type of risk response.

Contrasting views of risk versus uncertainty

Knight (1921) was one of the first economists to delineate the degree of knowledge in decision situations. Working from logical possibilities, Knight proposed three major categories: perfect knowledge, risk, and uncertainty. Perfect knowledge exists when the decision outcomes are known with certainty. Decision making is simple if perfect knowledge is available, but this is a rare occurrence.

The distinction between risk and uncertainty has focused primarily on objective versus subjective probabilities (see Chaps. 3, 4). Objective probabilities may be based either on the characteristics of the situation (e.g., the probability of a head in a fair coin toss is 0.5) or on observations of outcome frequencies in repeated trials. An illustration is deriving the probability of July rainfall from historic rainfall data.

In numerous farm situations objective probabilities are not available. A farmer may believe that laborers quitting during harvest may substantially reduce profit. Knowing the probability of each laborer interviewed being a potential quitter is desirable; however, no logical or empirical data exist to develop objective probabilities. Still, the farmer may use information about the job candidates to generate subjective probabilities about labor turnover.

Subjective and objective probabilities are distinguished by assumptions about prior information. Anderson et al. (1977) argue that all probabilities are subjective because the decision maker must subjectively assess whether any objective data are appropriate for the decision situation. For example, when agreeing to flip a coin to see who buys coffee at the local cafe, the farmer must judge the fairness of the coin to specify probabilities of the outcomes. All probabilities in decision making are to some extent subjective; thus the distinction between risk and uncertainty is unimportant.

Current popular usage implies little distinction between risk and uncertainty. Both terms stress potential variability of returns, but they differ from the traditional view in several ways. Risky situations occur when random variability in returns threatens the firm's survival. Risks are also associated with legal and human factors. For example, forward contracting to reduce price variability may be risky because of concern about the integrity of the contractor and lack of familiarity with contracting. The possibility of foregone profits is also a risk for farm operators. The purchase of land, if debt financed, increases the annual cash drain on the firm and increases potential variability of net cash income. In contrast, purchase of land also may reduce the risk that inflation will decrease a farmer's real net worth. Conversely, risk effects from a purchase of Treasury bonds are mixed because of their fixed nominal returns versus possible losses in purchasing power if inflation is higher than anticipated.

Sources of risk for the farm operator

Five major sources of business risk in agriculture are identified to better understand their effects on farmers and to evaluate farmers' risk responses: (1) production or technical risk; (2) market or price risk; (3) technological risk; (4) legal and social risk; and (5) human sources of risk. The financial risks that combine with these business risks to influence a farmer's total risk return are treated in Chapter 13.

Production or technical risk is random variability inherent in a farm's production process. Weather, diseases, and pest infestations lead to technical risk in crop and livestock production. Fire, wind, theft, and casualties are other sources of production risk.

Yield fluctuations are greatly influenced by weather and other uncontrollable factors. Table 8.1 illustrates differences in yield variability for

Table 8.1. Average yield and yield variability of selected crops

Crop	Average yield/ harvested acre	Standard deviation	Coefficient of variation
Tippecanoe County, Indiana (1960–78)			
Corn (bu)	84.0	15.5	18.5
Soybeans (bu)	27.1	4.3	15.9
Wheat (bu)	38.2	5.7	14.8
Thayer County, Nebraska (1951–76)			
Dryland corn (bu)	34.4	16.8	48.9
Irrigated corn (bu)	92.4	7.7	8.3
Dryland sorghum (bu)	52.7	13.3	25.3
Irrigated sorghum (bu)	86.0	13.2	15.4
Dryland alfalfa (tons)	2.2	0.6	25.5
Irrigated alfalfa (tons)	3.8	0.6	16.2
Dryland soybeans (bu)	19.9	4.2	20.9
Winter wheat (bu)	27.5	4.6	16.9

Sources: Patrick 1979; Bravo-Ureta and Helmers 1980b.
Note: Effects of yield trend have been removed.

Table 8.2. Average yield and yield variability of wheat in selected areas

Area	Average yield/ harvested acre	Standard deviation	Coefficient of variation
Columbia Basin project, Washington (1965–79)	76.5	10.7	14.0
Whitman County, Washington (1965–79)	48.8	8.0	16.5
Tippecanoe County, Indiana (1965–79)	38.2	5.7	14.8
Boone County, Missouri (1965–79)	49.9	16.5	33.2
Brown County, Nebraska (1961–76)	21.0	8.8	42.1
Southwest Oklahoma (1962–79)	28.1	17.2	61.1

Sources: Young et al. 1980; Patrick 1979; Flood 1981; Bravo-Ureta and Helmers 1980b; and Persaud 1980.

Note: Effects of yield trend have been removed.

selected crops in two geographic areas. Tippecanoe County in northwestern Indiana is representative of the central Corn Belt. After removing the trend effect in yield, the coefficients of variation for the three major crops are quite similar. In contrast, crops raised in the dry land conditions of Thayer County in southern Nebraska vary more than similar crops in Indiana. Substantial differences in variability also occur among the various types of crops. The effects of irrigation in increasing and stabilizing yields are also illustrated by the Thayer County data.

The yield variability of a specific commodity, such as wheat, can differ widely over a broad geographic area. As shown in Table 8.2, irrigated wheat in the Columbia Basin has relatively high, stable yields. Yields are lower and less stable under the rainfall conditions of Indiana, Washington, and Missouri. As is typical of wheat-growing regions in the Great Plains, yields are lower and less stable in the drier areas of Nebraska and Oklahoma.

The variability of yields also differs over time as indicated in Table 8.3 by coefficients of variation of Illinois corn yields for the 1927–75 period. The poorer weather conditions of the 1930s are indicated by the relatively high coefficient of variation for that decade. In contrast, benign weather in the 1960s resulted in a markedly lower coefficient of variation. Recent yield variability is indicated by the substantially higher coefficient of variation

Table 8.3. Coefficients of variation of Illinois corn yields

Time period	Coefficient of variation
1927–75	19.97
1930s	33.13
1940s	19.31
1950s	21.83
1960s	15.95
1970–75	21.48

Source: Sonka 1978.

Note: Effects of yield trend have been removed.

for the period 1970–75. The corn blight of 1970 and the poor weather conditions of 1974 contributed to the increased risk.

Market or price risk can occur for purchased inputs and saleable commodities. Table 8.4 reports data on price variability for selected farm inputs and commodities. Short-run fluctuations in input prices can cause considerable income losses and cash shortfalls. Availability of specific inputs is another market risk for farmers. In the longer run, concern about input price variability, interest rates, and relative price movements affects the farmer's decisions about enterprise selection, investments in durable assets, and other components of strategic planning. Greater volatility of inflation and interest rates have brought new sources of risk that influence long-run decision making by farmers.

A major source of concern for farmers is the variability of commodity prices. Information on seasonal price patterns and long-run trends exists for many commodities. However, in the 1970s increasing price instability became a greater source of risk to farmers. Table 8.5 illustrates the increased level of within-year price variability experienced by soybean producers in Illinois in the early 1970s.

For the years 1965–71 the annual differences in the highest and lowest monthly average price averaged $0.48/bu. However, for 1972–79 this difference increased to $2.60/bu. The months with the highest and lowest prices also varied from year to year.

Technological risk is the potential that current decisions may be offset by technical improvements in the future. Investments in durable assets may

Table 8.4. Price variability of selected farm products and inputs, 1960–78

Item	Average annual price	Coefficient of variation
Corn (bu)	2.60	17.9
Soybeans (bu)	6.23	20.1
Oats (bu)	1.59	13.6
Wheat (bu)	3.55	28.6
Hay (tons)	53.98	9.6
Hogs (cwt)	45.09	16.1
Cattle (cwt)	50.37	11.8
Milk (cwt)	10.59	7.0
Eggs (doz)	0.69	13.8
Turkeys (lb)	0.45	16.0
Anhydrous ammonia (tons)	241.00	31.7
Diesel fuel (100 gal)	40.00	12.6
Soybean oil meal (tons)	189.00	30.4
Feeder cattle (cwt)	82.00	142.0
Feeder pigs (cwt)	90.00	90.9

Source: Patrick 1979.
Note: Prices are expressed in 1978 dollars using the index of prices paid by farmers for commodities, services, taxes, and farm wages.

Table 8.5.   Highest and lowest monthly average soybean prices received by Illinois farmers, 1965–79

	High ($)	Low ($)	Difference ($)
1965	2.93	2.33	0.60
1966	3.57	2.75	0.82
1967	2.83	2.44	0.39
1968	2.60	2.34	0.26
1969	2.61	2.25	0.36
1970	2.89	2.40	0.49
1971	3.26	2.83	0.43
1972	4.04	2.95	1.09
1973	10.20	4.18	6.02
1974	8.21	5.23	2.98
1975	6.32	4.35	1.97
1976	6.79	4.55	2.24
1977	9.30	5.26	4.04
1978	6.80	5.58	1.22
1979	7.57	6.33	1.24

Source: *Ill. Agric. Stat.,* various issues.

be subject to dramatic technological change. The rapid change in confinement swine facilities during the late 1950s is an example. Technological uncertainty is generally greater for buildings, equipment, and other fixed structures that are less mobile than farm machinery.

Technological risks are not limited to farm technologies. For example, improvements in monitoring devices to measure residuals of feed additives in livestock products cause concern for livestock producers and lead to changes in production practices. Technological developments in transportation, processing, and other nonfarm sectors can also affect farm incomes.

Legal and social risks may increase as farms grow larger and more dependent on nonfarm sources of capital. Marketing techniques, like forward contracting, that respond to risks from price variability may bring new legal risks. Government policies also impact on a farm's operating environment. Examples include government price and income support programs, as well as tax, trade, credit, and environmental policies. Unanticipated changes in these policies are important sources of risk for farmers.

Human sources of risk are associated with the labor and management functions in farming. Health problems of key operators can severely disrupt farm performance. Changing objectives of individuals and family members may affect a farm's long-run viability. Human uncertainty has likely contributed to the mechanization of agriculture for machine inputs that are considered more dependable than labor inputs.

All these sources of risk may have short-run and long-run effects on farm businesses. Variability in annual net cash flows may disrupt the business due to cash shortfalls. As Table 8.6 shows, income variability differs substantially among regions and types of farms during the 1965–79 period.

These risks may also cause variations in net worth and other long-run performance measures of the farm business. For many farmers, short- and long-run goals may conflict in specific decision situations. Thus both aspects of uncertainty should be considered in evaluating risk responses.

Risk responses by farmers

Two types of risk responses are available to farmers. One concerns actions for reducing the effects of risk on the farm business. The other involves changes in a farmer's decision process.

In general, an action is considered risk reducing if, when repeated numerous times, it lowers the variability and expected level of income compared to alternative actions. If an action both reduces income variability and increases expected income, it is unclear whether such a decision is made to increase profit or reduce risk. (It may, however, be a very good idea.) This discussion focuses on a farmer's actions that reduce expected income to achieve greater income stability.

Risky decisions occur when at least some of the consequences are not known. Typically, this uncertainty arises because of the interval between the decision point and the final outcome. Often the farmer can select strategies that allow learning as time progresses. Delaying part of the fertilizer application until after the corn crop emerges gives more timely information

Table 8.6. Variability of real farm labor income, 1965–79 for selected states and types of farms

State and type of farm	Mean income	Standard deviation	Coefficient of variation
Kansas farms	18,013	21,376	118.7
Michigan			
Specialized dairy	15,765	12,057	76.5
All farms	15,423	13,811	89.6
Illinois			
Northern grain	27,246	21,744	79.8
Southern grain	23,408	12,354	52.8
Northern hog	31,513	30,744	97.6
Southern hog	29,624	18,295	61.8
Northern beef	9,954	24,699	248.1
Indiana (per operator)			
Hog	42,573	29,380	69.0
Dairy	22,024	7,679	34.9
Crop	34,867	27,704	79.5
Crop-Hog	40,472	30,430	75.2
State	36,390	24,996	68.7

Source: Derived from annual farm record summaries in the selected states.

Note: Concepts of labor income (or returns to labor and management) differ among states, but are consistent over time for a state. Incomes have been inflated to 1979 dollars by the index of prices paid by farmers for commodities, interest, taxes, and wages.

about price and weather conditions. In situations involving expensive inputs or volatile output prices, the farmer may use flexible strategies that incorporate learning.

ACTIONS TO REDUCE RISK. The farmer's actions to reduce risk are categorized by the production, marketing, and financial organizational areas of the farm business (Boehlje and Trede 1977).

Production Responses. Enterprise selection greatly affects the variability of cash flows. The variability of yields and farm incomes differs substantially among regions and enterprises (Tables 8.2, 8.6). The risk averse farmer might select a more stable region (the Corn Belt instead of the Great Plains) or enterprise (dairying instead of feeding cattle) in order to reduce income variability. However, the farmer's preferences, abilities, experience, and opportunities also affect such a decision. Thus, risk reduction is only one of several factors affecting enterprise selection.

Another production strategy involved in enterprise selection is diversification. Diversification involves combining enterprises to reduce the variability of total returns. To illustrate, let P_A and P_B be the proportion of resources used for the production of enterprises A and B, and σ_A^2 and σ_B^2 be the respective income variances. The variance of total returns, σ_T^2, is given by $\sigma_T^2 = P_A^2 \sigma_A^2 + P_B^2 \sigma_B^2 + 2 P_A P_B c \, \sigma_A \, \sigma_B$ where c is the correlation coefficient for the incomes of A and B. The correlation coefficient varies between plus and minus one. Positive values of c indicate returns that vary in the same direction and negative values indicate variation in opposite directions. Although the greatest reduction in total variability occurs if c is negative, some reduction in risk will generally occur from diversification unless enterprise returns are perfectly correlated. In general, risk is further reduced by diversification as the correlation between enterprises takes on lower values. Adding more enterprises would generally further reduce risk, but the marginal risk reduction becomes smaller as the number of enterprises increases.

Hanson and Thompson (1980) found that Minnesota famers who combined cash grain and beef feeding had lower variability of cash income in the 1966–77 period than specialized producers. Similarly, Patrick (1979b) showed the variability of average gross income from a combination of corn, soybeans, and wheat on Indiana farms was lower than a corn and soybean combination or specialization in corn. However, addition of wheat as the third enterprise reduced the standard deviation of income by only about one-half as much as the addition of soybeans as the second enterprise.

Although not designed specifically to analyze enterprise diversification, several studies have used MOTAD and quadratic programming procedures (Chaps. 9, 10) to derive expected income-variance efficiency frontiers for various farming situations. Solutions along the risk efficient set indicate the differences in variability associated with alternative crop mixes and production organizations.

Based on 1969–76 data, Schurle and Erven (1979b) found that changes in crop mixes could reduce the coefficient of variation (CV) of gross margins (gross income minus variable production expenses) for grain farms in northwestern Ohio from .31 to .22. This reduction in risk came with a 28.6 percent reduction in the expected level of total gross margin. By introducing a specialty crop, tomatoes, along with grain the CV could be reduced from .31 to .29 with no decline in the expected gross margin. Moreover, other combinations of tomatoes and grain would increase the expected gross margin by almost 25 percent above the maximum for grain production alone, although risk would increase as well, as indicated by a CV of .41.

Using a similar model for a west-central Indiana farm for the 1965–79 period, Shurley (1980) found that changes in crop combinations alone could reduce the CV from a high of .545 to .381, with a 4.5 percent reduction in gross margins. For an irrigated farm in eastern Wyoming, Held and Zink (1982) found that cropping changes reduced the CV from .628 to .471, with a reduction of 23.4 percent in the gross margin for the 1968 to 1978 period.

Livestock enterprises are also commonly included in production diversification, but may require additional resources. Held and Zink (1982) found adding livestock to the irrigated crop farm increased the gross margin by 7 percent and reduced the CV from .628 to .420. Additional changes in enterprise combinations reduced the CV of returns from .420 to .266 with a gross margin reduction of 28.4 percent. For a southwestern Oklahoma ranch, Persaud and Mapp (1980) found that changes in enterprise combination could reduce the CV from .614 to .357 with a reduction of 37.5 percent in the gross margin. Jibben and Allen (1979) and Woolery and Adams (1980) indicated that diversified land use combined with livestock feeding provided opportunities to increase net income and reduce relative variability of farm income in South Dakota and Wyoming. In contrast, Shurley (1980) found that adding a farrow-to-finish hog enterprise to an Indiana cash grain farm actually increased the CV of gross margins, after adjusting for the additional fixed costs associated with hogs.

Opportunities for enterprise diversification are often limited by resources, climatic conditions, and market outlets. Relatively high, positive correlations among enterprise returns in local areas may also diminish the gains in risk efficiency from diversification. Furthermore, economies from larger sizes of operations have favored increasing specialization in production. This increased specialization has commonly been accompanied by greater investment, increased fixed costs relative to variable costs, and reduced flexibility in production.

Geographic dispersion of cropland is another form of diversification that has been used extensively in the Great Plains and to lesser degrees in other regions. This strategy involves operating cropland located over a wide geographic area to minimize losses associated with the highly localized, severe storms and other hazardous events. If storms move from the southwest to northeast, for example, then cropland could be dispersed from the northwest to southeast to reduce damages. Gains from reduced risk must be compared with the increased costs of operating geographically dispersed tracts of land.

Selection of technical practices may also respond to uncertainty. These practices serve as informal insurance schemes. Often farmers may invest in excess machinery capacity to offset unfavorable weather. Some livestock producers maintain feed reserves to offset drought. Costs of the additional machinery, carrying feed reserves, and feed deterioration must be compared with possible loss due to risk. Antibiotics in livestock feed, insecticides in crop production, and other chemicals may be routinely applied even though not always required. These practices may reduce yield variability even if expected returns are lower. Tenant farmers may overmechanize and stabilize output to reduce the risks of losing their leased acreage. Farmers can diversify their production practices too. Planting several varieties of seed may reduce possible losses from weather, insects, or disease. Indeed, greater diversity in production practices may have facilitated the specialization in crop and livestock production that has occurred in recent decades.

Supplemental irrigation may be used to reduce the risk of drought. However, unlike other informal insurance strategies, substantial capital investment and financing may be required. Irrigation is a specialized farming practice that requires considerable managerial skills and experience. Because of these capital and managerial requirements, irrigation requires careful analysis as a risk response.

Substituting capital inputs for labor could respond to the risks associated with hired labor. Where hired labor is essential, some farmers adopt incentive plans and extensive fringe benefits to avoid losing key personnel.

Marketing responses. Farmers may reduce price variability by selecting enterprises with a low expected price variability (Table 8.4) and by maintaining eligibility for government programs. Inventory management and forward pricing are other means of reducing price variability. These responses are commonly combined with investments in market information and learning that improve the quality of expectations on market conditions and related events.

For nonstorable commodities, production may be timed to sell output periodically during the year. Spreading sales over time, as is common in livestock production, results in price averaging over the marketing period and reduces the variability of expected returns. Spreading sales is essentially diversification over time rather than over enterprises. Investment in on-farm storage for grain has been substantial in the Corn Belt and other areas. It provides flexibility for farmers to sell storable commodities throughout the year. Patrick et al. (1980) interviewed 91 Indiana farmers about their marketing practices. Seventy percent of the farmers spread their sales of corn, with 31 percent of those farmers selling corn six or more times in any one year. Fifty-eight percent of the farmers spread their sales of soybeans, but less so than corn. Spreading sales can insure that an individual roughly achieves the average price received by all farmers in that year. A disadvantage of spreading sales, however, is the lost possibility for achieving above average prices.

Totally spreading sales does not allow farmers to utilize their information and marketing skills. Thus many grain farmers make only a partial commitment to spread sales. Several midwestern farmers indicate a policy of selling part of their commodity every period of the year. In each period (typically two to three months long), the farmer uses information and marketing skills to time the sales. Specialized newsletters, market reports, and forecasts are available to farmers and others; however, Just and Rausser (1981, 207) found "surprising accuracy in the futures markets prices in comparison with the econometric forecasts."

Other marketing alternatives allow farmers to price their commodity prior to delivery. Forward contracting and hedging on the futures market are two such methods. Forward contracting determines a selling price for a specified future delivery. In the Indiana study, 64 percent of the farmers partially forward contracted their soybean crop. Thirty-eight percent of the farmers contracted more than 25 percent of their expected production. About 50 percent of the farmers contracted part of their corn crop, with almost 60 percent of these farmers contracting 25 percent or less of expected production. These farmers were protected from the possible price reductions (and increases) between the contract and delivery dates. Forward contracting prior to harvest also introduces some flexibility in marketing and raises concerns about yield risk in meeting the contract commitment.

Hedging on the futures market is used less by farmers, at least in the Midwest, than forward contracts. Thirteen percent of the farmers in the Indiana study hedged part of their corn crop in 1979; and 12 percent hedged part of their soybean crop. Basis risk is a major distinction between hedging and forward contracting. The basis is the difference between the futures price and the local market price. Although a normal basis pattern exists in each locality, that pattern can vary and this risk is borne by the contractor. Other disadvantages of hedging are the limited availability of suitable contracts, the discrete size of contracts, brokerage fees, and potential margin calls. For small- and medium-sized farming operations, forward contracting is more popular than hedging because less management time and skill are involved.

Several studies have evaluated routine hedging and forward contracting as grain farmers' responses to price risk (Bolen et al. 1978; Klinefelter 1979; Shurley 1980). In comparing strategies for Illinois farmers, Bolen et al. reported that spreading crop sales among various dates before and after harvest was at least as effective as hedging in reducing income variability. Both Klinefelter and Shurley used MOTAD programming models to evaluate alternative marketing strategies. Based on historic performances of specified strategies, these studies often found that routine hedging or forward contracting may not greatly reduce price risk. Lutgen and Helmers (1979) as well as Shurley found interactions between production and marketing decisions.

Leuthold and Peterson (1980) indicate, however, that selective hedging of swine contracts may effectively reduce price variability. Unlike the grain marketing studies that attempted to find the optimal marketing strategy over a period of years. Leuthold and Peterson used varied hedging strategies.

Contracts that fix both the price and quantity for future delivery bring additional risks because of the contract commitment. McKinnon (1967) shows how the correlation between a farmer's expected price and output, together with the relative variabilities of market price and yield, jointly determine an optimal level of contracting. As the proportion of contracted to expected production increases, the total of price and production risk decreases and then increases. For cotton producers in Texas, Barry and Willmann (1976) have shown that this pattern of risk change is reflected in access to credit and borrowing costs, which in turn affects other production and marketing choices.

Several other studies also explored optimal hedging for risk averse farmers using the mean-variance portfolio model. The conceptual foundations for this approach were developed by Johnson (1960), Stein (1961), and Ward and Fletcher (1971). Heifner (1972) developed a minimum risk model for hedging that was applied to cattle feeding and various grain storage situations. Peck (1975) studied the use of hedging in an expected utility maximization framework for egg producers, based on various forecasts in placing those hedges. She showed that the level of risk aversion was not significant in optimal hedging, unless risk aversion was very low, and found that hedging could substantially reduce income variation when compared with nonhedging. Berck (1983) also used portfolio theory to explain the hedging behavior of California cotton growers in which speculation and cross hedging could occur simultaneously with varying levels of crop production, credit use, and other activities. His results showed that the high costs of hedging and the opportunity to reduce risk through crop diversification substantially influenced the optimal hedge at planting time and yielded relatively low levels of hedging that were consistent with farmers' actual practices. Finally Peterson (1983) used a mathematical programming approach to evaluate the joint effects of multiple, indivisible hedges for inputs and outputs in a cattle feedlot with a sequence of cattle acquisition, feed purchases, and cattle sales, and different assumptions about the risk perceptions of the decision maker. His results showed the importance of basis risk, expectations, and levels of risk aversion in the optimal hedging strategy, although the high comparability between discrete and continuous solutions indicated that contract size issues in cattle hedging are of relatively minor importance.

Farmers may also contract to purchase inputs rather than purchase in the spot market. For example, livestock producers may hedge purchased feed to reduce price variability. Contracting may also assure quantity and quality of inputs and facilitate coordination among individuals. For example, feedlot operators may offer feeder cattle purchase contracts to ranchers, reducing the price risk for both parties. Although input contracting has been used primarily by agricultural processors, some opportunities exist for agricultural producers, especially with larger, capital-intensive operations.

Participation in government commodity programs is another marketing response to risk for many farmers, with studies by Kramer and Pope (1981) and Musser and Stamoulis (1981) focusing on the risk efficient effects. Kramer and Pope's results for a representative California farm indicated that the participation decision is strongly sensitive to the farmer's level of risk aversion and subjective beliefs, as well as to differences in farm size. Musser and Stamoulis' results for a representative farm in Georgia under the 1977 farm legislation also showed that participation tends to dominate nonparticipation in risk efficiency terms except for higher expected incomes in some of their model specifications.

Marketing decisions also involve learning because new information becomes available during the marketing period. In highly efficient commodity markets the new information is quickly reflected in commodity prices. Effective risk responses should utilize this information to adjust marketing options to changing conditions. Government price and income policies, such as deficiency payments and storage programs, also affect prices and price variability both within a given year as well as over time. Farmers need to develop skills in marketing and processing market information to effectively use these strategies.

Financial responses. As farms become larger and more specialized, use of production strategies such as enterprise diversification to reduce risks has diminished. Also volatility of commodity prices increased the need for marketing responses to risk, even though these strategies do not completely eliminate price variability. As income fluctuations due to business risk increase, financial responses to risk become increasingly important. Gabriel and Baker (1980) demonstrate the interrelated impact of business and financial risk on the farm firm. Utilizing the risk balancing concept, a farmer may adopt financial strategies to offset increasing production and market risk, or vice versa.

An important financial measure of the firm's ability to survive shortfalls in net income is its liquidity position. With rising land values many farmers experience increasing solvency. However, their financial position also may be less liquid. One financial response to risk is maintaining additional liquidity. Liquid assets are categorized by the time required to liquidate an asset and the discount in sale proceeds resulting from a forced sale (Van Horne, 1983). Savings accounts are liquid assets because they can be quickly converted to cash and their liquidation costs are low. Other assets may not meet these criteria. Liquidating a tract of land on short notice generally involves a substantial discount in sales value. Therefore, land is considered an illiquid asset.

Holding liquid assets may be costly because they typically earn lower returns. Productive assets and real estate generate higher expected returns than do cash or near-cash items. When inflation rates are increasing, liquid assets tend to decline in real value. Maintaining the real value of assets is desirable, but this typically involves conversion to less liquid forms. Another source of liquidity is the farmer's credit reserve. A credit reserve is the farm's unused borrowing capacity (Barry and Baker 1971). It can provide additional loans to cope with cash flow problems.

Liquidity is substantially affected by the investment and financing programs for durable assets. Utilizing long-term financing to lower annual payments may reduce cash requirements for the farm business. Spreading debt commitments may also affect the farm's credit reserve in times of income shortfalls. To maintain liquidity, it is important to match the debt repayment structure with the income-generating pattern of the purchased asset.

Sonka and Dixon (1978), building on work by Jones (1978), investigated the impact of alternative liquidity positions on farmers' borrowing capacity. Their results indicated that lenders' responses to loan requests are greatly influenced by the farmer's liquidity position. Greater liquidity increases the farmer's ability to withstand adverse income situations.

Held and Helmers (1981) and Patrick (1979a) investigated the effects of alternative levels of debt on survival and growth of farm firms over time with simulation models (Chap. 11). Held and Helmers found that increasing the maximum ratio of equity capital to total assets from 40 to 55 percent increased the probability of survival sharply for dry-land Nebraska wheat farmers; but, the increases in survival probability with still higher equity requirements were limited. Slower growth in net worth was associated with equity requirements above 50 percent. Patrick also found that the probability of firm survival decreased with increasing leverage, but in some instances very high allowances on leverage allowed Indiana farmers to survive compared to more restrictive borrowing constraints that forced their failure. Slower growth in net worth was associated with equity requirements of less than 30 percent. (Chapter 13 further illustrates the effects of leverage, financial risk, and responses to risk on a farm's financial performance.)

Leasing of assets is another way to maintain liquidity in the farm business. Leasing avoids debt commitments, adds to liquidity, and can provide flexibility in operations. Farmers have not used long-term leasing of machinery and equipment to the extent of the nonfarm sector, but recent tax law changes provide additional incentives for farm finance leasing.

Land is commonly leased on a cash or share basis and allows farmers to invest more in intermediate assets instead of less liquid farm real estate. Cash rents can be adjusted during adverse conditions. However, in a study of farmers in the El Paso Valley of Texas, Richardson and Condra (1981) found that a straight cash-lease farm operation has little chance of survival and success. In contrast, share rental of land allocates production and market risks between the operator and landlord. Crop-share leases are highly risk efficient financing plans because perfect positive correlation can be attained between an operator's crop return and his rental obligation. Held and Helmers (1981) found that share rental by Nebraska wheat farmers, rather than purchase, more than doubled the probability of firm survival. Net worth accumulation was only slightly less than with a combination share-rent and purchase-expansion option. Cash or share leasing of land does have the risk of losing control of the leased land when the contract expires, a risk not present with land ownership.

Insurance is another financial response to risk that provides a specialized source of liquidity. Commercial insurance can often be a more cost-effective means of maintaining a reserve of funds to offset a loss compared to an individual creating and holding his own reserve. Patrick et al. (1980) found that over 95 percent of the Indiana farmers interviewed had liability, fire, theft, life, and medical insurance, but less than half had hail or crop insurance. The Federal Crop Insurance (FCI) program has been modified to make it more attractive to producers (see Chap. 16). Kramer (1981) found that corn farmers in Virginia would have received more in FCI benefits over a 17-year period than they would have paid in premiums for the highest level of the coverage. Lemieux et al. (1982) analyzed the FCI program in the Texas High Plains and found that participation increased the size of farm, after-tax net present value of income, and ending net worth.

Farmers who assign low probabilities to yields below 75 percent of normal may not participate, but lenders may encourage crop insurance as a part of specific financing arrangements.

Integrated strategies: Agricultural producers face a variety of types of risks and have many risk reducing actions available. Comprehensive risk management strategies that integrate several of these actions are necessary in dealing with these multiple sources of risk. Most grain and livestock producers have only limited opportunities for diversifying enterprises and production practices. Marketing responses like spreading sales, forward contracting, and hedging are being used by increasing numbers of farmers, but they do not eliminate market risk. Financial responses are also used to build the farm's capacity to bear risks in production and marketing and to cope with financial risks as well. A comprehensive strategy integrating production, marketing, and financial responses should reduce risk more than can the individual responses to risk. Which integrated strategy is best for an individual producer depends on the available resources, goals and risk attitudes, equity position, financing available, weather conditions, market availability, and other factors. As these factors change, the best strategy is also likely to change.

DECISION PROCESS AS A RISK RESPONSE. Uncertainty modifies the decision process that is, itself, a response to risk. Uncertainty also creates a need for additional information to improve expectations about future events. In the Bayesian framework (Anderson et al. 1977) the difference between the expected value of the optimal strategy without the information and the Bayes strategy with additional information is the value of information. Conklin et al. (1977), for example, estimated the value of a perfect frost forecast as $3.18/day/acre for the frost season of Oregon orchardists. In addition, Rister and Skess (1982) found positive values associated with outlook information for postharvest marketing strategies for south Texas grain sorghum producers.

This section considers risk and uncertainty in the decision process. Two simple procedures for generating probabilities are also discussed.

Incorporating risk and uncertainty. The decision process presented earlier did not explicitly consider uncertainty. The third and fourth steps of the process are: (3) analyze alternatives and determine probable outcomes, and (4) decide which alternative to select. These steps are altered when uncertainty is considered.

Nelson et al. (1978) specify five components of a decision model under uncertainty: (1) alternatives the farmer is considering; (2) uncertain events; (3) outcomes (or payoffs) expected for the respective alternatives and events; (4) each event's probability; and (5) a decision rule or criterion for evaluating alternatives. Specifying alternatives also occurs in decision making under certainty. However, explicit specification of uncertain events is a major addition to the process. These events are beyond a farmer's control. In decision making under certainty only the most likely outcome is considered; however, with uncertainty the entire range of outcomes for each alternative is considered. This process is more elaborate and costly for decision makers but more useful too.

Estimating probabilities of events is a challenging task that is unfamiliar to many decision makers. But farmers have considerable information accumulated through experience, technical knowledge, forecasts, etc. to help in estimating the probabilities of various events. Moreover the farmer makes decisions as if the likelihood of the events involved were known.

Several types of decision rules for risk analysis were reviewed in Chapter 5. These included maximizing expected income, the expected utility model, and safety-first models. These decision rules are unique to each decision maker and may best be unspecified. Each farmer can evaluate the characteristics of the probability distributions for the alternatives that appear most important. Combining this information with nonmonetary considerations should lead to an appropriate choice. Decisions are intended to yield good outcomes. Good decisions, however, do not insure good outcomes (Anderson et al. 1977) due to the effects of risk. A good decision is consistent with the decision maker's expectations and preferences, not just a decision that works out well. Unfortunately, a good decision can result in undesirable outcomes; and, a poor decision can yield favorable outcomes.

Eliciting subjective probabilities. Acquiring information and evaluating decision alternatives are not costless activities. Efficient procedures that capture the major impacts of uncertainty are desired. Development of appropriate probability estimates is a difficult task for farmers. The farmer could directly specify the probability of each possible event. But, this procedure is unsatisfactory if individuals give biased responses (Tversky and Kahneman 1974; Thaler 1980).

A set of probabilities must satisfy the following consistency conditions (Anderson et al. 1977): (1) the probability of any individual event must be between zero and 1.0, inclusive; (2) the probability of two or more mutually exclusive events occurring is the sum of the probabilities of each individual event; and (3) the sum of the probabilities of all possible events must equal 1.0. The direct elicitation of probabilities from a decision maker may not satisfy these three conditions. Thus, simple procedures have been developed to translate a decision maker's beliefs about future events into probability statements. The strength-of-conviction method and a triangular-distribution technique are relatively easy to explain and use.

The strength-of-conviction method requires the following four steps to generate a set of probabilities:

1. Divide the range of possible events into a small number of logical groups. If the range of one event appears too large, subdivide the category and repeat the process.

2. Specify the decision maker's strength of conviction about the relative occurrence of each event on a numeric scale (i.e., a scale of 0 to 10, with 0 implying that the event cannot occur and 10 implying certainty).

3. Sum the degrees of conviction for all events.

4. Find the subjective probability of each event by dividing the degree of conviction for that event by the sum calculated in (3).

For example, a farmer who is purchasing feeder pigs desires to specify a probability distribution of hog prices. The process for specifying this distribution is summarized as follows:

Events, Output price category (P)	Degree of conviction for each price category (0–10)	Probability of each price category
$P > \$54/\text{cwt}$	1	$1/15 = .07$
$\$48/\text{cwt} \leq P < \$54/\text{cwt}$	6	$6/15 = .40$
$\$42/\text{cwt} \leq P < \$48/\text{cwt}$	5	$5/15 = .33$
$P < \$42/\text{cwt}$	3	$3/15 = .20$
TOTAL	15	$15/15 = 1.00$

This farmer's personal beliefs about future prices is now expressed by probabilities. The farmer believes a price between $48 and $54 is most likely, but not much more likely than a price between $42 and $48. A price greater than $54 is possible, but very unlikely. If these price categories are expressed as point estimates the farmer's expected market price can be estimated.

Output price category (P)	Point estimate
$P > \$54/\text{cwt}$	$57/cwt
$\$48/\text{cwt} \leq P < \$54/\text{cwt}$	$51/cwt
$\$42/\text{cwt} \leq P < \$48/\text{cwt}$	$45/cwt
$P < \$42/\text{cwt}$	$40/cwt

The expected market price is a weighted average of each point estimate multiplied by the probability of its price category.

Expected market price $= (.07 \times \$57) + (.40 \times \$51) + (.33 \times \$45) + .20 \times \$40) = \$47.24.$

In addition the variance is a weighted average of the squared deviations of each point estimate from the expected value. Thus

$$\text{variance} = (.07)\,(57 - 47.24)^2 + (.40)\,(51 - 47.24)^2$$
$$+ (.33)\,(45 - 47.24)^2 + (.20)\,(40 - 47.24)^2 = 24.46.$$

The standard deviation is $4.95 = (24.46)^{1/2}$. In this fashion the conviction method yields information about both the expected value and variability of the subjective probability distribution.

The triangular-distribution method requires less information to estimate the probability distribution (Cassidy et al. 1970; Anderson et al. 1977). Thus, it is simpler to use, but less accurate. The distribution for hog prices is plotted in Fig. 8.1. The four points describe a probability distribution that is concentrated in the upper $40 range.

The distribution is approximated by the dotted line *LHM,* which has a triangular shape. Use of the triangular distribution requires three items from the farmer: (1) the most likely value to occur (*M*), (2) the lowest possible value (*L*), (3) the highest possible value (*H*). Based on these values and requiring that all probabilities sum to 1.0, relatively simple formulas can be used to calculate a cumulative distribution that is useful for decision making. To calculate the probability (P_i) of a value of X being less than X_i, one of two formulas is used.

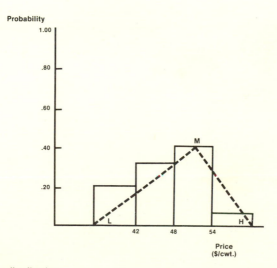

FIG. 8.1.   Price distribution.

(1) For a value $X_i \le M_i$, $P_i = (X_i - L)^2/(H - L)(M - L)$
(2) For a value $X_i \ge M_i$, $P_i = 1.0 - (X_i - H)^2/(H - L)(H - M)$

The triangular distribution is illustrated for two farmers who are considering forward contracting of stored corn for May delivery. The forward price is \$3.25/bu and both farmers agree that this is the most likely price in May. One farmer, Mr. Smith, believes the May price could range from a high of \$3.80 to a low of \$3.00/bu. The second, Mr. Johnson, believes that the price could range from \$3.60 to \$2.60/bu. Using formulas 1 and 2, cumulative probability distributions for each farmer are shown in Fig. 8.2.

If the specified situations were to occur a large number of times, formula 3 could be used as a simple method to approximate an average value.

$$(3) \ \text{Average} = \frac{L + M + H}{3}$$

Thus Mr. Smith's average price is \$3.35/bu and Mr. Johnson's is \$3.15. In addition, the probability distributions of Fig. 8.2 show a 65 percent chance for Mr. Johnson that the May price will be less than \$3.25 contract price. Mr. Smith, however, feels that the chance of a cash price less than \$3.25 is only 31 percent. Thus these farmers may develop different forward contracting strategies even though they agree on the most likely price. In many cases, specification of the expected range of outcomes and translation of

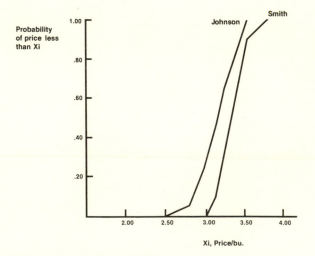

FIG. 8.2. Cumulative probability distribution.

these expectations into a probability distribution for risk analysis aids the decision process.

The triangular distribution based on formulas 1 and 2 is sometimes tedious to use. However, these formulas can be programmed on microcomputers and programmable calculators for easier use. Several extension uses of these decision aids already have occurred. As more of these aids become available and as more farmers acquire services of electronic equipment the usefulness of probabilistic planning concepts will also increase.

Summary

Farmers face (1) production or technical risk, (2) market or price risk, (3) technological risk, (4) legal and social risk, and (5) human sources of risk in the agricultural production process. A farmer's response to risk may be in production, marketing, or the financial organization of the farm business. Effects of these responses are discussed and it is suggested that an integrated strategy may be more effective in dealing with multiple sources of risk. Techniques available to analyze these strategies are discussed in Chapters 9 through 11.

A second type of risk response is a modification of the decision process. An expanded decision process considers the uncertain events that can occur, outcomes expected, probabilities of each event's occurrence and a procedure for ranking alternatives. Two relatively simple methods of deriving subjective probability information useful in this expanded decision process are illustrated.

CHAPTER 9

Methods of
risk analysis
for farm firms

HARRY P. MAPP, JR., AND **GLENN A. HELMERS**

STATIC ECONOMIC ANALYSIS is based on the simplifying assumptions of certainty about the environment and an objective of profit maximization. Introduction of risk extends these concepts to include the decision maker's perception of risk and his or her attitude toward risk. A number of approaches have been developed to analyze risk at the firm level; the literature in this area is extensive. This chapter introduces alternative methods of risk analysis, presents the appropriate models, and discusses their advantages and disadvantages. In addition, empirical studies are reviewed that apply these methods to analyze the production, marketing, and financial alternatives of farmers under risky conditions.

Mean-variance analysis and quadratic programming

Mean-variance (EV) analysis has served as the conceptual framework for many risk analyses in agricultural economics. The foundations of the EV model were presented in Chapters 5 and 6. Here we establish its use in quadratic (risk) programming.

EV analysis bases the selection of risky prospects on the means and variances of their probability distributions. This concept originated in portfolio theory to explain diversification as a rational choice by decision makers. Markowitz (1959) conceived the portfolio selection problem in a

Harry P. Mapp, Jr., Oklahoma State University, and
Glenn A. Helmers, University of Nebraska.

quadratic programming framework and specified the objective to minimize portfolio variance for alternative levels of expected returns

$$\text{Minimize } V(Z) = \sum_{i=1}^{n} \sum_{j=1}^{m} q_i \sigma_{ij} q_j \tag{9.1}$$

subject to

$$\sum_{i=1}^{n} q_i U_i \geq M \tag{9.2}$$

$$\sum_{i=1}^{n} q_i = 1 \tag{9.3}$$

$$q_i \geq 0 \text{ for } i = 1, \ldots, n \tag{9.4}$$

where q_i = the proportion of each risky investment i; U_i = the expected return for investment i; σ_{ij} = the variance-covariance matrix; and M = the expected income level. The system is solved iteratively through parametric variations in M to define a set of risk efficient (minimum-variance) solutions.

Freund (1956) was the first to apply quadratic programming to a farm firm problem. Freund's model contained four production activities and several resource constraints for a representative farm in North Carolina. He found that the introduction of risk into the programming model reduced both the level and standard deviation of net revenue; moreover, diversification was explained as a rational choice of expected utility maximizers. Quadratic risk programming has since been applied in many other studies to evaluate optimum farm organizations under conditions of risky choice. Examples include studies by Barry and Willmann (1976); Johnson (1979); Musser and Stamoulis (1981); Scott and Baker (1972); Lin et al. (1974); and Adams et al. (1980).

In matrix notation the model is typically formulated as

$$\text{Maximize } U'X - \lambda X' \sigma X \tag{9.5}$$

subject to

$$AX \leq B \tag{9.6}$$

$$X \geq 0 \tag{9.7}$$

where X = the activity levels; U = the expected returns associated with each activity; B = the resource restrictions; σ = the variance-covariance matrix of activity returns; and λ = the risk aversion coefficient.

Except for the objective function, the model resembles a linear program (LP) with A, X, and B corresponding to their LP counterparts. Data based on either objective or subjective concepts of probability are needed to estimate the variance-covariance matrix. For a problem with four activities and three restrictions, the model is formulated as:

$$\text{Max } [U_1,\ U_2,\ U_3,\ U_4] \begin{bmatrix} X_1 \\ X_2 \\ X_3 \\ X_4 \end{bmatrix} - \lambda [X_1,\ X_2,\ X_3,\ X_4] \begin{bmatrix} \sigma_{11} & \sigma_{12} & \sigma_{13} & \sigma_{14} \\ \sigma_{21} & \sigma_{22} & \sigma_{23} & \sigma_{24} \\ \sigma_{31} & \sigma_{32} & \sigma_{33} & \sigma_{34} \\ \sigma_{41} & \sigma_{42} & \sigma_{43} & \sigma_{44} \end{bmatrix} \begin{bmatrix} X_1 \\ X_2 \\ X_3 \\ X_4 \end{bmatrix}$$

subject to

$$\begin{bmatrix} a_{11} & a_{12} & a_{13} & a_{14} \\ a_{21} & a_{22} & a_{23} & a_{24} \\ a_{31} & a_{32} & a_{33} & a_{34} \end{bmatrix} \begin{bmatrix} X_1 \\ X_2 \\ X_3 \\ X_4 \end{bmatrix} \leq \begin{bmatrix} b_1 \\ b_2 \\ b_3 \end{bmatrix} \text{ and } \begin{bmatrix} X_1 \\ X_2 \\ X_3 \\ X_4 \end{bmatrix} \geq 0$$

In this formulation, λ is varied parametrically to derive the efficient frontier. When $\lambda = 0$, or $\sigma = 0$, the problem is reduced to a linear program.

Quadratic risk programming, as an expected utility approach, is consistent with the existing body of decision theory. The objective function corresponds to a quadratic utility function having expected income and variance of income as the objects of utility. The decision maker's risk attitude is expressed by the risk aversion parameter. If the decision maker is risk neutral, $\lambda = 0$ and expected income is maximized. As risk becomes increasingly important, the risk aversion coefficient increases and risk efficient farm plans are identified. Generally, the higher the risk aversion, the more diversified are the risk efficient portfolios. Other factors, however, can still yield a diversified portfolio. For example, various constraints may yield diversity in the portfolio apart from risk considerations. Diversity can also arise for firms operating in less than perfectly competitive markets.

Some of the limitations often cited for quadratic risk programming apply in most approaches to risk analysis. Specifying the risk aversion coefficient is arbitrary, yet critical for determining a risk efficient farm plan. One might derive the entire efficient frontier and present the set of farm plans to a farmer. If the focus is on measuring risk aversion, the farmer might reveal his degree of risk aversion through selection of an optimal plan from the risk efficient set. However, this approach is only valid with a model that fully captures the relevant risk responses for the decision maker. Alternatively one might vary the risk aversion parameter until the difference between a farmer's actual plan and a farm plan on the efficient frontier is minimized (Brink and McCarl 1978).

Estimation of the variance-covariance matrix presents numerous meth-

odological pitfalls (see Chaps. 3, 4, 10). Ideally, variance-covariance relationships should be based on the subjective evaluation of the decision
maker. Except for Lin et al. (1974), few empirical studies have taken this
approach. Rather, objective measures of variability based on historical data
have dominated the literature. Key decisions include identifying the relevant
sources of risk; collecting the appropriate data as in the case of crop yields
and prices; selecting the appropriate length of the historical series; identifying the appropriate price series and accounting for the effects of inflation;
and constructing the cost of production series.

In addition, one must distinguish between known patterns of variation
(trend, cyclical, seasonal) and random variation. Some believe that producers base their plan on the long-term mean of a historical series of returns
and that any deviation from the mean is a random event (Thomas 1971;
Love 1972). Measuring variability as variance (squared deviations about the
mean) is consistent with this view. Others have approximated the expected
outcomes based on linear or polynomial trends (Smith 1972). Random variation is then measured as deviations from the trend line. Another approach
is to measure the unexpected variation as deviations from the expected
component of a moving average (Brink and McCarl 1978; Persaud and
Mapp 1980). Other approaches (Young 1980) include measuring the random
component in terms of first differences of the data series (Jones 1969);
utilizing first through kth order differences (Tintner 1940; Carter and Dean
1960; Wildermuth et al. 1971; Mathia 1975; Yahya and Adams 1977) and
using autoregressive integrated moving average (ARIMA) models (Bessler
1977; Ibrahim and Williams 1978), a moving weighted autoregression
model (Klein 1978), or a moving weighted linear time trend model (Calvin
1979).

Despite its problems and limitations, quadratic risk programming has
had numerous applications in empirical analysis. Scott and Baker (1972)
used quadratic programming to derive a risk efficient set of farm plans for a
central Illinois cash grain farm. The production alternatives included corn,
soybeans, oats, wheat, and land conservation. The analysis allowed the
farmer to choose a production plan from the efficient set based on his own
risk attitude.

Lin et al. (1974) utilized quadratic programming to develop risk efficient sets for a panel of California farms. They tested the hypothesis that
farmers' operational decisions are more consistent with utility maximization
than with profit maximization by evaluating farm plans under maximization of profit, expected utility, and lexicographic utility, respectively. The
expected utility formulations most accurately predicted actual and planned
crop patterns, followed by the lexicographic formulation and profit maximization.

Musser and Stamoulis (1981) used quadratic programming to model a farm firm in order to analyze the effects on risk efficiency of participation in the Food and Agriculture Act of 1977. The basic model included important policy provisions of the act: loan rate, deficiency payments, set-aside, voluntary diversion, and disaster payments. Data were synthesized to estimate the variance-covariance matrix of incomes for commodities covered under the act. The study provided empirical support for the widely held view that the government's commodity programs reduce farmers' risks.

A number of portfolio analyses using the mean-variance model have focused on credit risk, asset illiquidity, asset fixity, credit reserves, portfolio risk, and other financial choices for farmers. In reviewing farm applications of portfolio theory, Robison and Brake (1979) observed a tendency to describe portfolio choices along EV frontiers and allow costless transition from one portfolio to another and among individual assets. This simplification ignores asset illiquidity and asset fixity, whose effects may significantly change the economic incentives for portfolio revisions.

Barry et al. (1981) used the mean-variance portfolio model as a conceptual framework for combining credit risks with other financial and business risks to determine total risk. They demonstrate that credit reserves, valued in part for their role in risk aspects of financial management, are themselves subject to risk. If credit becomes too volatile, it loses value as a source of liquidity and farmers are forced to seek other costly sources. Thus, they argued that credit risk must be accounted for in farmers' total portfolio risk and in risk and liquidity analysis at the firm level.

Barry and Willmann (1976) developed a multiperiod risk programming model to evaluate forward contracting and other financial choices for farmers who are subject to market risk and external credit rationing. The model derived sets of EV efficient farm growth plans that reflected the influence of contracting on income stability, levels of credit, and income growth. The results indicated that the lender's credit responses could modify the producer's contracting plans and the rate of income growth.

Whitson et al. (1976) modeled a ranch operation with multiperiod quadratic programming in order to evaluate the risk return effects of vertically sequenced production and marketing strategies. The results indicated that retention of calf ownership through different finishing stages either on pasture or by custom feeding in commercial feedlots could significantly influence both the level and variability of income growth. Thus vertical production alternatives in ranch planning appeared effective in risk management but should not be evaluated independently of other risk responses.

Johnson (1979) used multiperiod quadratic programming to integrate short-run production and marketing and long-run investment and financial decisions into a common framework. The model allowed responses to risk through variations in farm size, diversification of crop and livestock production, and adoption of alternative cash selling and hedging options. The study's results suggested that farmers use scale adjustments, including variations in the levels of investments and credit use, rather than diversification in managing risk. Johnson argued that an integrated analysis of the production, marketing, investment, and financial strategies is essential in risk management.

Minimization of total absolute deviations (MOTAD)

The MOTAD model was introduced in Chapters 5 and 6 as a decision rule that provides a linear alternative to quadratic programming in deriving a risk efficient set. The basic concept is to minimize total (or negative) absolute deviations about expected income, subject to constraints on expected income and other resources (Hazell 1971). Re-solving the model for parametric variations in expected income yields a MOTAD efficient set. The linear solutions closely approximate the quadratic solutions and may offer cost and computational advantages in conducting the analysis.

For a problem involving four activities, three constraints, and the minimization of negative gross margin deviations for a five-year period, the MOTAD model is specified as:

Minimize
$$F_1X_1 + F_2X_2 + F_3X_3 + F_4X_4 - \lambda[d_1^+ + d_1^- + d_2^+ + d_2^- + d_3^+ + d_3^-$$
$$+ d_4^+ + d_4^- + d_5^+ + d_5^-]$$

subject to
$$a_{11}X_1 + a_{12}X_2 + a_{13}X_3 + a_{14}X_4 \leq b_1$$
$$a_{21}X_1 + a_{22}X_2 + a_{23}X_3 + a_{24}X_4 \leq b_2$$
$$a_{31}X_1 + a_{32}X_2 + a_{33}X_3 + a_{34}X_4 \leq b_3$$

and
$$d_{11}X_1 + d_{12}X_2 + d_{13}X_3 + d_{14}X_4 - d_1^+ + d_1^- = 0$$
$$d_{21}X_1 + d_{22}X_2 + d_{23}X_3 + d_{24}X_4 - d_2^+ + d_2^- = 0$$
$$d_{31}X_1 + d_{32}X_2 + d_{33}X_3 + d_{34}X_4 - d_3^+ + d_3^- = 0$$
$$d_{41}X_1 + d_{42}X_2 + d_{43}X_3 + d_{44}X_4 - d_4^+ + d_4^- = 0$$
$$d_{51}X_1 + d_{52}X_2 + d_{53}X_3 + d_{54}X_4 - d_5^+ + d_5^- = 0$$
$$x_j, d_h^+, d_h^- \geq 0$$

where X_j and F_j are the level and expected income, respectively, of the jth activity, the d_j represent the negative deviations of income, a_{ij} is the technical requirement of the jth activity for the ith constraint, b_i is the ith constraint level, and λ is a scalar.

If objective data are used to specify the variabilities of return and other factors, the data requirements for MOTAD and quadratic programming are similar. Data on yields, prices, and costs of production must be obtained to determine the series of gross margins or net returns. Unlike quadratic programming, the MOTAD approach does not require a variance-covariance matrix. However, MOTAD does consider the covariance relationships among activities. Deviations from the mean of the series for each activity are summed across all activities. Positive deviations in one activity may cancel out negative deviations in another activity, thus accounting for the correlation between these activities.

Risk measures based on subjective concepts of probability are more difficult to model using the MOTAD approach. The time series of absolute deviations would need to be formulated from subjective measures — a difficult task at best. If the time series could be obtained subjectively, the length of the series would be limited, thus tending to overestimate the variability involved due to the fewer number of observations. Perhaps one could elicit subjective probability distributions, or joint distributions, and sample them randomly in order to create a representative time series.

The MOTAD approach has been used in a number of studies. Brink and McCarl (1978) specified a MOTAD model for 38 Corn Belt farmers using individual farm data and negative deviations from expected returns as the measure of risk. A set of farm plans was developed for each farmer by parameterizing the scalar λ. The farmer's risk aversion coefficient was identified as the value of λ that minimized the difference between the risk efficient plan and the farmer's present plan. The majority of farmers had risk aversion coefficients that were zero or less than 0.25, significantly less than in some other studies.

Mapp et al. (1979), developed a MOTAD model for a typical farm situation in southwestern Oklahoma and utilized the risk efficient farm plans in a simulation model to evaluate the effects of alternative economic futures. The analysis simulated the potential effects of slower growth rates for land values, increased costs of production, and alternative beginning equity levels on the viability of the farm firm. The chance of farm failure (bankruptcy) increased substantially when the initial ratio of equity to assets was below 45 percent and land values increased only 4 percent annually.

Gebremeskel and Shumway (1979) developed a MOTAD model to investigate risk reducing forage and cattle management strategies. The model accounted for forage quality and was used to determine forage species, fertilization rates, herd size, and the degree of on-farm integration for solutions in a MOTAD efficient set. By integrating statistical decision theory with the programming model, annual calf marketing strategies were derived and evaluated based on observable data for predicting subsequent calf prices and forage yields.

Persaud and Mapp (1980) developed a MOTAD model to evaluate risk management strategies for farmers in southwestern Oklahoma. The model's marketing activities included forward contracting of wheat sales and wheat storage and subsequent periodic sale on a monthly basis throughout the year. Forward contracting and periodic marketing of wheat appeared in several risk efficient farm plans.

Simulation analysis

Simulation is an analytical technique that models the reality of a system of relationships. It is widely applied to solve military, industrial, behavioral, and economic problems. In agriculture, simulation analysis is used to model plant and animal growth processes, growth and intergenerational transfers of the farm firm, risk and survival prospects, supply and demand relationships, multiobjective decision processes, and many others (Anderson 1974). In economic analysis, few relationships are known with certainty. Simulation is a flexible technique that can easily incorporate stochastic variables.

A simulation model may have many attributes: (1) it may be deterministic or stochastic; (2) it may involve single or multiperiod events; (3) it may be programmed to maximize or minimize a linear or nonlinear objective function, search for an optimal solution, or be nonoptimizing; (4) it may represent part or all of a complex process; and (5) it may be behavioral or mathematical.

Flexibility in model design is both an advantage and a disadvantage of simulation. The system and design of the model are determined by the researcher. Simulation models rarely have a preexisting structure, as occurs with the coefficients, constraints, and objective functions of linear and quadratic programming. Each problem is uniquely modeled. Once a firm is simulated, the model can sometimes be adapted to solve or analyze other problems. However, few simulation models in agricultural economics have been generalized and documented for modification and reuse.

ELEMENTS OF FIRM SIMULATION MODELS. The steps in constructing simulation models are: (1) model formulation, (2) synthesis, (3) verification/validation and (4) experimentation. In the formulation stage, the problem is identified and research hypotheses are formulated. The model's structure is determined, including information flows, decision rules, feedback loops, and input-output requirements. Stochastic variables must be identified and incorporated for risk analysis. The model's output should be designed to yield the key measures needed for statistical analysis. The simulation model will not have an objective function unless one is specified by the researcher. In many risk applications, researchers have simulated the impacts of uncertain yields and prices on net farm income, net worth, short- and long-term credit requirements, or consumption in a given year. The organization of production is usually specified in advance. However, decision rules can be specified to determine an organization of production.

Simulation models may contain LP components to determine optimal production plans and to simulate the organizations under risky conditions (Chien and Bradford 1976; Richardson and Condra 1981). Where time and risk are important, the cumulative effects of yield and price variability on net income, ending net worth, and farm survival may be evaluated. Model output may include average ending net worth and its standard deviation, the coefficient of variation of net worth, and the rate of farm failures.

In the synthesis step, the model is specified in detail, including the stochastic variables (prices, yields, rainfall, temperature, net income, hail, etc.), the choice of distributions, collection of data, examination of serial dependence, and estimation of covariances. Risk analysis in a multiperiod model requires appropriate specifications of future economic events. For example, the general inflation rate, farm input and output prices, and changes in farmland values must be considered carefully. If nonequilibrium conditions are simulated over an extended period, the outcomes may be artificially driven by the economic assumptions. The correct specification of inflation is important in simulation models, although the danger of misspecification also holds for programming models.

The verification/validation step considers the model's technical accuracy and realistic portrayal of stochastic events. Verification includes the "debugging" of apparent inconsistencies and determining if subroutines are performing correctly. Validation involves determining how well the model simulates reality. One validity test compares the model's result with observed behavior. For example, do the yields, prices, or net returns generated by the model have the proper maximum, minimum, mean, and standard deviation? Validation often requires subjective appraisal, gauging results against historical changes if the model reproduces historical observations, or checking the model's performance against expected theoretical changes. The experimentation stage subjects the model to a range of values of the key variables. One might simulate the potential impact on net farm income of 1000 combinations of stochastic yields and prices for several crop or livestock activities. The impact of risk responses such as all risk crop insurance, disaster or deficiency payments, or hedging and forward contracting, may be evaluated under different assumptions about beginning net worth, critical debt to equity ratios, or future economic conditions.

Probabilistic results may be presented to the decision maker to show the likelihoods that risk management strategies will maintain income above a critical level. An elicited utility function or subjective evaluation by the producer may be used to select desirable outcomes, or stochastic dominance criteria may be used to identify risk efficient farm plans.

Simulation offers the potential for modeling feedback phenomena and adaptive control processes that characterize many responses to risk. Adaptive control describes the process of altering decisions based on new information or revised decision criteria. The new information is fed back into the model in order to revise the solutions. Thus information and learning are important in simulation analysis. Some studies incorporating Bayesian concepts have emphasized the value of information under risky conditions (Eidman et al. 1967; Carlson 1970; White and Eidman 1971; Baquet et al. 1976).

STOCHASTIC SPECIFICATIONS. The specification of stochastic variables in simulation models is an important part of risk analysis. If a variable is normally distributed, the probability distribution is completely specified by the mean and variance. Given the mean and variance, "canned" computer routines can generate hundreds or thousands of random normal values from the distribution. Stochastic crop yields may follow a normal distribution, although the possibility of negative yields then exists. This problem could be overcome by truncating the distribution so that negative yields equal zero. Prices are not likely to follow a normal distribution.

For nonnormal distributions many probability distributions are possible: uniform, lognormal, binomial, triangular, geometric, Rayleigh, Weibull, Cauchy, Poisson, Pascal, Erlang, chi-square, t, F, gamma, beta, Stacy, and others. The uniform distribution is used in generating random normal deviates to simulate a normal distribution. The lognormal distribution has the desirable property of generating only positive values for a random variable. The triangular distribution is attractive for generating stochastic prices; it is specified by the maximum, minimum, and modal (most likely) values. Frequently, farmers can specify the maximum expected wheat price (perhaps the target price), the minimum expected price (perhaps the loan rate), and the most likely price (perhaps the current price or last year's price). With these parameters, one can specify values for the appropriate triangular distribution.

When several crop enterprises are modeled, their yields are likely not independent. For positive or negative correlation, an assumption of yield independence is inappropriate. For normally distributed yields, the procedures for generating normally distributed and "appropriately correlated" random events involve: (1) estimating the variance-covariance matrix, (2) factoring the matrix into upper and lower triangular A matrices, and (3) generating random variables using the upper triangular A matrix and the means and variances of each correlated random variable (Clements et al. 1971). If enterprise prices are correlated, the analyst could generate a set of prices that follow triangular distributions but have the appropriate correlations. The correlation matrix can be combined with triangular distributions to generate triangularly distributed and appropriately correlated random variables. These procedures have been used in simulation analyses of national policy alternatives (Richardson 1978) and in firm-level studies of farm growth and survival (Hardin 1978; Richardson and Condra 1981).

OPTIMIZING SIMULATION MODELS. Simulation is not an optimizing technique. It is generally used to simulate a range of outcomes without focusing specifically on maximizing or minimizing criteria. However, in risk analysis, researchers are frequently interested in identifying actions that will be optimal according to some criteria. An example is identifying strategies with the highest expected income under stochastic conditions or strategies to reduce the probability of income below a disaster level or an unacceptably low level. Both sets of strategies would be optimal for the stipulated criteria.

The optimal set might be identified in several ways. One approach is to simulate a set of outcomes for the key variables and then fit a regression equation(s) to the data that represents the optimizing criteria. Levels of the key variables that maximize the decision criteria are found with differential calculus. Another approach uses "hill-climbing" techniques that systematically vary the levels of the key variables while searching the response surface. When varying the variables will no longer increase the performance measures, the solution is considered optimal. If the same optimum solution is obtained from several starting points, then a global optimum likely is obtained. Search techniques, such as the "box complex procedure," are applied to solve a number of constrained optimization problems (Swann 1974; Richardson et al. 1979), including some risk analyses at the firm level (Harris and Mapp 1980)

In many farm-level studies researchers have little knowledge about the risk attitudes of the decision maker. Because estimating individual utility functions is difficult and often unreliable, alternative approaches are sought. Stochastic dominance criteria have had increasing use in recent years because of their flexibililty and less restrictive assumptions regarding the nature of the individual utility function (see Chap. 6). These criteria can be used to order the simulation results into efficient and inefficient sets for a more orderly selection of an optimal solution by a decision maker.

Solution reliability and sensitivity in risk analysis models

Researchers have expressed much concern about the sensitivity of risk efficient farm plans to changes in risk measures, constraints, and technical coefficients. Schurle and Erven (1979a) view solution sensitivity as a weakness of the MOTAD approach; they question the quality of decisions made using the efficient frontier. They developed a MOTAD model for a 600-acre Ohio farm that produces corn, soybeans, wheat, mechanically harvested tomatoes, and cucumbers. Additional activities included hiring labor, machinery capacity, and field time associated with spring planting and fall harvesting. Risk efficient farm plans derived by the model were compared with farm plans slightly off the risk efficient frontier. Substantial differences were found among the activities and activity levels, although the differences in risk were relatively small. This finding raised concerns about the predictive accuracy of the MOTAD model.

Persaud and Mapp (1980) explored the risk efficiency effects of variability in net returns measured as deviations from the mean of a series and deviation from equally weighted moving averages in a MOTAD framework. Substantial differences existed in production activities, expected net returns, and relative variability of returns for these variability measures. Adams et al. (1980) investigated the sensitivity of QP solutions to alternative specifications of the return and risk parameters. The resulting crop mixes were highly sensitive to the parameter specification. All the income and risk formulations yielded efficient frontiers with considerable diversification. However, results obtained from shorter time series on income expectations more closely approximated the actual cropping patterns in the area. These differences in optimal farm plans that result from different risk measures hamper making specific farm level recommendations.

Johnson and Boehlje (1981) argue that the validity of using alternative techniques, such as MOTAD, should depend upon how well they approximate expected utility solutions rather than how closely they approximate QP solutions. They argue that for some symmetric distributions, MOTAD is as valid from the standpoint of theory as QP in solving expected utility problems. However, under stipulated conditions, including normal distributions and quadratic utility functions, the use of sample rather than population values may cause differences in MOTAD and quadratic programming results (Johnson and Boehlje, 729)

None of these studies documents clearly that solution sensitivity is a problem unique to QP or MOTAD models. In addition, they fail to offer definitive recommendations beyond exercising caution in using and interpreting risk efficient farm plans. Due to a general scarcity of adequate data, a number of risk analyses have involved farms with few production, marketing, and financial activities and constraints. However, failure to specify completely the resource situation and constraint set may contribute to solution sensitivity. Farmers operate in a multiattribute environment in which many forces, choices, preferences, and events influence behavior and performance. Focusing on risk alone is an abstraction that will yield highly sensitive solutions to changes in risk characteristics. Increasing the complexity and richness of the activity and constraint set should reduce the sensitivity of the solution to variations in risk measures and other parameters. However, the richer the model, the more difficult it is to associate model performance and solution sensitivity with risk and other model characteristics.

Concluding comments

This chapter has focused on methods of risk analysis for farm firm research. Methods discussed included quadratic risk programming, minimization of total absolute income deviation, and simulation analysis. A number of earlier approaches, such as focus-loss constraints or maximum admissible loss (Boussard and Petit 1967), marginal risk constraint (Chen and Baker 1974), dynamic programming (Burt 1983), and game theory approaches (McInerney 1967, 1969; Kawaguchi and Maruyama 1972) were not discussed. Studies that incorporate risk, but use other linear programming approaches (Thomas et al. 1972; Simmons and Pomareda 1975; Neiuwolt et al. 1976) were also not considered.

These methods all have advantages and disadvantages. No one model or approach to risk analysis is best at the firm level. The appropriate model depends upon the specific problem, objectives of the research, data availability, and cost and computational considerations.

CHAPTER 10

Applications I: risk programming

WESLEY N. MUSSER, HARRY P. MAPP, JR.,
AND **PETER J. BARRY**

RISK PROGRAMMING MODELS are standard methodology for analysis of risk management strategies for farm firms. These models use different forms of mathematical programming techniques to derive either a risk efficient set of farm portfolios or an optimal farm portfolio for a given level of risk aversion. Quadratic programming (QP) and the MOTAD formulation of linear programming are the most commonly used programming models. As alternative specifications of portfolio theory (Markowitz 1959), QP is used when portfolio variance is minimized and MOTAD when the absolute deviation is minimized for alternative levels of expected returns. As discussed earlier (Chaps. 5, 6, 9), the LP solutions closely approximate the QP solutions and may offer cost and computational advantages in conducting the analysis.

In this chapter the formulation of programming models for risk analysis in farm firms is described. The next section introduces a generalized risk programming model and discusses concepts and methodological issues fundamental to model formulation. Both QP and MOTAD models are discussed. Then an empirical crop diversification model is presented for a Georgia farming situation with assumptions, data requirements, and results being discussed.

Wesley N. Musser, University of Georgia; **Harry P. Mapp, Jr.,** Oklahoma State University; and **Peter J. Barry,** University of Illinois.

Specifying risk programming models

As shown in Chapter 9, the general form of a quadratic risk programming model using matrix notation is

$$\text{maximize } U'X \;-\; \lambda X'\sigma X \tag{10.1}$$

subject to

$$AX \;\leq\; B \tag{10.2}$$

$$X \;\geq\; 0 \tag{10.3}$$

where X = activity levels; U = expected returns associated with each activity; B = resource restrictions; σ = variance-covariance matrix of activity returns; and λ = a risk aversion coefficient. A unique optimum for this problem is associated with a particular level of λ, and an expected value–variance (EV) frontier is derived by parameterizing λ.

The objective function is the theoretical equivalent of maximizing expected utility in situations where expected utility is a function of expected income and variance of income for a risk averse decision maker. When λ = 0, the risk neutral decision maker maximizes expected returns, which is equivalent to the LP solution to the programming problem. As the decision maker becomes more risk averse (λ increases), the risk efficient farm plans generally have lower levels of variance relative to the respective levels of returns. This form of objective function is theoretically appropriate if the utility function of a decision maker is quadratic or if the activity net returns follow a multivariate normal distribution that is fully specified by mean and variance. The QP approach also closely approximates more general formulations of expected utility problems (Levy and Markowitz 1979). The Wolfe (1959) QP algorithm, which is used in many QP software packages, including QPF4360 (Cutler and Pass 1971), specifies the objective function of QP differently than (10.1)

$$\text{Minimize } -LU'X \;+\; X'\sigma X \tag{10.4}$$

where L is a scaler parameter. Defining $L = 1/\lambda$, (10.4) equals the product of $-L$ and (10.1). Thus (10.4) is equivalent to (10.1). Using (10.4), an EV frontier is obtained by parameterizing L from 0 to $+\infty$.

GENERALIZED RISK PROGRAMMING MODEL. The specifications of activities and constraints are very similar for QP and LP. An activity is included in X for each viable management alternative in the firm's production, marketing, and financial choice set. A constraint level is included in *B* for each finite resource or limiting factor. To facilitate discussion of problems in formulating activities and constraints, a generalized risk programming model (GRPM) is outlined in Table 10.1.

The first set of activities in the GRPM represents the production and marketing of crops and/or livestock. Marketing may occur as cash sales at harvest or as periodic sales from storage, and may also involve forward contracting or hedging. Differences exist between QP and LP in formulation of linkages between production and marketing activities and in modeling intermediate products, which are discussed in subsequent sections. The next set of activities in the GRPM represents the acquisition of operating inputs. These inputs may be purchased at planting time, purchased prior to planting (possibly involving contracting or hedging), rented or leased, or acquired from the model's production activities. Interactions between the input acquisition activities and the production-marketing activities are important but are complex to model. The financial activities relate production, marketing, and input acquisition to on-farm and off-farm investment, borrowing, consumption, and taxation. These interrelationships add realism to the model but have some fundamental complexities as well.

The constraint set includes upper limits on beginning and ending cash balances, operating inputs, farm capital, credit capacity, consumption, and taxation. The constraint set should be as rich as possible, within the bounds of computational capacity, to insure realism in the risk efficient farm plans and reduce the sensitivity of solutions to slight changes in risk measures or constraints.

A key component of the QP model is the variance-covariance matrix, presented in Table 10.1. Each activity in the model is, in concept, subject to variation and correlation with other activities and thus contributes to the model farm's total risk. Diagonal elements are the variances for each activity. Off-diagonal elements are covariances between the respective activities. Thus the production activities are correlated with each other as well as with the activities for marketing, input acquisition, investments, borrowing, and so on. Similarly, the financial activities may be correlated with input acquisition, as well as with production and marketing. All of these variance-covariance relationships may influence a firm's risk position. Estimation of the variance-covariance matrix requires a number of methodological assumptions discussed in earlier chapters. A later section of this chapter provides further discussion.

One aspect of the variance-covariance matrix is the correlation reversal among certain activities. As indicated in the GRPM, covariances among income-generating activities and among cost-generating activities are entered directly into the QP with their estimated signs (positive or negative). In contrast, covariances between income-generating and cost-generating ac-

Table 10.1. Outline of a generalized risk programming model (GRPM)

Constraint	Produce and market			Acquire operating inputs			Invest		Borrow	Consume and tax	Relation	Level
	Enterprise 1	Enterprise 2	Enterprise 3	Input 1	Input 2	Input 3	On farm	Off farm	Borrow	Consume and tax		
	X_1	X_2	X_3	X_4	X_5	X_6	X_7	X_8	X_9	X_{10}		
Objective	U	U	U	$-U$	$-U$	$-U$	U	U	$-U$		$=$	Max
Beginning cash				A	A	A	A	$-A$	$-A$		$\leq$	B
Ending cash	$-A$	$-A$	$-A$						A		$\leq$	B
Operating inputs	A	A	A	$-A$	$-A$	$-A$					$\leq$	B
Farm capital	A	A	A				$-A$				$\leq$	B
Credit	$-A$	$-A$	$-A$	A	A	A	$-A$	A	A		$\leq$	B
Consume and tax	$-A$	$-A$	$-A$	A	A	A	A	A	A	A	$\leq$	B
Variance-Covariance Matrix												
X_1	σ_1^2											
X_2	σ_{21}	σ_2^2										
X_3	σ_{31}	σ_{32}	σ_3^2									
X_4	$-\sigma_{41}$	$-\sigma_{42}$	$-\sigma_{43}$	σ_4^2								
X_5	$-\sigma_{51}$	$-\sigma_{52}$	$-\sigma_{53}$	σ_{54}	σ_5^2							
X_6	$-\sigma_{61}$	$-\sigma_{62}$	$-\sigma_{63}$	σ_{64}	σ_{65}	σ_6^2						
X_7	σ_{71}	σ_{72}	σ_{73}	$-\sigma_{74}$	$-\sigma_{75}$	$-\sigma_{76}$	σ_7^2					
X_8	σ_{81}	σ_{82}	σ_{83}	$-\sigma_{84}$	$-\sigma_{85}$	$-\sigma_{86}$	σ_{87}	σ_8^2				
X_9	$-\sigma_{91}$	$-\sigma_{92}$	$-\sigma_{93}$	σ_{94}	σ_{95}	σ_{96}	$-\sigma_{97}$	$-\sigma_{98}$	σ_9^2			
X_{10}	$\sigma_{10,1}$	$\sigma_{10,2}$	$\sigma_{10,3}$	$-\sigma_{10,4}$	$-\sigma_{10,5}$	$-\sigma_{10,6}$	$\sigma_{10,7}$	$\sigma_{10,8}$	$-\sigma_{10,9}$	σ_{10}^2		

tivities enter a QP with the opposite of their estimated sign. This change in sign reflects the reversal in the preferred correlation relationship between these activities. That is, a higher correlation between income-generating and cost-generating activities is preferred because it tends to stabilize income and reduce risk. In contrast a lower correlation between two income-generating or two cost-generating activities has a greater stabilizing effect. The mathematical relationship between the sum of two activities illustrates this relationship: $\text{Var}(\pm ax_1 \pm bx_2) = a^2 \text{ Var } x_1 + b^2 \text{ Var } x_2 \pm 2ab \text{ Cov } x_1x_2$. The signs of the variance terms in the sum would be positive for both income- and cost-generating activities. However, to specify ab in the objective function, the covariances must be entered with a reverse sign when the activities are in the different groups.

The outline in Table 10.1 represents a single period formulation of the risk programming model. A multiperiod quadratic program, which accounts for risk and returns over time, would consist of one large matrix with years represented by submatrices of technical coefficients along the main diagonal and off-diagonal elements representing transfers of assets, liabilities, and other interyear effects (e.g., Barry and Willmann 1976; Kaiser and Boehlje 1980; Johnson 1979). The objective function would then represent the summation of each year's linear and nonlinear entries (variances and covariances) over all years in the planning period valued either at present or at the end of the model horizon. Each annual submatrix would contain its own variance-covariance matrix. If appropriate, covariances could also be specified among years to reflect interyear relationships. In this fashion, the multiperiod quadratic program would yield risk efficient production, marketing, and financial plans for each year in a planning period, under different levels of risk aversion. (For further treatment of the concepts, methods, and potential problems of multiperiod analysis for both certainty and risk programming applications, see Hirshleifer [1958], Hillier [1963], Cocks and Carter [1968], Boussard [1971b], and Weingartner [1977].)

Due to the complex relationships in the GRPM most applications of quadratic (risk) programming have concentrated on a subset of the model's components. Many studies have focused on organizing production under risk conditions or a combination of production and marketing activities. These subsets of activities and constraints can be easily lifted from the generalized model and analyzed separately.

Specification of the objective function. Some important methodological question for a risk programming study include the appropriate definition of net returns and the estimation procedure for expected returns, variances, and covariances. Most such analyses focus on developing short-term plans. With an objective of profit maximization under certainty, fixed costs are ignored in the short run. Thus, net returns are usually defined as gross margins (gross receipts minus cash operating costs) per unit of activity. However, fixed costs are relevant for decisions in a short-run risk programming analysis if the decision maker's utility function is specified to have net income (net of fixed costs) as the object of utility (Anderson et al. 1977). To avoid the arbitrary allocation of fixed costs among enterprises, the objective function can be based on gross margins, and the fixed costs can be subtracted from the solution values of the linear objective function before the EV frontier is constructed. If a unique solution is sought, the fixed costs can be entered as a separate activity.

The choice between subjective and historical estimates of expected returns, variances, and covariances is a controversial one. Decision theorists, including Anderson et al. (1977), prefer subjective measures (see Chaps. 3, 4). While subjective estimates of expected returns are normally available and used in LP models, subjective estimates of variances and covariances are difficult to obtain and have questionable accuracy. Most applications of risk programming have utilized historical data. Lin et al. (1974) are an exception although they were unable to successfully elicit subjective covariances.

For either subjective or objective estimates, the variables that contribute to the variance of net income must be identified. In short-run production situations, most costs are nonstochastic at the beginning of the production period. Many inputs are used in predetermined quantity and can be purchased before the beginning of production. If all inputs are nonstochastic, the variance-covariance matrix of net returns equals the variance-covariance matrix of gross revenue under the standard statistical theorem that Var $y = a^2$ Var x when $y = ax + b$ with y and x being random variables (Anderson et al. 1977). Under many production decisions, an assumption that the relationship holds is quite reasonable.

In other planning situations, however, some or all of the inputs may be stochastic. Examples include the costs of fertilizer and chemicals, costs of borrowing, feed costs, prices of land and machinery, and so on. Then variances and covariances must be estimated, based on historic frequency concepts or subjective evaluation. Moreover, the estimation approach may differ depending on whether input acquisition is specified as a separate set of activities or combined with the production and marketing activities.

Use of historical data also requires decisions on the appropriate level of aggregation for yield and price data, the appropriate length of time series, and detrending procedures before estimating the variance-covariance matrix. Annual yields are generally available by crop at county and state levels. In some areas, data from crop reporting districts are available. Although desirable, historical data by crop at the farm level are rarely available. Thus, county average yields are mostly used in empirical studies even though they underestimate farm-level variability.

The county yield data implicitly assume averages for soils, production practices, fertilizer and chemical applications, and management for the county. It might be desirable to include a production activity for each crop on several different soil types under conventional and reduced tillage technology for several dry-land and irrigated production situations; however, this degree of detail is virtually impossible to attain. As a result, using a county yield series for each crop reduces the richness of the activity and constraint set and contributes to a highly sensitive QP solution. In some cases, experimental data may be available.

County average output is not available for livestock on an enterprise level. Thus farm level or experimental data must be used, or livestock production can be specified as nonstochastic. Price data are generally published for each crop and livestock activity by month and for the marketing year. The data are weighted by marketings or unweighted, in nominal dollars, and may be at the state level or for intrastate regions. Most analyses have used seasonal average prices; however, studies analyzing sale at harvest versus periodic marketing have used average prices for the respective months of the marketing period.

Generally, the longer the data series, the greater the likelihood that yield trends exist and that the price series may have experienced trend, seasonal, and cyclical variations. It is desirable to remove these known sources of variation from the historical data and measure variances and covariances based on unexplained (random) variation (see Chap. 3). Analysts should be aware that the variance-covariance matrix and the risk efficient farm plans selected by the QP model are sensitive to the length of data series and the detrending method.

Production and marketing linkages. In a LP analysis, separate production and marketing activities are usually specified for each crop and livestock activity. The production activity contains the appropriate crop yield as well as the input requirements and their costs. The marketing activity contains the price appropriate for each method of marketing or time of the year. Transfer activities link production and marketing together. The LP model then selects the combination of production and marketing that maximizes net returns.

Such an approach cannot be used in QP. Specification of variance of net income in QP requires that the activities be additive rather than multiplicative. Separate marketing and production activities have a multiplicative effect on net income and are therefore inconsistent with QP. Instead each activity must combine production and marketing. As in Table 10.1, different marketing strategies are modeled with separate activities. For example, to model production of winter wheat with possible sales at harvest and each month during the ensuing marketing season, twelve joint production-marketing activities are needed. Each activity would have an expected gross margin series, perhaps based on a historic series of yields times the appropriate prices minus costs of inputs, storage, and transportation. The variance-covariance matrix estimated from this historic series of gross margins would reflect the appropriate activity relationships and avoid the multiplicative variance problem.

Contracting and hedging. Modeling the risk aspects of marketing alternatives such as forward contracting and hedging presents some unique problems. Heifner's (1966) study of hedged and unhedged storage of wheat, corn, and soybeans was an early QP application involving marketing decisions. Barry and Willmann (1976) analyzed risk efficient farm plans based on cash sales at harvest and preharvest forward contracts of cotton and grain sorghum. Musser et al. (1980) considered alternative purchase and sale times for backgrounding of beef cattle. Eddleman and Moya-Rodriguez (1979) considered cash forward contracting and cash sales of soybeans at harvest and from storage. Klinefelter (1979) analyzed various forward contracting and cash sales of corn and soybeans. Persaud and Mapp (1980) also considered forward contracting and cash sale alternatives for several crops. Most of these studies did not analyze all of the risk management strategies available to farmers. Only Persaud and Mapp had both marketing and production decisions for a number of different enterprises endogenous to the model. Barry and Willmann considered two enterprise alternatives and Musser et al. analyzed different production-marketing alternatives for one enterprise.

Modeling of the risk effects of preharvest forward contracts and hedges presents a special methodological problem in risk programming models. Previous studies have created a time series of gross returns for these activities by multiplying detrended historical forward prices and detrended historical yields. This procedure implicitly assumes that the farmer can deliver any level of production at the contract prices, abstracting from yield uncertainty involved in preharvest contracting. If the expected yield is forward contracted, as these activities assume, deviations from this yield must be accommodated in the cash markets or elsewhere in the marketing plan. McKinnon (1967) has argued that the variance of net income must reflect the joint effects of price and yield risk in forward contracting.

This problem can be accommodated in a risk programming model by accounting for market behavior when the actual yield does not equal the contracted quantity. The gross returns series for preharvest contracts can be constructed as

$$GM_t = P_{ct}Y_{ct} + P_{mt}(Y_y - Y_{ct}) - IC_t \qquad (10.5)$$

where GM_t = gross revenue per acre from a preharvest contracting strategy in year t, P_{ct} = contracted price per unit in year t, Y_{ct} = quantity per acre contracted in year t, Y_t = actual per acre yield in year t, P_{mt} = actual market price per unit at delivery, and IC_t = input costs per acre in year t.

For example, a wheat farmer might contract 50 or 60 percent of expected production. Thus, Y_{ct} could be specified as 50 percent or 60 percent of the expected yield per acre. Separate activities could be included for other levels of contracting. If yields exceed the contracted level, gross margins equal gross receipts for the contracted yield (Y_{ct}) times contracted price (P_{ct}) plus gross receipts for the yield above the contracted level ($Y_t - Y_{ct}$) at the market price (P_{mt}) minus production costs (IC_t). In years when actual yields are below the level contracted, ($Y_t - Y_{ct}$) is negative and the producer does not have sufficient product to satisfy the contract. The farmer must purchase the shortfall at the market price (P_{mt}) to satisfy the contract. The contracted price and yield will be received, but gross margins are reduced by the value of the shortfall and the input costs.

The reconstructed series of gross margins (GM_t) based on (10.5) thus serves as the basis for estimating risk and return measures for forward contracting. However, price assumptions must still be made for P_{ct} and P_{mt}. For each commodity, a set of practices exists that can be characterized as typical for producers and contractors. For wheat producers, a number of contracts are negotiated in mid-March when farmers have an intuitive estimate of expected production. Elevator operators, for example, might base the contract price offered on the July wheat futures price at Kansas City on the second Friday in March adjusted for transportation to the Gulf, or this futures price might be discounted by \$0.10/bu to provide a safety margin for the elevator operator. The contract will specify the quantity of grain to be delivered. Market price at the delivery time would be appropriate for P_{mt}. Decisions on deflating or detrending prices should be consistent throughout the analysis.

Modeling the effects of hedging on risk and returns is more complex because futures contracts have more uncertainty than forward contracts. For grain producers or elevator operators, seasonal grain inventories may be hedged by selling futures contracts when grain is placed in storage. Normally the hedge is lifted by buying back the futures contracts when stored grain is sold rather than settling the futures contracts by delivery. However, the possibility of basis risk may not allow hedging to totally reduce the farmer's price risk.

To illustrate, let a cash and futures position be represented by activities X_1 and X_2, respectively, in a risk programming model. Assume these activities have the same expected return, the same variances (σ_1^2, σ_2^2), and covariance σ_{12}. The covariance may be expressed as $\sigma_{12} = c\sigma_1\sigma_2$, where c is the correlation coefficient. The total risk, σ_T^2, from a portfolio of cash and futures positions is

$$\sigma_T^2 = \sigma_1^2 X_1 + \sigma_2^2 X_2^2 - 2X_1 X_2 c \sigma_1 \sigma_2$$

In the absence of basis risk, the cash and futures position are perfectly, positively correlated ($c = 1$); that is, they move together and reduce the risk of a hedged position. As basis risk increases, however, the correlation between X_1 and X_2 declines, indicating a greater degree of risk associated with hedging. In formulating the risk program to include hedging on futures markets as a risk response, the important data needs are the variances of cash and futures prices for the commodities and their covariances.

An important limitation of this approach is its failure to account for the sequence of the storage decisions as new price information is generated during the year. Large-scale grain operators frequently vary storage operations in response to changes in the basis. Sequential decisions could be included by solving the model iteratively for each decision period in the storage year. Average revenues for the storage activities would be replaced by their predicted values based upon the best information available in each decision period. Variances and covariances of revenues would be replaced by variances and covariances of the prediction errors; thus both market risk and estimation risk would be involved (see Chap. 3).

One would expect both forward contracting and hedging to reduce price risk for the producer relative to open market sales. As risk aversion becomes more important to a producer, one or more of the available contracting or hedging strategies should become more appealing. Often, contracting and hedging involve use of credit or require approval by lenders. If so, the relationships between the model's marketing and financial components need to be considered.

Acquiring operating inputs. The second set of activities in the GRPM involves the acquisition of inputs. They are linked to the production and marketing activities with constraints. As in LP, input acquisition activities are sometimes combined with production activities and other times separated from the production activities to provide accounting relationships in the model solution.

Modeling the purchase of indivisible inputs, such as tractors and equipment, also presents problems in QP, as it does in LP models. Integer, nonlinear programs are available to solve such problems, but computational capacity is limited. An alternative approach is to solve the risk programming model twice, with and without the indivisible asset, and compare the risk efficient sets (Robison and Barry 1980).

Modeling intermediate products, most importantly livestock feed, in QP varies from LP formulations. If part or all of the livestock feed is produced on the farm, linking the activities for feed and animal production with transfer rows will not reflect the risk in gross margins attributed to variability in feed production. Gross margins will fluctuate with feed production because either livestock output or feed purchases must change to maintain a constant level of livestock output. The absence of methods to accommodate this problem has contributed to the lack of emphasis on livestock in risk programming models.

Two recent studies have included methods to model the risk implications of feed availability. Gebremeskel and Shumway (1979) developed MOTAD constraints that included deviations in actual forage production for each production period, along with hay sales and purchase activities, to provide digestible energy for a constant beef gain. The hay-balancing activities had entries in the linear objective function and the deviation matrix. Woolery and Adams (1980) modeled the alternative management practice of adjusting livestock production to reflect levels of feed production. The livestock activities jointly represented livestock and feed production, with the variance-covariance relationships calculated from a time series of net revenues.

A comprehensive analysis of crop and animal production could include joint feed-livestock activities with either (1) all purchased feed, (2) market transactions to adjust feed production, and (3) adjustment of animal output to feed production. The time series of gross margins used to calculate the risk measures would subtract feed purchase from gross revenue, add or subtract transactions for deviations in feed production from their expected values, and use livestock output consistent with variable feed production.

Resource uncertainty. Standard formulations of risk programming assume resource supplies are nonstochastic. As in LP models, the resource constraints, B, in (10.2) reflect the expected value of resource endowments to the firm. This assumption abstracts from important sources of risk for many firms. For example, field time availability is an important component of risk in crop production in the Midwest, and has received some research attention (Boisvert and Jensen 1973; Edwards and Boehlje 1980). Other examples of important sources of resource uncertainty include grazing days in livestock pastures and irrigation water availability.

Recently, Paris (1979) has extended risk programming to accommodate resource uncertainty. Defining the expected values of resource quantities as B and variance-covariance matrix of quantities as σ_s, the generalized risk programming program is as follows:

$$\text{maximize } u'x - \lambda x' \sigma_x x - \lambda Y' \sigma_s Y \qquad (10.6)$$

subject to

$$AX - 2\lambda \sigma_s Y \leq B \qquad (10.7)$$

$$X \geq 0, \ Y \geq 0 \tag{10.8}$$

where σ_x is a variance-covariance matrix of X, Y is a vector of dual values on the constraints, and other variables are as defined previously. For solutions of this problem with RAND QPPF4/360 (Cutler and Pass 1971), σ_s must be estimated and dual variables Y included in the solution. More efficient computations are possible with other algorithms (Paris 1979).

One application of this framework concerns the impact of risk on selection of soil conservation methods (Kramer et al. 1983). Both income and resource risk are important in use of reduced tillage. Reduced tillage reduces field time and mitigates the effect of resource uncertainty. However, reduced tillage may result in more production risk and, therefore, income risk than conventional tillage because of other responses to environmental conditions. Thus, generalized risk programming would be important in analyzing this problem.

This generalized risk programming model has several empirical limitations. As formulated, the model is limited to uncertainty in resource endowments. The risk in quantities of purchased operating inputs, such as hired labor, cannot be represented in this framework. Furthermore, estimation problems exist for both σ_x and σ_s. Historical data on resource supplies are not available to estimate σ_s. Kramer et al. (1983) used weather data to synthesize their time series of field time availability. The problem with σ_x is potentially more serious. Since historical yield data reflect historical variation in resource availability, estimation of σ_x with standard methods using historical data results in double counting the components of yield risk. Paris implicitly accommodates this problem in assuming that price is the only stochastic influence in σ_x. Attributing output risk solely to the risk in resource supplies ignores the effects of weather and other environmental variables on output (Dillon 1977, 104).

Financial responses to risk. Another set of activities in the GRPM in Table 10.1 concerns financial responses to risk. Included are activities for off-farm investment, borrowing, consumption, and taxes that are linked to other activities with cash, capital, credit, and other constraints. These activities allow an interaction among financial, production, and marketing responses to risk for a comprehensive analysis of risk management.

Financial responses to risk are discussed in detail in Chapter 13. Unlike other responses to risk, financial responses largely increase the capacity of the farm to bear risk, through the liquidity provided by credit and cash reserves, rather than reducing the incidence of risk. With these components in the model, risk efficient plans for higher levels of risk aversion may include higher levels of liquidity. Furthermore, the risk programming results can indicate the trade-offs among liquidity, diversification, and contracting, and other risk responses for decision makers with different levels of risk aversion. In addition, including information about lender responses, as expressed through credit availability or costs of borrowing, adds realism and may influence other types of risk response. For example, if holding liquid reserves (credit) becomes riskier, then other risk responses may be more preferred.

The investment activities in Table 10.1 permit growth in production capacity and allow extension of the model for multiperiod analysis. As previously discussed, the multiperiod model resembles a polyperiod LP model with the addition of risk information on the variance-covariance matrix for selected activities in each period. Even for a single period model, the methodology developed in the firm-growth literature for LP models can be used to specify the model. Land and machinery investments add to production capacity, may require loan financing, and influence the credit reserve through their effects on the firm's assets and liabilities. Debt servicing requires principal and interest payments that in turn affect annual income and taxes. Short-term borrowing uses nonreal estate credit and requires later payment of principal plus interest. Family consumption may be specified as a constant amount or by a declining marginal propensity to consume. Income taxes may be specified according to a progressive tax structure. Real estate and nonreal estate credit provided by land and machinery collateral and income expectations are represented in right-hand side values and constraint coefficients for the investment-financing activities. Procedures for estimating exogenous cash requirements have been developed in the firm-growth literature (Baker and Bhargava 1974). Estimation of the constraint levels for initial cash, the line of credit, and the impact of management alternatives on debt limits can occur through a survey of lenders (Barry and Willmann 1976; Barry et al. 1981).

MOTAD MODEL SPECIFICATION. A MOTAD model may be solved by an LP algorithm with the objective of minimizing total absolute income deviations subject to a set of linear resource constraints and to a constraint on expected gross margins (see Chap. 9). A MOTAD model is specified similar to QP except that a deviations matrix replaces the variance-covariance matrix. The general structure of a MOTAD model that minimizes total negative gross margin deviations is presented in Table 10.2. The basic production, marketing, and financial activities and constraints discussed for the QP model are also appropriate for the MOTAD. Rather than using the sum of squared deviations about the mean (variance) as the measure of risk or variability, MOTAD uses the sum of the total absolute deviations from the mean or expected gross margins. MOTAD may have cost and computational advantages for large risk programming problems and its results are generally similar to the QP results.

Table 10.2. Outline of a MOTAD model

Constraint	X_1	X_2	X_3	...	X_m	d_1^-	d_2^-	d_3^-	...	d_t^-	Relation	Level
Objective						1	1	1		1	=	minimize
Beginning cash	$-A$	$-A$	$-A$		A						≤	B
Ending cash	A	A	A		A						≤	B
Operating inputs	A	A	A								≤	B
Farm capital	A	A	A								≤	B
Credit	$-A$	$-A$	$-A$								≤	B
Consume and tax	$-A$	$-A$	$-A$		A						≤	B
Year 1	D_{11}	D_{12}	D_{13}	...	D_{1n}	1					≥	0
Year 2	D_{21}	D_{22}	D_{23}	...	D_{2n}		1				≥	0
Year 3	D_{31}	D_{32}	D_{33}	...	D_{3n}			1			≥	0
.											.	.
.											.	.
Year t	D_{t1}	D_{t2}	D_{t3}	...	D_{tn}					1	≥	0
Gross margins	U	U	U	...	U						=	λ

Table 10.3. Linear tableau of empirical model for Georgia

	Corn	Cotton	Peanuts	Tobacco	Wheat	Soybeans	Oats	Grain sorghum	Hired labor 1	2	3	4	5	Right-hand side
Linear objective function	68.29	168.14	1432.90	2178.07	31.15	141.96	10.79	21.16	-2.80	-3.00	-3.00	-2.60	-2.90	
Cropland	1.00	1.00	1.00	1.00	1.00	1.00	1.00	1.00						≤182.6 acres
Peanut rotation			1.00											≤60.9 acres
Cotton rotation		1.00												≤91.3 acres
Peanut and cotton rotation		1.00	1.00											≤121.8 acres
Tobacco allotment				1.00										≤21.0 acres
Labor														
Jan.–Feb.	.56	.56	.56					.56	-.9					≤440 hr
Mar.–Apr.	1.67			25.00						-.9				≤435 hr
May–June	.24	2.00	2.18	25.00	1.58	1.67	1.58	2.23			-.9			≤390 hr
July–Aug.			.24	75.00	.24	.24		.24				-.9		≤435 hr
Sept.–Oct.	1.72	1.00	4.22		2.22	1.58	2.22	1.58					-.9	≤385 hr

Applications of QP and MOTAD models

We illustrate the use of QP and MOTAD in evaluating cash crop enterprises under conditions of risk in a south Georgia farm situation. The enterprises include corn, soybeans, wheat, oats, peanuts, and tobacco, all specified on a per acre basis. Peanuts and tobacco production involve mandatory government allotments and specialized equipment. Cotton production requires specialized harvesting equipment and good management because of pest problems. In the model, management and equipment are assumed adequate to produce any combination of these enterprises.

An activity is specified for each feasible production/marketing alternative (see Table 10.3). Each crop is assumed marketed at harvest. The model farm does not participate in voluntary government commodity programs, even though maximum acreages are specified for the allotments of tobacco and peanuts. Model constraints include cropland, tobacco and peanut allotments, rotational requirements, and resident labor. Labor hiring increases the labor constraint only by 0.9 hr to reflect loss of supervisory time. Constraints are not included for investment, borrowing, consumption, or taxes. Thus, the model assumes that machinery capacity and financial capital are not limiting resources, and the interactions among production/marketing activities, financial constraints, and risk attitude are not considered. Thus the model focuses solely on enterprise diversification as a response to risk.

Data based on 1978 technical relationships and prices were used to develop the objective function values presented in Table 10.3 (Stamoulis 1979). The variance-covariance matrix for the Georgia model was originally based on time series data from 1958 through 1977. However, this time frame included three different regimes of government programs that influenced the degree of price stability. Until the mid-1960s, farm programs were based on relatively high price supports that resulted in the government's accumulation of large stocks of commodities. Lower relative price supports in the mid-1960s and early 1970s then allowed prices to fluctuate more freely. Finally, the increased importance of international trade in the 1970s subjected agricultural prices to still greater fluctuations. Because price volatility was greater in the 1970s, deriving risk measures based on data from the two earlier periods would likely underestimate the price component of the variance-covariance matrix. Thus, the price series were based on nominal prices per unit for the 1973–77 period.

The risk information for the model was developed under the assumption that input costs were all nonstochastic. Multicounty per acre crop yields were multiplied by the price per unit to derive gross returns per acre of each activity for the 1973–77 period. Linear regression was used to adjust the gross revenue series for trends. Gross revenues were regressed on

time and the regression residuals, representing unexplained or random variation, were used to estimate the variance-covariance matrix presented in the
top portion of Table 10.4. The presence of negative covariances between
several activities suggests that enterprise diversification should be a desirable risk response for this farm.

A deviations matrix was also estimated for solution of a MOTAD
Model for comparative purposes. In this empirical application, the deviations in gross revenue were calculated around time trends. Thus, the regression residuals from the detrending regressions were used as estimates of
deviations, which are presented in the bottom portion of Table 10.4. Even
though variances and covariances are not estimated in a MOTAD model,
the positive and negative deviations in the time series represent the same
data used for the variance-covariance matrix in the QP model and therefore
account for the interrelationships among activities.

The QP and MOTAD models were solved parametrically using RAND
QP and LP-MPSO, respectively, and the results are summarized in Table
10.5.

The highest return solution (solution 7) yields gross margins of about
$82,842 for both the QP and MOTAD models. Moreover, the risk efficient
farm plans are identical for both models. Each return-maximizing solution
contains 60.9 acres cotton and peanuts, 21.0 acres tobacco, and 39.8 acres
soybeans. The variance of the QP solution is similar to the variance of the
MOTAD solution using a formula presented by Brink and McCarl (1978).

Under standard portfolio theory, the return-maximizing solutions
should be specialized rather than diversified. However, standard portfolio
theory includes only one constraint, financial capital, while several resource
constraints are effective in most farm situations, including this empirical
model. If cropland was the only constraint, the maximum profit solution
would specialize in tobacco that has the highest expected profit per acre.
However, the tobacco allotment limits the acreage of tobacco. Similarly, the
peanut allotment limits the peanut acreage, and the rotational constraint
limits cotton acreage so that soybeans are included on the residual acreage.
Thus multiple resource constraints in farm situations may result in diversified solutions even under a profit-maximizing objective.

Solutions are reported for several changes of basis points for the QP
and MOTAD models. Because the change of basis points differ for each
model, the levels of expected returns for comparable QP and MOTAD
solutions do not exactly correspond. As the expected values of gross
margins decline, the respective crop activities and acreages reported in Table
10.5 differ slightly for the QP and MOTAD models. In solution 4, for
example, the QP solution has fewer acres of wheat (98.5 acres vs. 126.3
acres) and tobacco (17.4 acres vs. 21.0 acres) than the MOTAD solution,
but the QP solution has a larger acreage of cotton and peanuts. The vari-

Table 10.4. Variance-covariance and net returns deviations matrices for Georgia model

	Corn	Cotton	Peanuts	Tobacco	Wheat	Soybeans	Oats	Grain sorghum
Variance-covariance matrix for QP model								
Corn	1587.381	1177.340	1452.215	4963.415	64.000	719.803	82.925	659.228
Cotton		3053.608	−521.197	−7327.787	324.903	41.480	134.544	455.824
Peanuts			3527.965	11,861.662	−231.521	488.620	56.258	657.516
Tobacco				71,651.891	−1137.506	5123.678	−134.228	2206.509
Wheat					45.196	11.147	9.774	19.822
Soybeans						711.740	3.583	290.838
Oats							7.899	34.324
Grain sorghum								275.160
Net return deviations matrix for MOTAD model								
1973	−42.990	−3.813	−68.647	−269.789	2.576	−21.320	−1.594	−18.536
1974	35.790	−34.131	59.526	−431.164	−4.785	39.068	−.747	15.266
1975	14.988	17.429	64.984	−25.750	−3.308	−23.496	2.840	7.768
1976	34.612	82.786	−33.960	−162.836	10.667	15.067	2.937	12.810
1977	−42.401	−62.271	−21.904	27.211	−5.150	−9.319	−3.436	−17.308

Table 10.5. Parametric QP and MOTAD solutions for Georgia model

Solution number	Expected net returns		Sum of negative deviations MOTAD	Variance		Cotton		Peanuts		Tobacco		Wheat		Soybeans	
	QP	MOTAD		QP	MOTAD	QP	MOTAD	QP	MOTAD	QP	MOTAD	QP	MOTAD	QP	MOTAD
	($1000)					(acres)									
1	16.178	17.596	2.175	1062.3	1486.7	7.0		7.7	7.3	3.4	5.2	171.4	102.1		
2	23.714	24.498	3.086	2895.0	2990.8			11.7	10.3	5.8	7.3	158.1	144.9		
3	49.181	45.642	6.666	18783.9	13954.9	51.4	20.1	6.7	8.5	17.4	17.4	107.1	136.6		
4	51.649	52.598	7.725	21054.1	19724.0	55.1	28.0	11.6	7.2	17.4	21.0	98.5	126.3		
5	71.596	73.790	13.273	46167.9	55326.7	87.0	37.6	34.8	31.7	21.0	21.0	39.8			92.4
6	82.666	82.783	15.771	75399.9	78111.5	61.6	58.6	60.3	60.9	21.0	21.0			39.8	42.1
7	82.843	82.842	15.851	76000.9	78905.9	60.9	60.9	60.9	21.0	21.0	21.0			39.8	39.8

ances associated with the QP solution (21054) and estimated for the MO-TAD solution (19724) are reasonably close even though variance estimates for the individual commodities, particularly wheat and tobacco, differ considerably.

As the expected net returns decline, acreages shift to wheat with the lowest variance and away from tobacco with the highest variance. Tobacco also has high returns, but the risk averse decision maker trades off expected income for lower variance. Moreover, wheat is negatively correlated with tobacco and peanuts. The lower income levels have fewer activities in the risk efficient solutions than the highest expected net return plan. Portfolio theory would suggest more diversity rather than less in the lower income solutions, but the results here are mostly explained by the constraints. Nonetheless, the four lowest expected return solutions for QP and the three lowest for MOTAD do demonstrate a diversified risk response—none of the allotment or rotational constraints are effective for these solutions.

In another application of the Georgia QP model, a longer data series and different detrending procedure were used to estimate the variance-covariance matrix. In this research, oats were included in the return-maximizing solution and the lowest risk solution included oats, peanuts, cotton, and soybeans (Musser and Stamoulis 1981). As in other studies and with other analytical techniques, risk programming results are sensitive to the data series, detrending assumptions, and richness of the activity and constraint set.

Concluding comments

This chapter described the formulation of risk programming models that incorporate activities for production, marketing, input acquisition, investment, credit, consumption, and taxation. QP and MOTAD models were emphasized, along with an empirical application to a Georgia farm. Results show similar risk efficient farm plans for QP and MOTAD for the various levels of expected returns. Changes in risk efficient farm plans are explained by portfolio theory and model constraints.

These models may be applied as risk efficiency criteria without estimating the decision maker's risk preferences. Variations in the risk aversion parameter in a QP model or expected net returns in a MOTAD model allow the researcher to derive the risk efficient frontier. Decision makers can then reveal their risk return trade-offs by selecting a desired farm plan from the efficient set. The modeling approach is consistent with existing portfolio theory and with expected utility maximization under assumptions of normally distributed returns or quadratic utility.

Applications of QP and MOTAD require numerous methodological assumptions, many of which affect the risk efficient solutions. These models have been criticized for solution sensitivity; however, the sensitivity problem is no more severe than for other analytical techniques. LP solutions are also sensitive to the data assumptions, constraints, and other model specifications. The same is true for QP and MOTAD.

QP and MOTAD appear well suited to analyzing production and marketing strategies at the farm level. Diversification, contracting, and periodic marketing may provide favorable risk return trade-offs for risk averse decision makers. Incorporating credit and liquidity considerations, investment alternatives and consumption for one or more periods adds further realism to the model and results.

Modeling some risk responses, such as hedging, is difficult because of basis risk and changing market conditions within the marketing period. An approach is presented for handling basis risk in risk programming models. Multiperiod risk programming may be used to develop risk efficient growth plans over a finite planning horizon. Computational inefficiencies and concerns about solution sensitivity have been largely overcome, making QP and MOTAD models of continuing usefulness for risk analysis at the firm level.

11

Applications II: Simulation

ODELL L. WALKER AND GLENN A. HELMERS

THIS CHAPTER PROVIDES an overview of methods and applications of simulation in analyzing firm performance under conditions of risk. Results of simulation analysis are presented for various situations involving farm growth and survival. The emphasis is on the modeling procedures, data needs, and interpretation of the simulation results. The models show the diversity of simulation approaches, yet also indicate that the common characteristics of simulation studies are made unique to each study's setting and purpose.

Farm growth and survival problems

The life cycle of the proprietory family farm is well known. The beginning farmer faces problems of resource acquisition and capital scarcity that restrict the beginning farm size. However, institutional, technical, and economic factors push the desired size of farm upward. The beginning phase is critical for survival of the farm business, but so is later growth in size to achieve income aspirations and gain operating efficiencies. Thus the realities of farming bring periodic growth pressures throughout the life cycle. In the last phase, terminating the farm business, meeting retirement goals, and achieving intergenerational transfers present major challenges.

The discussion to follow focuses on the established farm. Simulation studies are reported on: (1) expansion by land acquistion; (2) alternative management strategies; (3) effects of beginning equity, farm expansion, and credit limits on farm growth and survival; and (4) the effects of loan ar-

Odell L. Walker, Oklahoma State University, and Glenn A. Helmers, University of Nebraska.

rangements and debt constraints on farm growth and survival.

The objective of these studies is to better understand factors affecting the growth and survival of farms under a risk setting. Simulation is used as an experimental tool with no emphasis on optimization. Thus decisions about enterprises, production practices, resource mixes, and financial arrangements are usually predetermined for each simulation run, so that impacts on growth and survival can be evaluated.

These microanalyses are not designed for aggregation to regional or national levels. However, microsimulation studies contribute to policy analysis and to extension and classroom teaching. The microanalyses of policies and environmental factors are important, timely products of simulation models. Changes in policies and environmental conditions can occur quickly. Simulation provides a useful framework for studying the firm's adjustment from one equilibrium position to another as a result of policies that cause changes in model parameters. Simulation can easily perform experiments on a wide range of future scenarios.

In sensitivity analysis the analyst studies how departures from equilibrium among key variables may influence the firm's financial performance and decision making. High levels of inflation, in particular, have hampered model construction. For example, periodic differences between rates of growth of land values and rates of growth in current returns to farmland warrant analyses of their independent effects on a farm's financial performance. However, simulation as well as programming models must closely examine the interrelationship of these types of variables; the relationship between land values and farm commodity prices is an example. Departures from equilibirum conditions are primarily short-run phenomena; hence, severe restraints are needed on modeling disequilibrium conditions.

The risk analyses discussed here show how various responses to income variability influence prospects for firm survival. The process of firm failure is difficult to simulate because many farms are discontinued before financial insolvency occurs. Other farms avoid termination by partial liquidation of assets. Failure occurs here when the firm reaches a stated criterion for insolvency. Partial liquidation of assets at stress times is not allowed. In practice, a higher incidence of recovery would likely occur due to a wider range of methods for responding to risks.

Oklahoma simulation studies

A FARM INVESTMENT SIMULATION MODEL. The planning, growth, or decision type (Johnson and Rausser 1977) simulation in the Oklahoma studies incorporates the effects of variation in yields and prices on annual variability of farm income. Prices and yields are assumed to be triangularly distributed, trended, and correlated. The model can also use normally distributed variables. Two kinds of outcome variables are estimated (Fig. 11.1). Annual cash flows over a specified time horizon are used to estimate the net present value of the firm and to derive annual balance sheets. For present value analysis, cash flow includes the terminal value of assets. Balance sheet information accounts for the effects of capital transactions, financial transactions, and inflation.

The cash flow and balance sheet data provide the basis for analyzing the profitability and financial feasibility of investments and the growth potential of the farm operation, given the economic environment, the farmer's financial obligations, initial financial position, and the pattern of income over the model horizon. The model reports the minimum and maximum values, mean, range, median, mode, standard deviation, and coefficient of variation of both output variables and input variables.

YIELD AND PRICE DISTRIBUTIONS. Careful attention is needed in simulating the firm's physical and economic environment. Trends, cycles, random shocks, and secular change affect performance. In this study polynominal

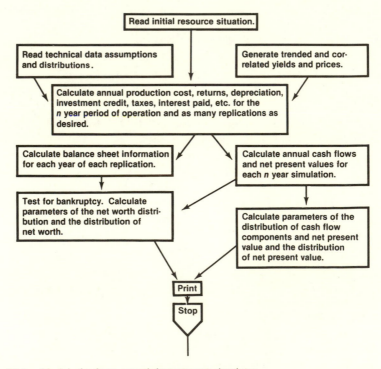

FIG. 11.1. Model of a farm growth-investment simulator.

functions of time up to fifth order were fitted to data series for county yields and state average prices received by farmers. County yield data provide the only comparable yield series available across farming areas and states. These data may underestimate the variation experienced on individual farms. Actual farm data from records or experiments could be employed if available.

Using matrix notation, the model's yield equation is represented by

$$Y = \bar{Y} + A_Y W_Y \tag{11.1}$$

and the price equation is

$$P = \bar{P} + A_P W_P \tag{11.2}$$

where Y and P are yields and prices used in the model, $\bar{Y}$ and $\bar{P}$ are expected yields and prices from the estimating procedure discussed above, A is an upper triangular matrix derived from the variance-covariance matrix (Clements et al. 1971) and W is a vector of random normal deviates. The W matrix is generated by a random number subroutine. When the triangular distribution is assumed, a matrix of correlation coefficients is used to derive the upper triangular matrix.

Any appropriate prediction of Y or P can be used in conjunction with the random normal deviates and A matrix. In some cases, no yield trend may occur over the years and crops used. Livestock prices followed cyclical patterns based on the work of Franzmann (1971). Because the entry point in the cattle price cycle may strongly affect financial performance over time, the same entry points are chosen for each simulation run. Effects of different entry points are illustrated in a later study (Held and Helmers 1980).

Annual cash flow. Annual net cash flow is the sum of agricultural sales, operator off-farm income and other family income minus production expenses for crops and livestock, interest on annual capital, other interest, loan payments, family living costs, and nonfarm expense. Family consumption and nonfarm expenses increase from a fixed level at a specified rate. A positive cash flow earns interest at a specified rate. A negative cash flow is offset by borrowing. Borrowing is constrained by a minimum ratio of equity to owned assets. If cash flow is negative and borrowing capacity is exhausted, the firm has failed (not survived). However, the simulation continues and results are used in the statistical analysis. An alternative is to evaluate performance only for the survivors.

Net present value. The annual net cash flows are discounted to net present values at a discount rate specified by the user. The net present value analysis is used in evaluating new investments, such as adding 160 acres of land to the farm operation. The maximum bid price for land is the difference between the farm's net present value with and without the investment. Sensitivity analysis of maximum bid prices to changes in various model parameters can also occur.

Income taxes. The effect of income taxes on annual net cash flows needs special attention in simulation models. Depreciation is calculated by the straight line method, the double declining balance method, or both. Investment tax credit may be carried forward for seven years but not back. Capital gains on land are taxed at the end of the horizon to account for their contingent liability on the firm's net worth.

Balance sheet. The firm's assets include cash and intermediate-term and long-term assets. The values of intermediate- and long-term assets change each year to reflect the effects of inflation, depreciation, and transactions. The inflation rates for machinery and land are specified by the user. The firm's liabilities include beginning values of intermediate- and long-term debts plus other term debt acquired during the model horizon.

Input data. The analysis incorporates a subjective evaluation of the possible variation in product prices and yields. A triangular distribution is completely specified by the minimum, maximum, and most likely values for each product price and yield. Values of land, buildings, fences, and improvements must be specified along with loan arrangements and interest rates, a length of planning horizon, and loan maturities.

Machinery sets are adjusted for the cropping plan and the size of model farm. Labor requirements are calculated outside the model for alternative organzations and sizes of farms. Size economies or diseconomies are reflected in requirements for hired labor by each enterprise. Only the amount of hired labor is included in enterprise costs.

The model farm. The specific study centers on north central Oklahoma, which is part of the winter wheat region of the Great Plains. This region is characterized by high levels of mechanization, relatively flat to rolling lands, high adaptability to winter wheat, a fairly stable wheat yield, a strong tendency to monoculture, and relatively large farms. Climatological factors cause some intraregional variation. For example, winter wheat pasture is available in the southern area.

The initial farm situation described in Table 11.1 owns 640 acres and rents 640 acres. An additional 160 acres is purchased in year 1 to demonstrate its effects on annual cash flows and other performance measures.

Fifty percent equity is assumed and annual rent for land is $25.00/acre. Crop enterprises are wheat, grain, sorghum, and alfalfa. Livestock enterprises are winter grazing of stockers on wheat pasture and winter plus spring grazing of stockers on wheat pastures. All of the acreage is cropland except for roads and farmstead. The farm's balance sheets before and after the land purchase are shown in Table 11.1.

LAND PURCHASE. The simulation experiment tests the effects of alternative treatments over a 20-year period on various measures of financial performance. Table 11.2 shows the levels of variables used in selected simulation runs. The runs are alternative treatments for estimating outcomes of the land investment. Table 11.3 summarizes results for these runs. The mean net present value for the base runs (run 1) is greater for the current farm than for the expanded farm. Thus, the maximum bid price for land is less than the $800 price used to obtain results in Table 11.3. The current farm fails 2 out of 100 times while the expanded farm fails 7 out of 100 times for the base run. Thus, addition of the land at an $800 price adds to farm risk.

All of the alternative runs improve the profitability of the land investment. The results from run 2 (Table 11.3) indicate that a more favorable market for agricutural products enhances income expectations and reduces variability in farm income. A land inflation rate of 12 percent results in higher ending net worth and net present value, and lower income variability (run 3). Removing the capital gains tax obligation in year 20 has a modest positive effect on ending net worth (run 4).

One hundred sets of prices and yields were generated for the simulation runs using (11.1) and (11.2). Net present values for each run are ranked from most to least favorable for the farm's economic success. Results for

Table 11.1. North central Oklahoma model: Resource situation and land purchase (balance sheet)

	Current farm year 0 value	Proposed situation beginning year 1 (160 acres land added) value
Assets		
Intermediate	81,165	81,165
Long term	572,000	710,000
Total	$653,165	$791,165
Liabilities		
Machinery	40,582	40,582
Buildings and land	286,000	424,000
Total	$326,582	$464,582
Net worth	$326,583	$326,583
Equity (%)	50	41.3
Leverage ratio	1	1.42

Table 11.2. Selected simulation experiments for a land investment analysis

Run (experiment)	Description	Land inflation rate (%)	Price trend (%)	Input cost trend (%)	Land loan interest rate (%)	Other interest rates (%)	Equity (%)	Discount rate (%)
1	Base run	6	2	3	8.5	8.5	41	7.5
2	Equal trends in costs and prices	6	3	3	8.5	8.5	41	7.5
3	Higher land appreciation rate	12	2	3	8.5	8.5	41	7.5
4	No adjustment for capital gain tax liability in year 20	6	2	3	8.5	8.5	41	7.5

Source: Hardin 1978.

Table 11.3.   Ending net worth and net present values under selected simulation experiments

Run	Minimum	Mean	Maximum	Standard deviation	Coefficient of variation
Current farm					
Ending net worth					
1	$356,629	$1,189,289	$2,021,388	$372,937	31
Net present value					
1	−198,129	231,732	666,942	187,050	81
Expanded farm					
Ending net worth					
1	419,231	1,315,789	2,206,397	406,306	31
2	999,402	1,789,015	2,553,322	335,443	19
3	4,250,427	5,146,159	6,173,600	415,069	8
4	427,436	1,356,320	2,284,516	419,771	31
Net present value					
1	−289,129	206,419	691,597	208,897	101
2	96,894	387,100	825,895	187,003	48
3	617,632	1,115,607	1,598,470	208,063	19
4	−270,898	216,146	709,987	211,837	98

Source: Hardin 1978.

the 1st-, 10th-, 50th-, 90th-, and 100th-ranked runs were used in estimating maximum bid prices for land (Hardin 1978). The break-even bid prices were $975, $883, $765, $693, and $559/acre, respectively, compared to the $800 asking price. The break-even land prices make the difference between the net present value of the current and expanded firm equal to zero. Break-even analysis can also analyze the chance of investment success for other asking prices. For example, the buyer who pays $883 has a 10 percent chance of achieving a higher net present value and a 90 percent chance of a lower net present value. An investor following a safety-first rule that requires a 90 percent chance of positive net present value will bid a maximum of $693/acre.

Break-even land prices were much higher in runs with more favorable prospects for farm income. The optimistic analyses assumed that product and input price trends were 3 percent, wheat yield increased 2 percent per year, and rates of gain for stocker cattle increased 0.5 percent per year. From best to worst, the maximum bid prices for land were $1,197, $1,053, $920, $789, and $718. The safety-first rule allows a bid of $789 for a 90 percent chance of a positive (higher) net present value for the land investment.

OPERATING AND MARKETING STRATEGIES. The simulation model was used in a north central Oklahoma study to evaluate effects of several risk responses on farm growth and survival. The risk responses include crop-share rent, product diversification, crop insurance, government farm programs, sequential sales, forward contracting, and hedging.

Selected economic factors. This simulation approach has a base run with many failures in order to measure effects on the failure rate of alternative strategies and conditions. The base run (Table 11.4), using the assumptions described in note a, gives an expected ending net worth of $372,500, compared to a $326,582 beginning net worth. The wide range from minimum to maximum ending net worth indicates that chances of failure due to fluctuations in financial performance are relatively high. Thirty-six firm failures out of 100 runs were observed. All runs—with and without failures—were included in the results.

A higher beginning equity substantially improved the prospects for survival and ending net worth. Run 2, with 100 percent equity rather than 50 percent equity, improved annual cash flow by reducing interest paid on loans for land, machinery, and carry-over of operating debt. No firm failures occurred.

Improved prices for agricultural products (run 3) and higher inflation rates for land (run 4) increased expected outcomes and decreased risk. The

Table 11.4. Ending net worth under alternative economic futures and risk strategies, north central Oklahoma farm

| | Ending net worth | | | Standard | Farm |
Run	Minimum	Mean	Maximum	deviation	failures
		($1000)			
1. Base[a]	−421.2	372.5	1249.0	334.2	36
2. 100% beginning equity	710.0	1318.2	1849.3	218.3	0
3. 3% product price trend	57.7	785.5	1440.8	284.8	9
4. 7% land inflation	653.1	1446.8	2323.2	334.2	1
5. 0.3 = min. ratio of equity/L.T. assets	−421.2	372.5	1249.0	334.2	53
6. Multiple enterprise plan[b]	−377.2	409.5	1289.9	341.7	33
7. All risk crop insurance	−505.2	281.7	1123.5	334.6	46
8. Disaster payments	−320.1	419.2	1249.0	317.8	27
9. Crop insurance and disaster	−423.4	329.3	1123.5	320.8	41
10. Crop share	−131.3	525.7	1238.7	277.7	13

Source: Walker and Hardin 1979.

[a]The base assumptions were: 2 percent annual product price increase, 4 percent annual input price increase, 4 percent annual land inflation, 50 percent beginning equity and minimum equity to assets = 0.2. Runs 2–5 include changes in the base assumptions. Runs 6–10 use base assumptions.

[b]All other runs had only wheat and one winter stocker per two acres. This plan has 50 percent wheat, 25 percent sorghum, 25 percent alfalfa, and one stocker per four acres. Correlations among the enterprises are:

Yield					Price			
							Nov.	Mar.	Alfalfa
Stocker	Wheat	G.S.	Alfalfa		Wheat	G.S.	stockers	stockers	hay
1.0	.17	.14	.33		1.0	.72	.14	−.21	.58
	1.0	.39	.52			1.0	−.08	−.33	.65
		1.0	.03				1.0	.76	−.28
			1.0					1.0	−.43
									1.0

inflation rate did not affect the standard deviation because the value of land is added to ending net worth. However, the annual revaluation of land builds credit and, thus, growth potential, by increasing the firm's ability to fulfill minimum equity requirements.

In run 5 a more stringent credit constraint increased farm failures to 53 in 100. Other results for run 5 were not affected because all failures were included in the statistical analysis.

Risk strategy results. Runs 6 through 10 show results for the alternative risk responses. A diversified crop plan is used in run 6. Correlations among enterprises are shown in note b. All risk crop insurance is purchased every year in run 7. Run 8 evaluates the disaster provisions of the Food and Agriculture Act of 1977. Run 9 includes both crop insurance and disaster payments. Run 10 uses crop shares rather than cash rent as occurs in run 1.

The enterprise mix for the base plan specializes in wheat and stocker cattle, which is characteristic of the area. Using ending net worth as the measure of plan profitability, the multiple enterprise plan in run 6 is slightly more profitable than the base plan. It also decreases firm failures and increases the minimum ending net worth. Simulation provides a multiyear dimension for evaluating the effects of diversification. The cumulative effect of unfavorable events on net worth could cause the diversified plan to have a higher ending net worth than the specialized plan. This result would be counter to the usual case of expecting specialized plans with higher risk to have greater expected profits.

Run 7 imposed all risk crop insurance for wheat. Insurance premiums were $3.00/acre; and indemnity was paid for yields below 16.5 bu/harvested acre. The payment is 16.5 minus the actual yield times $2.50/bu. The lower expected net present value and ending net worth, relative to the base run, is partially due to the cumulative effects of insurance premiums on cash flow. Hence, lower returns and higher failure rates result from crop insurance in this analysis.

Run 8 reflects the impact of disaster payments available through the 1977–81 farm program. The disaster payment program resembles the insurance program, although it has no premium. Participation raises the expected and minimum values of ending net worth, and reduces the standard deviation and number of failures. Results of run 9 with a combination of insurance and disaster payments demonstrate the poor performance of crop insurance for the model farm.

Results of run 10 indicate that crop-share arrangements on leased acreage increase the expected and minimum values of ending net worth. Hence, in this case, crop shares appear preferable to cash rent for risk averse or risk neutral farmers.

Nebraska simulation studies

EQUITY, EXPANSION, AND BORROWING LIMIT TRIALS. The simulation model used in the Nebraska studies was developed by Held and Helmers (1980). It differs from the preceding model in that farm growth decisions are endogenously determined. That is, an expansion alternative is chosen within the model depending on the firm's financial situation. The model user may exclude some expansion alternatives if desired. The firm may expand by purchasing land in 320-acre units in alternate years. Other alternatives are to rent, combine rental and purchase, or not expand acreage. A decision to rent versus purchase depends on (1) average cash flow being positive over previous years (year 1 to present) and (2) availability of borrowing capacity. Given the option, land will be rented when average cash flow for all previous years is negative. After expansion occurs, the model replaces old machinery with new machinery as needed to operate the larger farm.

The model portrays a 960 acre wheat-fallow farm in the Nebraska Panhandle. Simulations are for 15 years with 100 replications. Only trials that meet the financial criterion of a 0.4 equity to asset ratio are summarized in the results. In contrast, summaries of results for the Oklahoma model included both survivals and nonsurvivals.

Projected yields and prices are based on anticipated trends, cycles if appropriate, and random shocks. The procedure for generating trends and random shock is similar to the Oklahoma study. In that study, linear trends were replaced with polynomial functions if cycles were detected. The Nebraska studies used three cyclic patterns for wheat prices and yields. Fig. 11.2 shows the three cycles for wheat price excluding seasonal variation. Model one reflects an annual price oscillation; the cyclical pattern in model two decreases in early years of the simulation, increases in middle years, and decreases in later years. Model three is the opposite of model two. These cycles allow evaluation of survival and growth at different entry times.

Simulation experiments and results. All combinations of price and yield models were used in evaluating results of farm expansion programs, equity levels, internal credit constraints, and land appreciation (Table 11.5). Expansion by purchase offered the greatest expected ending net worth; however, a relatively high rate of business failure occurred. Rental yielded higher rates of survival, average rate of return, and average net cash flow (run 2). Renting significantly increased survival rates over the purchase alternative while only moderately reducing ending net worth. A no-expansion alternative yielded a high (98 percent) survival rate, but the lowest ending net worth.

The level of beginning equity strongly affected results for each expansion alternative. The equity trials assumed the same beginning assets but

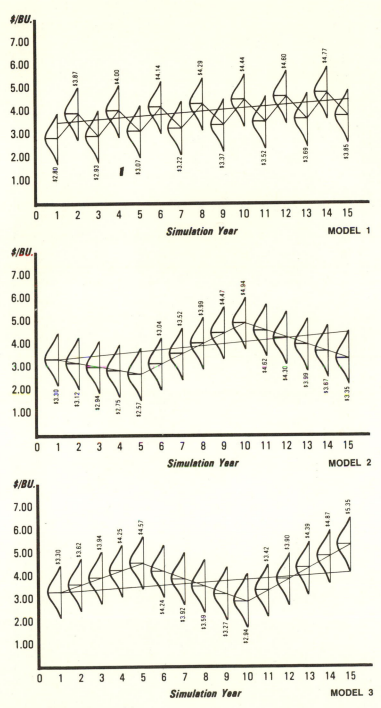

FIG. 11.2. Wheat price models.

Table 11.5. Growth and survival of a wheat-fallow farm in the Nebraska Panhandle, under selected model variations, 15 years

Run	Rate of survival (%)	Ending net worth in year 15 ($1000)	Average net farm income ($1000)	Net farm income ($1000)	Owner equity in year 15 (%)	Avg. rate of returns (%)	Ending acreage[a] in year 15 (acres)	Average net cash flow ($1000)
(Alternative expansion alternatives, land at $375/A, land appreciating at 4%, 65% beginning owner equity)								
Expansion alternative								
1 Purchase	20	711.0	20.0	1.8	.46	.046	2208(1248)	−25.6
2 Share rental	99	654.7	39.5	1.1	.84	.06	2880	2.2
3 Combination	85	677.0	34.3	1.3	.67	.056	2880(399)	−9.6
4 No expansion	98	429.1	11.0	1.8	.59	.033	960	−16.4
(Alternative beginning equities, 4% land appreciation, combination expansion)								
Beginning equity (%)								
5 50	74	558.3	32.7	1.3	.67	.061	2880(117)	−10.9
6 65	(See run 3 above)							
7 80	99	804.4	34.5	1.4	.64	.051	2880(769)	−10.6
(Alternative levels of borrowing at 4% land appreciation, buy land alternative)								
Equity for borrowing limit (%)								
8 40	(See run 1 above)							
9 45	65	644.9	18.0	1.8	.49	.044	1861	−23.0
10 55	94	497.7	13.0	1.9	.54	.038	1246	−18.8
11 65	98	429.1	10.9	1.8	.59	.033	960	−16.4
(Alternative land price increases, buy land alternative)								
Land % increase								
12 0	2	378.9	33.8	.98	.45	.069	1920	−9.4
13 4	(See run 1 above)							
14 8	40	1589.0	4.9	9.6	.50	.035	2736	−48.2

Source: Held and Helmers 1980.

a Acreage in parentheses denotes purchased acreage during the 15 years. The initial farm size was 960 owned acres.

different levels of indebtedness. For the equity trials, only the buy-rent alternative is shown in runs 5, 6, and 7 (Table 11.5). The model farm's survival rate ranged from 74 percent survival at 50 percent equity to 99 percent survival at 80 percent equity.

If the owner limits borrowing in order to provide liquidity for a rainy day, survival rates increase at the expense of lower expected ending net worths and average rates of return for survivor farms (runs 8–11). Thus, the internal limit on credit is considered a choice between, for example, a 0.65 chance of $644,900 ending net worth or a 0.94 chance of $497,700 ending net worth. Maximizing the expected value of ending net worth favors the latter choice; however differences in farmers' risk aversion could lead to other choices.

The effect of land appreciation on growth and survival shown in Table 11.5 (runs 12–14) is not surprising. A zero rate of appreciation leads to almost certain firm failure. An 8 percent rate of land appreciation improves survival and ending net worth about twofold over a 4 percent appreciation rate. Increases in land values also favor survival through their positive effects on credit reserves.

Indiana simulations

FINANCIAL SPECIFICATIONS, FARM GROWTH, AND SURVIVAL. Patrick (1979a) simulated a representative Indiana farm under conditions of price and yield variability in order to determine the effects of different loan arrangements and debt to equity levels on farm growth and survival. The model was an extension of a behavioral model developed at Purdue by Patrick and Eisgruber (1968). The set of growth, production, and loan alternatives includes externally imposed constraints such as availability of additional land and internal restraints on farm financial arrangements and labor. An optimal choice from the set of alternatives occurs within the model, in contrast to the previous simulation models. A multiple-goal function is used with the following weights: family consumption 0.4, net worth accumulation 0.25, risk aversion 0.25, and work-leisure preference 0.10. Minimum standards are established for each goal and alternatives are evaluated in a satisficing framework. The optimal plan meets all minimum standards and has the highest weighted level of satisfaction.

Land and input prices increase at a 6 percent annual rate and farm product prices increase at a 5 percent annual rate. A positive trend in productivity also occurs. Family consumption is a lagged function of disposable farm income. If cash flow difficulties arise, funds for loan repayments and operating expenses can be borrowed for a one-year term. However, the firm is terminated if such borrowing occurs in three consecutive years.

Three loan repayment plans, debt to asset ratios, and farm sizes were considered. The repayment plans were (1) equal principal payment – declining total payment; (2) fully amortized – equal payment; and (3) fully amortized – equal total payment with a reserve fund-insurance program (Baker 1976), each with a 9 percent annual interest rate. The levels of debt/assets allowed were 0.50, 0.70, and 0.90.

Farm product prices and crop yields were assumed to vary. Livestock production varied independently of crop yields. A variance-covariance matrix for crop yields was derived from Purdue agronomy farm data for the 1951–77 period. Correlations are based on relationships among annual average prices received by Indiana farmers during the 1951–1977 period, expressed in 1977 dollars. Simulated product prices are not permitted to fall below 70 percent of a specified current price.

Three farm situations were modeled: (1) a low-resource, full-tenant farmer with net worth of $41,600 and initial debt to asset ratio of 0.49; (2) an intermediate-resource situation with a net worth of $141,970 and debt to asset ratio of 0.47; and (3) a high-resource situation with a net worth of $406,370 and a debt to asset ratio of 0.32. Each farm had 400 acres initially. Land could be purchased in 80 acre tracts with one year between purchases. Land was also available in 40, 80, and 120 acre tracts on 50-50 share leases. The farms were simulated for 20 years with 25 replications.

Results. Table 11.6 shows the operator's average net worth and capital investment after 20 years of simulation under the three loan repayment plans for the low- and intermediate-resource situations. In both cases, the average annual growth rate for net worth exceeded the annual inflation rate of 6 percent. The low-resource farm purchased no land and the loan repayment plan had little effect on the results. Avoidance of a long-term debt commitment substantially improved the firm's survival prospects. Net worth growth for the 90 percent debt level is more than double the growth for the 50 to 70 percent debt limits. Hence, the level of debt is a more important growth factor than the loan repayment plans.

The intermediate-resource farm with a maximum debt ratio of 50 percent experienced no difference in survival rates under the three loan repayments. However, the net worth growth was highest under the equal principal payment plan. Because this plan required larger cash payments in early years than amortized loans, family living levels were reduced. Frugal living forced the farm family to accumulate net worth faster; higher net worth in turn provided the basis for greater expansion. When the maximum debt level increased to 70 percent, the probability of firm survival decreased under all loan repayment plans for the intermediate-resource situation. The average net worth growth and operator capital investment of the surviving

Table 11.6. Effects of various loan repayment arrangements and maximum permitted levels of debt

Type of loan repayment		Low initial resource farms Maximum debt permitted (%)[a]			Intermediate initial resource farms Maximum debt permitted (%)[a]		
		50	70	90	50	70	90
Equal principal payments	Net worth ($1000)	190	191	411	927	1434	1412
	Coefficient of variation (%)	13.2	14.6	54.6	6.4	8.8	12.0
	Capital investment ($1000)	263	267	1109	1378	1915	1881
	Coefficient of variation (%)	6.5	10.7	39.3	14.8	8.1	14.3
	Survival probability (%)	100	100	100	92	64	72
Fully amortized loans	Net worth ($1000)	184	184	464	770	1470	1555
	Coefficient of variation (%)	13.5	14.7	57.5	12.6	16.0	14.3
	Capital investment ($1000)	273	267	1450	1267	2446	2742
	Coefficient of variation (%)	13.8	10.0	42.2	21.8	15.7	16.2
	Survival probability (%)	100	100	100	92	56	68
Fully amortized loans with insurance	Net worth ($1000)	199	194	421	747	1493	1483
	Coefficient of variation (%)	15.8	20.9	80.4	15.0	15.1	21.5
	Capital investment ($1000)	261	262	1141	1093	2524	2529
	Coefficient of variation (%)	7.2	14.2	66.0	22.4	12.7	24.6
	Survival probability (%)	100	96	96	92	88	76

Source: Patrick 1979.

Note: Inflation rates of 6 percent annually for land, farm costs, and nonfarm prices and 5 percent annually for agricultural product prices are assumed. The initial net worth of the low resource farmer, $41,600, would grow to $133,417 after 20 years at the 6 percent rate of inflation. The initial net worth of the intermediate resource farm, $141,970, would grow to $455,317 after 20 years at a 6 percent rate of inflation.

[a]Ratio of debt to intermediate or long-term assets (as appropriate) × 100.

firms increased sharply. The net worth accumulations under the three repayment plans are similar. Capital investment under the equal principal payment program is lower.

Increasing the maximum debt to 90 percent had unexpected results for the intermediate-resource farm. Under the equal principal payment and fully amortized loan programs, the probability of survival increased as the maximum debt level increased. Typically the nonsurviving farms at the 70 percent debt level purchased land and then encountered cash flow difficulties that forced liquidation. The increase in maximum debt to 90 percent caused some farmers to finance expansion of their livestock operation. As a result net worth accumulation and capital investment increased under the fully amortized loan program.

These results suggest that the financial organization of the farm has a strong bearing on risk management. Debt levels and repayment plans strongly influence the probability of farm survival and growth. However, relationships among debt level, repayment plan, and a firm's resource position are complex. These results indicate that increasing the maximum debt levels may not always decrease the probability of firm survival. In some cases, greater debt capacity had no effect; in other cases, it increased the rate of survival because of enterprise mix and expansion choices. With only a few exceptions, higher levels of debt allowed surviving firms to achieve greater growth in net worth and capital investment. Extending the repayment period generally increased the probability of survival; however, the effects on net worth and capital investment were mixed.

Other studies

Simulation was used by Mapp et al. (1979) to evaluate farm plans derived from a MOTAD model. The simulation procedure complemented the MOTAD model by evaluating the cumulative effects of the farm plan over time. Dean et al. (1980) analyzed the effect of government risk management programs on farm survival and growth, with emphasis on effects of substituting all risk crop insurance for the disaster program. Their results showed that the cash flow effects of paying insurance premiums each year could significantly influence the impact of crop insurance on farm survival and growth. Lutgen and Helmers (1979) used the Nebraska farm simulator to generate risk income relationships for combinations of production and marketing alternatives on an east central Nebraska farm. Richardson and Nixon (1981) have developed a farm level income and policy simulation model (FLIPSIM) in cooperation with USDA. The model offers considerable promise and flexibility for the kinds of analyses described in this chapter.

Summary

These methods and applications of simulation illustrate the simulation concepts discussed in Chapter 9. The farm simulation models used in Oklahoma, Nebraska, and Indiana demonstrate how the initial resource situation, financial organization, and various alternatives in risk management influence farm growth and survival under risk. The Oklahoma farm simulator reflects one approach to defining and designing model components, developing stochastic and other data, using the model experimentally, and analyzing results of experimental runs. The Nebraska model illustrates some alternative approaches, including provision for internalizing farm expansion choices within the model rather than treating them externally. The Purdue model makes an internal optimal choice from among a wide range of decisions using a multiple-goal function in a satisficing framework.

The variables investigated in these simulation models include: (1) prices, yields, and land values; (2) equity levels; (3) farm enterprises; (4) government program participation; (5) share renting versus cash renting land; (6) marketing strategies; and (7) borrowing limits. The results show the usefulness of simulation as a tool in farm analysis. Other model formulations, variables, and applications, which relate to a particular problem and draw on the analyst's own knowledge and interests, are clearly applicable in farm simulation studies.

12

Educational programs for risky decision making

ODELL L. WALKER, A. GENE NELSON, AND CARL E. OLSON

THE CONCEPTS, TOOLS, AND EMPIRICAL FIND-INGS reported in preceding chapters demonstrate that decision makers at all levels can develop effective approaches for dealing with uncertainty. However, a large gap exists between the concepts and methods of risk analysis, and those practiced in farm and farm-related decision making (Walker and Nelson 1977). Extension economists and other educators must integrate these approaches into their educational programs and provide the material to their clientele. In this chapter we suggest educational approaches to risk analysis that are grounded in modern decision theory and conditioned by teaching experiences and the specific problem setting.

The educational decision setting

Professionals interested in risk analysis are quick to advocate educational attention to the dynamic-stochastic environment of commercial agriculture. However, extension workers and classroom teachers must decide how to allocate scarce educational resources between nonstochastic approaches to planning and the more complex approaches to planning under

Odell L. Walker, Oklahoma State University; A. Gene Nelson, Oregon State University; and Carl E. Olson, University of Wyoming.

uncertainty. Each decision maker must also consider the various decision-making approaches and allocate scarce managerial resources accordingly in an environment that places time limits on decision making. The educator, extensionist, and decision maker must fix priorities and identify important problems in which the tools of decision making under uncertainty pay highest dividends. For example, risk should be considered when making decisons about major capital investments; management of cost, price, and yield variability; and other key determinants of economic success for farmers.

The educator must start at the audience's level. The farmer audience in extension usually has a strong intuitive understanding of problems under uncertainty yet limited knowledge of formal uses of probabilistic and economic analysis. The university audience usually has a stronger background in economic analysis but has a less complete understanding of the agricultural decision setting and lacks the practical experience that characterizes extension clientele. These two groups demand analytical concepts, models, data, and results that are accurate, complete, timely, cost-effective, understandable, and believable.

These attributes often have internal trade-offs. For example, when time is limited the decision approach may be more expensive (a consultant may be hired), less accurate, and less complete than might otherwise be desired. The decision maker must balance learning and decision costs against the potential returns from improved decisions.

Believability and understandability deal with psychological, pedagogical, and communicative factors in teaching and learning. Even experienced researchers have difficulty fully understanding the methodological approaches of a research colleague that arise from sophisticated models and measuring procedures. Analysts and decision makers like to check the data, the model, and the results, particularly if their own dollars or reputation are at stake. Sometimes it is easier to accept results from a model that is simple to understand and use than from a more complex model. To entice a decision maker to spend sufficient time on a dynamic-stochastic analysis, the potential return should outweigh the cost of learning and decision making.

Several analysts have addressed the farm-ranch decision setting and recommended approaches to teaching risk management (Dean 1966; Officer et al. 1967; Halter and Dean 1971; Walker and Nelson 1977, 1980; Holt and Anderson 1978; Nelson 1980; Musser et al. 1981b). Dean (1966) suggested three alternative "stopping points" for "prescriptive" efforts to help farmers make risky decisions: (1) define states and actions and present the payoff table in monetary terms; (2) add objective probabilities (either prior or both prior and posterior) to the payoff table; and (3) add objective probabilities to the payoff table and convert the payoff entries from monetary to utility values.

A USDA extension special needs project completed jointly by Oregon State University and Oklahoma State University was based on the following premises in developing an educational program about decision making under uncertainty (Walker and Nelson 1980):

1. There is a human tendency to ignore risks and uncertainties (Hogarth 1975). The educational program should help to identify, understand, and measure a decision maker's various sources of risk.

2. The greatest potential for helping farmers to improve the decision making process is through payoff matrix and decision tree concepts. Use of these concepts encourages the decision maker to consider all possible events and actions before focusing on the most serious or promising ones.

3. Decision makers can consider future events in terms of subjective probabilities. Educational materials should be developed to teach decision makers how to estimate and use probabilities in analyzing their decision alternatives.

4. Objectives differ among farmers with risk attitudes ranging from risk takers to strong risk avoiders. Priority should be given to helping decision makers recognize and understand their attitudes regarding risk, including how these attitudes are influenced by their financial position.

5. Decision makers seek to control the risks affecting their farm operations. Thus, risk control methods should be included in educational programs. Such methods guide the selection of alternatives for consideration in the payoff matrix and decision tree frameworks.

A later study by a subcommittee of Regional Research Project W-149 (Young et al. 1979; Walker and Nelson 1980) concluded that: (1) if decision models require information about risk aversion, farmers must be able to provide it; (2) objective measures of risk aversion and risk bearing ability are needed; (3) educational programs should provide information on alternative courses of action and objective probabilities; and (4) building payoff matrices and decision trees is a high priority in educational programs with farmers.

Conceptual base for educational programs

The concepts and tools discussed in earlier chapters are important components of decision making under uncertainty. Given enough time and study, most decision makers can master the tools; however, the educational setting usually does not provide sufficient time to fully develop these approaches. The long-term effort should incorporate as many concepts as are useful and cost-effective. Building on intuition and limited analytical backgrounds is the most successful approach in extension and undergraduate education. The modern decision theory framework based on a payoff matrix and decision tree meets these criteria.

Figure 12.1 outlines conceptual and factual needs and alternative approaches for implementing decision theory. Payoff matrix and decision tree formats are depicted at the top of Fig. 12.1. The types of knowledge required to build the components for actions, events, outcomes, probabilities, and decision criteria components are identified by arrows leading to the payoff matrix and decision tree. Other components might include the experiment and *strategies,* as in Bayesian analysis (Halter and Dean 1971). (The word *strategy* in the Bayesian context refers to conditional rules concerning which action to choose. For example, given the occurrence of result Z_1 in an experiment or forecast, the strategy might specify that Action A_1 be chosen. In other parts of this chapter, the word strategy refers to more abstract principles and concepts about classes of actions and probable results across events. For example, the concept of flexible action hypothesizes reductions in risk and expected returns as results.)

Table 12.1 contains parallel formulations of a payoff matrix and decision tree for a stocking-rate problem in a ranch operation. Although the

Table 12.1. Payoff matrix and decision tree for a ranch-stocking rate problem

Payoff matrix	Actions			
	A_1 Stock lightly	A_2 Stock moderately	A_3 Stock heavily	
States				$P_{(s_i)}$
S_1 (High rainfall)	5000	8000	14,000	.2
S_2 (Average rainfall)	4500	7500	6,000	.6
S_3 (Low rainfall)	4000	1000	−5,000	.2

Decision tree

Action	Rainfall state	Outcome ($)

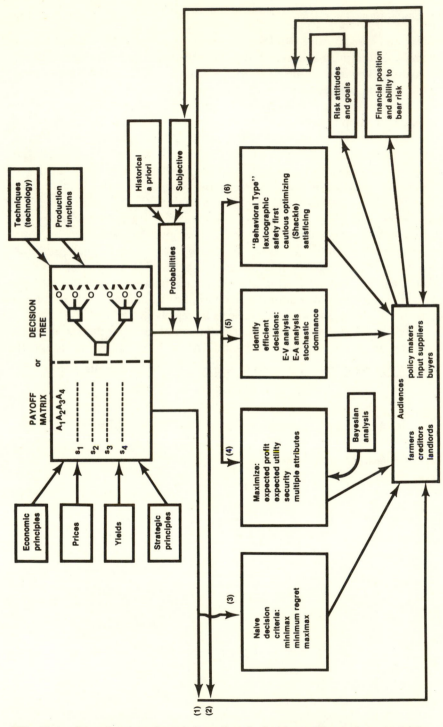

FIG. 12.1. Educational needs and alternatives in decision making under uncertainty.

events and actions are few, the problem illustrates the conceptual approach. The matrix should be as small as possible for the given decision problem, yet large enough to provide a realistic set of choices (Nelson et al. 1978). For hand calculations, only the most relevant actions are considered. Three stocking rates are used here. Variations such as whether to stock heavily and store or purchase feed during the grazing season are excluded. The three rainfall levels are representative of past growing seasons; the probabilties reflect rainfall records for the area. Information about price, disease, and pest events are not included; they could be added at the expense of greater complexity.

ESTIMATING PAYOFFS. Once the events and actions are specified, outcomes (payoffs) for each combination of action and event are calculated. The first task is to identify changes in costs and returns that are attributed to the action/event combinations. In a stocker operation with a fixed acreage of range, land costs are considered fixed. A short-term partial budget can be used, including only those cost and return items and parts of the business affected. Price expectations are established for the appropriate planning horizon. Variable items include stocker numbers, operating capital, and feed and other input costs. Rates of gain, death loss, veterinary expenses, forage and feed costs, interest, labor, and other items are estimated using appropriate production data for the empirical situation. Data sources may include experiments, rancher experiences, expert estimates, enterprise budgets, and ranch records.

Payoffs are usually estimated in monetary returns. For a short-term partial budget, the residual return to fixed resources, operator labor, and management is a basis for comparing each action, across all events. For a problem requiring a long-term partial budget, net farm income to operator's owned resources, labor and management, after depreciation, could be used. Return to operator's labor and management, return to equity, return to management, or net cash flow might also be estimated. Usually, total returns rather than returns per production unit must be estimated.

Budgeted payoffs for Action A_2 in Table 12.1 under all events are:

State		Action (A_2), $	
	S_1	S_2	S_3
Receipts	97,880	97,325	94,875
Expenses:			
cattle	81,750	81,750	81,750
forage	...	...	2,900
supplement	...	...	600
interest	7,500	7,500	7,500
veterinary	430	430	800
miscellaneous	200	145	325
Total expenses	89,880	89,825	93,875
Return to land, operator labor, fixed capital, overhead, management, and risk	8,000	7,500	1,000

Discounted cash flow techniques are applicable for comparing risky investments with different patterns of returns over time. If the stocking-rate problem is complex, linear programming or simulation or both can be used to estimate the payoffs for each combination of actions and events (Mapp et al. 1979).

ALTERNATIVE EDUCATIONAL APPROACHES USING DECISION THEORY. Figure 12.1 suggests six alternative approaches to educational programs using decision concepts and tools discussed in preceding chapters. Dean's suggestion that educators at least present payoff matrices is represented by arrow (1). A second possibility, arrow (2), is to express the information in probabilistic form using either historical or subjective probabilities. For subjective probabilities, interaction between the audience and the educator is essential in order to elicit actual expectations.

A third educational route, arrow (3), utilizes naive decision criteria without probabilities. Examples are the maximin, maximax, and minimum regret. These game theoretic decision criteria are subject to several criticisms (Halter and Dean 1971). The major criticism is that no probabilistic knowledge is assumed. The criteria ignore the experience of the decision maker, experiences of others, and use of scientific information in formulating subjective probabilities. However, these criteria may in fact reflect an implicit probability distribution. The maximin criterion, for example, implies that the probability of the least favorable event is one. Despite the severity of these criticisms, the naive criteria are still useful in introducing students and farmers to decision making concepts.

Approaches to risky decision problems that follow arrows (4), (5), and (6) use probabilities and a variety of decision rules. The maximizing approach of (4) includes maximizing expected monetary value. Maximizing expected utility would involve either assuming or elicting a utility function for the decision maker. Security or multiple goals could also be the object of maximization.

Comprehensive risk programming likely is not feasible for individual farmers; however, general results for regions or benchmark farms might occur as indicated by arrow (5). Stochastic dominance and other decision rules [arrow (6)] are directly applicable for the decision maker once he learns to use and evaluate these rules in relationship to his goals. Use of Bayesian analysis to revise probabilities might also be considered.

Table 12.2 provides alternative solutions to the ranch-stocking problem, using selected decision rules. The optimum action for each criterion is underlined. The first five decision rules demonstrate the varied actions that result from the naive criteria. The max $E(R)$ criterion uses the probabilities in Table 12.1. The safety-first rule maximizes returns subject to the provi-

Table 12.2. Alternative solutions to a ranch-stocking rate problem

Decision rule	Action		
	A_1	A_2	A_3
		Outcome ($)	
Maximin	4000	1000	−5,000
Maximax	5000	8000	14,000
Minimax regret	−9000	−6000	−9,000
Equally likely states	4500	5500	5,000
Most likely states	4500	7500	6,000
Max $E(R)$	4500	6300	5,400
Max $E(R)$ subject to: $P(0_{ij} < 1000) < .3$	4500		

sion that the chance of any payoff (outcome) being less than $1000 is less than .3. Actions A_2 and A_3 do not meet that provision.

Teaching materials and techniques

Examples of educational efforts to move the concepts and methods of risk analysis closer to the decison making stream are presented in this section. The USDA extension project conducted by Oregon State University and Oklahoma State University provided general teaching modules for introducing and illustrating decision theory concepts and decision analysis. (Additional information on the materials described can be obtained from Dept. Agric. Econ., Oregon State Univ., Corvallis.) These modules provide the basis for developing educational programs about risk assessment and management for different types of farmers and for different decision situations.

The five general teaching modules are self-contained packages of educational materials for use in teaching the general concepts of risky decision making. They use a slide-tape format with printed support materials such as workbooks and handouts. This format provides flexibility in the repeated delivery of the information. The slide-tape format allows for participation and feedback from the audience; it also enhances comprehension and retention of concepts. The modules are entitled: "Dealing with Risk in Making Farm Decisions: Introduction" (12 min.); "Guiding Risky Decisions with a Payoff Matrix" (22 min.); "Using Probabilities in Making Farm Decisions" (90 min.); "Considering Your Attitudes in Making Risky Decisions" (18 min.); and "Controlling Risk in a Farm Business" (49 min.).

The decision analysis modules apply decision making concepts to specific situations. An example is the computerized decision aid developed and field tested by Holt and Anderson (1978). It is used with farm audiences to analyze the decision to graze stocker cattle on wheat. Probabilities for different prices, yields, and cattle gains account for production and market risks. Actions, events, outcomes, and joint probabilities are specified in a decision tree format. The output provides the distribution of returns and the expected return for each alternative.

Farmers can develop data as a group or take turns in analyzing their own situations. Holt and Anderson report that opinions about appropriate data differed; thus, farmers appreciated having their own (or similar) situations analyzed. The interactive program on a portable computer terminal was considered essential in tailoring the analysis to individual farms. Farmers were very comfortable with the use of joint probabilities.

INTEGRATED PRODUCTION AND MARKETING PLANNING. Decision theory has been incorporated into extension programs on production and marketing in Michigan. Decisions considered in the workshops include crop mix, variety, fertility levels, and product pricing. Extension economists provide crop balance sheets for prior years. Given predicted acres planted and harvested for each crop, subjective probabilities for U.S. average yield and total production are estimated. Workshop participants are provided information on trends in corn yield and crop price patterns in unique years (e.g., a short crop year). The most likely yield is used in the crop balance sheet to estimate a price that will clear the market. This part of the exercise teaches concepts and techniques of probabilistic market analysis.

A computer program is used to evaluate the profitability of alternative mixes of corn and soybeans, based on expected product prices (Black and Chaffin 1971). The program may choose an optimal fertility program as well. Selection of corn and soybean varieties and timeliness factors are also modeled. Multiple runs of the program with different prices will generate a distribution of returns. In other production areas with greater yield variability, crop yields and pest control costs could also be treated as uncertain events. Finally, a decision tree is used to integrate the analysis of pricing and production alternatives (Fig. 12.2). The decision maker can choose a crop proportion and the percent of expected production to forward contract or hedge at planting. The probability column in Fig. 12.2 is the joint probability of yields and prices based on the farmer's own expectations.

RISK CONSIDERATIONS IN CROP SELECTION. A "what to grow" extension program in Minnesota utilizes the safety-first approach to account for the effects of risk in crop returns (Musser et al. 1981b). Estimates of the standard deviation of gross crop income per acre are used to develop lower confidence limits for crop net returns. The analytical method captures important features of decision theory and portfolio analysis in an extension setting.

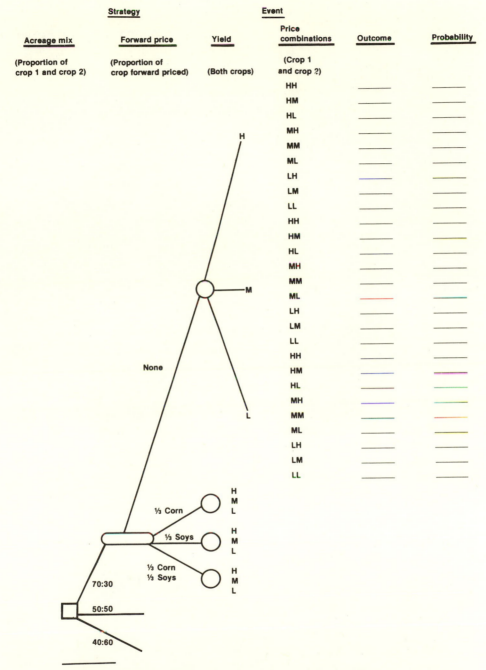

Strategy			Event		
Acreage mix	Forward price	Yield	Price combinations	Outcome	Probability
(Proportion of crop 1 and crop 2)	(Proportion of crop forward priced)	(Both crops)	(Crop 1 and crop 2)		

H = High, M = Medium, L = Low

Source: Private Communication, Roy Black, Dept. Agric. Econ, Michigan State Univ.

FIG. 12.2. Decision tree for crop mix and pricing problem under yield and price uncertainty.

Much of the Minnesota extension program involves interpreting and using crop budgets for the farming area. Risk terminology is explained and subjective estimates of crop riskiness are elicited. These rankings of crop riskiness are used during discussion of the empirical results described below. Objective estimates of crop standard deviations are presented based on historic time series analysis of state prices and county yields. Lower confidence limits (L) at the 10 and 25 percent levels are based on

$$L_i = E_i - Ks_i \qquad\qquad\qquad (12.1)$$

where E_i = expected cash returns for crop i, s_i = standard deviation of net cash returns for alternative i, and K = the number of standard deviations required for the desired probability that E_i is less than L_i, given the sample degrees of freedom. For example, for corn in southwest Minnesota, $E_1 = 84$, $s_1 = 42$ and the return at the 10 percent lower confidence limit is $28 (Table 12.3). Correlations of prices and yields within and among crops could also be considered, although these additions would complicate the calculations and teaching procedures.

TEACHING THE USE OF PROBABILITIES. Probabilistic information is a necessary part of risk analysis in decision making. Farmers have responded positively to the estimation and use of probabilities in extension programs. In a postworkshop mail survey in Oregon, 91 percent of the 44 responding farmers indicated that the probability information was useful to them. Of 61 farmers completing evaluation forms in Oklahoma, 64 percent felt that the treatment of joint probabilities was the "strongest point of the program" (Holt and Anderson 1978).

One problem is the lack of tested approaches for eliciting subjective

Table 12.3. Risk-returns analysis for selected crops by production region of Minnesota, 1980

Area and crop	Price	Yield	Weighted average net cash return	Standard deviation	10% risk level
	($)	(bu)	($)	($)	($)
South Central					
Corn	2.44	120	135	13	117
Soybeans	6.54	40	186	13	169
Wheat	4.20	60	177	29	138
Oats	1.54	90	65	6	58
Southwest					
Corn	2.32	90	84	42	28
Soybeans	6.40	23	95	28	58
Wheat	4.06	45	121	17	98
Oats	1.40	80	55	10	41

Source: Adapted from Musser et al. 1981.

Table 12.4.   Worksheet for assessing risk using triangular probability distribution

Your information:
1. Enter the *highest* price you can reasonably expect ....$___95___/cwt
2. Enter the *lowest* price you can reasonably expect ....$___60___/cwt
3. Enter the price you think is *most likely* to occur.....................$___77___/cwt
4. Enter the price you need to *break even* with cost ....$___70___/cwt

If line 4 is less than line 3 (otherwise go to line 11):
5. Subtract line 2 from line 1.......................................___35___
6. Subtract line 2 from line 3.......................................___17___
7. Subtract line 2 from line 4.......................................___10___
8. Square the number in line 7 ....___100___
9. Multiply line 5 times line 6 ....___595___
10. Divide line 8 by line 9..___.17___
    THIS IS THE PROBABILITY THAT THE PRICE WILL BE LESS THAN YOUR
    BREAK-EVEN PRICE

If line 4 is greater than or equal to line 3:
11. Subtract line 2 from line 1......................................._____
12. Subtract line 3 from line 1......................................._____
13. Subtract line 4 from line 1......................................._____
14. Square the number in line 13 ...._____
15. Multiply line 11 times line 12 ...._____
16. Divide line 14 by line 15.._____
17. Subtract line 16 from 1.00......................................._____
    THIS IS THE PROBABILITY THAT THE PRICE WILL BE LESS THAN YOUR
    BREAK-EVEN PRICE

probabilities. Several methods of elicitation have been identified (see Chaps. 4, 8): (1) direct estimation, (2) cumulative distribution approach, (3) use of the triangular probability distribution, and (4) assigning "weights" measuring strengths of conviction (Nelson and Harris 1978). Methods 3 and 4 have had the greatest attention in educational programs. These approaches are easily understood by producers and farm management students; but additional work is needed to verify their accuracy in eliciting the true beliefs of the decision maker.

A worksheet to simplify probability calculations for the triangular distribution is shown in Table 12.4. To illustrate, suppose a cattle producer requires a price of $70 to cover all costs. Based on the cattle producer's information, experience, and expectations, the triangular probability distribution of cattle prices is determined by three numbers: the "lowest possible" price at $60/cwt, the "highest possible" price at $95, and the "most likely" price at $77. The worksheet procedure finds the probability that the price received will be less than the break-even price of $70. For this example, the probability is 17 percent that the price will be less than $70/cwt. (Table 12.4).

A few pilot efforts are also underway to develop and disseminate probabilistic outlook information. Farmers, policymakers, and other outlook users would then have more comprehensive and accurate perceptions about the uncertainty associated with future commodity prices or other variables.

Probabilities provide a mechanism for pooling information from several experts and efficiently communicating it to users. The most extensive experience with the use of probabilities in outlook activities is weather forecasting (Murphy and Winkler 1979). Since 1965, forecasted precipitation probabilities have been routinely formulated and disseminated to the general public by the National Weather Service. Despite initial resistance, these probabilities are now an important and integral part of the service's public weather forecast.

The case for developing an operational program to formulate and disseminate probabilistic outlook information for agricultural commodities has been presented by Nelson (1980). Even recognizing the limitations of estimation methods, probability estimation is a skill that can be taught and developed, particularly among experienced forecasters such as outlook specialists. The operational program would include a survey of user needs, training programs for outlook specialists, and user educational programs. Further research is needed to develop elicitation techniques and to evaluate costs and benefits.

EDUCATIONAL PROGRAMS ON RISK STRATEGIES. Strategies such as forward contracting or hedging, using insurance, maintaining product and cost flexibility, planning for financial liquidity, diversifying enterprises and others described in Table 12.5 offer a problem-oriented setting for teaching the

Table 12.5. Examples of risks and risk strategies in farming and ranching

Production risk	*Financial risk*
Select low production risk enterprises	Keep adequate liquidity
Diversify business	Maintain credit reserve
Maintain cost flexibility	Negotiate longer loan repayment periods
Use risk-reducing production practices	Hold safe solvency position
Invest in extra machine capacity	Develop land leasing strategies
Disperse farm operation geographically	Incorporate to limit risk
Negotiate land lease arrangements	Obtain more accounting information
Maintain resource reserves	
Purchase crop insurance	*Technology risk*
Obtain additional information	Maintain flexibility
	Keep informed of new developments
Market risk	
Hedge on future market	*Legal risk*
Sell by forward contracts	Maintain insurance program
Spread product sales over time	Keep informed of new regulations
Maintain product and harvest cost flexibility	
Select low-price risk enterprises	*Human risk*
Diversify business	Plan back-up management
Negotiate land lease arrangements	Plan for loss of an employee
Forward price production inputs	Maintain insurance program
Obtain more outlook information	Plan for estate transfer
Casualty loss risk	
Obtain property insurance	

concepts of decision theory. The role of strategies in decision theory is to suggest relevant actions to be analyzed; for example, a flexible, diversified plan might be compared with a specialized plan. A 1975 survey of extension and classroom farm management specialists (Walker and Nelson 1980) indicated that much risk analysis is conveyed through an explicit focus on strategies in risk management. For example, economists in most states held workshops on hedging, contracting, and storage. When research on effects of a risk strategy is available, the educator can generalize the result to different types of farm situations. Research reported in Chapters 8, 10, and 11 included some evaluation of marketing, financial, and production strategies for specific farm situations. Other recent research on strategies is in the reference list.

Summary

A substantial gap exists between risk management practices of farmers and ranchers and risk management potentials inherent in the tools described in this book. This chapter suggests educational methods for teaching risk concepts within the extension and classroom environments. Several educational approaches are identified and examples are provided. All feature key components of modern decision theory and many are in a payoff matrix or decision tree format.

Experiences with these techniques indicate that extension and classroom audiences are receptive to studying the risk management concepts. However, educators and decision makers must allocate scarce teaching and learning resources carefully. The following priorities are suggested:

1. Use components (actions, states, outcomes, and probabilities) of decision problems under uncertainty to identify problems and organize analyses.

2. Develop payoff matrices or decision trees that supply information and ideas for solving important problems.

3. Improve use of information:

    a) Increase ability of farmers to observe and learn in an uncertain environment.

    b) Provide models for processing information, e.g., mathematical tools for formulating price or yield expectations.

    c) Teach probability concepts and procedures.

    d) Provide "objective" probabilities for key variables like prices, yields, frost, disease, and insects.

4. Assist decision makers to relate consequences of actions to their risk attitudes and to identify and choose appropriate decision criteria.

5. Provide feedback processes and adaptive mechanisms for use within and between decision periods.

PART 3

Financial dimensions of risk in agriculture

13

Financial responses to risk in agriculture

PETER J. BARRY AND C. B. BAKER

        A FIRM'S RISK RESPONSES contribute to risk averting goals by reducing the likelihood of business and financial risks, transferring risks to other economic units, and increasing the firm's capacity to bear the consequences of risk. Financial responses to risk are distinguished from those in production and marketing by their emphasis on a firm's risk bearing capacity. Their importance in agriculture is expressed by farmers' strong reliance on managing liquidity, leverage, and insurance.

        In this chapter we consider concepts, methods of analysis, and empirical studies involving financial responses to risk in agriculture. The following section uses a conceptual model to analyze the financial structure of farm businesses and to evaluate various financial responses to risk. The model then is extended to risk pricing of farm assets in a market equilibrium framework. Later sections of the chapter review empirical studies about financial responses to risk in agriculture.

Financial modeling and portfolio analysis

        The mean-variance portfolio model is an appealing framework for expressing a jointly optimal structure of enterprises, assets, and liabilities for a farm business. By optimal, we mean that the farm's production, marketing, and financial activities are organized to maximize expected utility for a risk averse investor. Linkages between these organizational areas

Peter J. Barry and C. B. Baker, University of Illinois.

are important and may strongly influence the optimal portfolio, including the firm's financial responses to risk.

The optimal farm portfolio is based on the following information: (1) the investor's desired trade-off (λ) in utility terms between the expected level ($\bar{r}_e$) and variance (σ_e^2) of returns to equity capital; (2) expected levels and variabilities of returns on farm and nonfarm assets; (3) expected levels and variabilities of the costs of liabilities (borrowed and leased capital); (4) correlations among and between returns and costs for assets and liabilities; and (5) a set of decision choices for structuring assets and liabilities. These informational requirements characterize any decision situation; they can be refined, extended, and enriched to fit the empirical setting.

The mean-variance approach is well known and much debated, especially about its limiting assumptions. It assumes either that an investor's utility function is quadratic reflecting preferences only toward the means and variances of the returns distribution, or that expectations are modeled by normal distributions, which are fully specified by their means and variances. If one of these conditions is met, then an expected utility maximizing choice of assets occurs among the mean-variance efficient set. In many applications, expectations are assumed normally distributed and the investor's utility function, in the relevant range, is approximated by the negative exponential $U(r_e) = 1 - e^{-2\lambda r_e}$, where r_e is the return to equity and λ is the degree of risk aversion. Maximizing the expected value of a negative exponential integrated over a normal density function, as is assumed for r, is equivalent to maximizing

$$E[U(r_e)] = E(r_e) - \lambda \sigma_e^2 \qquad (13.1)$$

where $E(r_e)$ and σ_e^2 represent a portfolio's expected returns and variance, respectively (Freund 1956). This expression directly accounts for means and variances and is equivalent to a nondecreasing utility function with constant absolute risk aversion.

The mean-variance approach has had widespread use in economic and financial analysis in agriculture (Robison and Brake 1979). Its strong foundations in microfinance theory (Tobin 1958; Markowitz 1959), explicit measures of risk, and rigorous demonstration (Tsiang 1972; Levy and Markowitz 1979) of its usefulness as an approximate method for portfolio selection make it widely accepted in financial analysis.

RISK-EFFICIENT PORTFOLIOS. The traditional portfolio model defines a *risk efficient set* as combinations of risky assets (or activities) that minimize variance for various expected returns. (See Barry [1983] for a similar description of this portfolio analysis.) In farming these risky assets are expressed as alternatives in production, marketing, and investment. In empirical analysis, the risk efficient set is also subject to other resource constraints and business requirements. Consider two activities, X and Y. Both generate risky assets having normally distributed rates of return with means $(\bar{r}_x, \bar{r}_y)$, variances (σ_x^2, σ_y^2), and covariance σ_{xy}. If P_x and P_y represent their respective proportions in the farm portfolio and $P_x + P_y = 1.0$, then the expected portfolio return $\bar{r}_{x|y}$ is

$$\bar{r}_{x|y} = \bar{r}_x P_x + \bar{r}_y P_y \tag{13.2}$$

and the portfolio variance is

$$\sigma_{x|y}^2 = P_x^2 \sigma_x^2 + P_y^2 \sigma_y^2 + 2P_x P_y \sigma_{xy} \tag{13.3}$$

The mean-variance (EV) efficient set is found by minimizing variance (13.3), subject to alternative levels of expected returns (13.2) and other resource constraints and business requirements. The EV efficient set is thus expressed by line XY in Fig. 13.1A. Its location depends on the expected returns and variances, and its shape depends on the correlation between X and Y. An optimal choice is the EV efficient portfolio that maximizes expected utility, as signified by the tangency with the investor's risk-return indifference curves.

This framework is extended to include financing by introducing a risk free asset (i.e., zero variance). Positive and negative holdings of the risk free asset represent lending and borrowing, respectively, at the risk free rate. Combining the risk free asset with the portfolios of risky assets yields the separation theorem in which the investment decision in risky assets is independent of the desired combination of risky and risk free assets (Tobin 1958). The result of the extension is an enlarged efficient set that combines the risk free assets with risky assets.

To illustrate, let the risk free asset have interest rate, i_d, as indicated by the intercept on the vertical axis in Fig. 13.1B. A line is drawn from risk free rate i_d through its tangency at A with the EV frontier of risky assets XY.

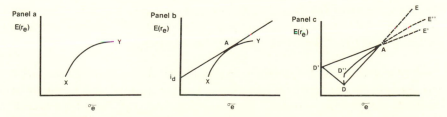

FIG. 13.1. Risk efficient sets for risky assets, risk free borrowing, and risky borrowing.

(Portfolio effects of risk free assets are expressed by standard deviations rather than variances. The effects on portfolio composition are the same in either case.) This line is the new risk efficient frontier. Any point on the line represents the proportion of the dominant risky portfolio, A, and the proportion of lending or borrowing at the risk free rate. A point to the left of A denotes an investor who holds the risk free asset in combination with portfolio A. A point to the right of A denotes an investor who expands investment in portfolio A with borrowed funds. The farther to the right, the greater are borrowing and leverage. An optimal structure of assets (investment) and liabilities (financing) is the portfolio along line i_dA that maximizes expected utility.

To illustrate numerically, suppose that portfolio A of risky assets has an expected return $\bar{r}_a = .15$, or 15 percent, and a standard deviation of $\sigma_a = .05$, or 5 percent. The interest rate on the risk free asset is $i_d = .10$, or 10 percent with a standard deviation of $\sigma_d = .00$.

The expected return to equity capital then is

$$\bar{r}_e = \bar{r}_a P_a + i_d P_d$$

where $P_a + P_d = 1.0$. P_a and P_d are the respective proportions of risky assets and the risk free asset in the total portfolio. However, since leveraging implies negative holdings of the risk free asset, the expression for returns to equity is modified to

$$\bar{r}_e = \bar{r}_a P_a - i_d P_d \qquad (13.4)$$

where $P_a - P_d = 1.0$

The standard deviation of the returns to equity is the weighted standard deviation of the risky assets:

$$\sigma_e = \sigma_a P_a \qquad (13.5)$$

Expected returns and risk measures are shown in columns 4, 5, and 6 of Table 13.1 for several levels of leverage. Higher leverage increases the expected returns to equity; but the standard deviation increases even faster. Thus total risk relative to expected returns increases with greater leverage, as indicated by the increasing coefficient of variation.

BUSINESS AND FINANCIAL RISKS. It is useful to distinguish the effects of business and financial risk on the firm's total risk. Business risk involves the variability (σ_a) of the returns to the firm's risky assets. It is independent of the financial organization. Financial risk arises from the financial claims on

Table 13.1.   Expected returns and risk measures for alternative leverage ratios

Debt to equity (1)	Proportions P_a (2)	P_d (3)	Expected return ($\bar{r}_c$) (4)	No interest risk σ_c^a (5)	CV[b] (6)	Interest risk σ_c (7)	CV (8)
			%	%		%	
0.00	1.00	0.00	15.00	5.00	.33	5.00	.33
0.25	1.25	−.25	16.25	6.25	.38	6.29	.39
0.50	1.50	−.50	17.50	7.50	.43	7.65	.44
0.75	1.75	−.75	18.75	8.75	.47	9.03	.48
1.00	2.00	−1.00	20.00	10.00	.50	10.44	.52
1.50	2.50	−1.50	22.50	12.50	.56	13.29	.59
2.00	3.00	−2.00	25.00	15.00	.60	16.16	.65
3.00	3.50	−2.50	27.50	17.50	.64	19.04	.69

[a]σ_c = standard deviation.
[b]CV = coefficient of variation.

the firm. (For simplicity, only financial risks associated with debt financing are considered in this analysis.)

The following analysis shows how business risk is magnified by financial risk to determine total risk to a firm's equity holders. We use a measure of financial leverage (P_a) to indicate the degree of financial risk. As leverage increases, so does total risk relative to business risk; the degree of increase is directly related to leverage, and thus financial risk.[1]

As Barry (1983) shows, business risk (BR) and financial risk (FR) combine to determine total risk (TR) in a multiplicative way:

$$(TR) = (BR)(FR) \tag{13.6}$$

Total risk is expressed by the coefficient of variation for equity holders (see column 6, Table 13.1)

$$(TR) = \frac{\sigma_e}{\bar{r}_e} = \frac{\sigma_a P_a}{\bar{r}_a P_a - i_d P_d} \tag{13.7}$$

Business risk is expressed by the coefficient of variation for risky assets

$$(BR) = \frac{\sigma_a P_a}{\bar{r}_a P_a} = \frac{\sigma_a}{\bar{r}_a} \tag{13.8}$$

---

1. The approach to delineating business and financial risk is adopted from Gabriel and Baker (1980). They derive an additive relationship between business and financial risk in determining total risk, which shows the absolute increase in total risk that is attributed to debt financing. The emphasis here, however, is on the percentage increase in business risk that is attributed to debt financing. Thus the two approaches are essentially the same, differing only in their measurement concepts.

Financial risk is then found by dividing total risk in (13.7) by business risk in (13.8)

$$\begin{aligned}
(FR) &= (TR)/(BR) \\
&= \frac{\sigma_a P_a}{\bar{r}_a P_a - i_d P_d} \Big/ \frac{\sigma_a}{\bar{r}_a} \\
&= \frac{\bar{r}_a P_a}{\bar{r}_a P_a - i_d P_d}
\end{aligned} \tag{13.9}$$

Substituting the expressions for business and financial risk into (13.6) yields

$$(TR) = \frac{\sigma_a}{\bar{r}_a} \cdot \frac{\bar{r}_a P_a}{\bar{r}_a P_a - i_d P_d} \tag{13.10}$$

The first term in (13.10) expresses business risk and the second term measures financial leverage, which is the index for financial risk. Higher leverage increases the second term, and thus increases total risk.

We illustrate with the numerical example using a debt to equity ratio of 1.0 ($P_a = 2.0$, $P_d = 1.0$). The coefficient of variation for BR is .333 = (5/15); the leverage measure is 1.50 = (.15)(2)/[(.15)(2) − (.10)(1)]. The coefficient of variation for total risk is then .50 = (.333)(1.50). Thus, leverage magnifies business risk 1.5 times in determining total risk.

Effects on total risk of changes in leverage, and thus financial risk, are easily evaluated using (13.10). Farmers may, for example, consider trade-offs between business and financial risks in responding to changes in risk or expected returns. A decline (increase) in business risk could lead farmers to accept more (less) financial risk as they restructure their assets and liabilities.

UNCERTAIN BORROWING COSTS. An assumption of risk free borrowing was more realistic before the 1980s when interest rates were lower, more stable, and subject to fixed rates on loans (Barry 1983). Even then, however, fluctuations in fund availability from some lenders along with lenders' nonprice responses to changes in farm performance tended to destabilize farmers' credit reserves. More recently, high volatile interest rates and greater use of floating rate loans have brought new sources of financial risk to consider in portfolio management. When borrowing becomes risky, its costs have an expected value with nonzero variance and covariances with returns on risky assets; portfolio risks generally increase and the separation theorem fails.

These effects on portfolio risk involve short sales, or negative holdings, of a risky financial asset with the proceeds of this borrowing activity used to expand investment in other risky assets (Fama 1976). This process is illustrated in Fig. 13.1C where risky borrowing or lending is represented by asset D. Short sales of D and leveraging of investment in A extends the portfolios along the dashed lines above A^2. A reversal now occurs in the effects of the correlation relationship between assets for short versus long positions. The correlation between returns on short and long positions in two assets is the negative of their correlation when both are held long. Thus leveraging brings greater risk for lower levels of correlation between assets that are held short and long.

The expected return to equity for a leveraged investor, subject to uncertain borrowing costs, is the expected returns to risky farm assets less the expected cost of borrowing

$$\bar{r}_e = \bar{r}_a P_a - \bar{i}_d P_d \tag{13.11}$$

Variance of returns to equity is the sum of the variances on the returns to assets and the costs of borrowing less their covariance, each weighted by the proportions of assets and debt

$$\sigma_e^2 = \sigma_a^2 P_a^2 + \sigma_i^2 P_d^2 - 2P_a P_d \sigma_{ai} \tag{13.12}$$

The negative sign in (13.12) indicates the inverse relationship between the covariance and portfolio variance. Returns to a farmer's equity will be stabilized by a strong correlation between asset returns and borrowing costs. In contrast, opposite movements in asset returns and borrowing costs will destabilize returns to equity.

To illustrate we include risky borrowing costs in the numerical example used earlier. Besides the previous data, let the standard deviation of borrowing costs be $\sigma_i = .03$ or 3 percent and assume a zero covariance ($\sigma_{ai} = .00$). The impacts of risky borrowing on total risks and the coefficients of variation are shown in columns (7) and (8) in Table 13.1 for the various levels of leverage. Risky borrowing adds more to total risk as leverage increases, although the actual increase depends on the variances and covariances. In general, the amount of increase in total risk will be relatively small for the range of leverage measures that characterize most farms.

PORTFOLIO ADJUSTMENTS UNDER RISK. The portfolio model provides an integrated framework for expressing an optimal organization of assets and

---

2. The shape of the line is determined by the correlation between D and A. Perfectly positive correlation results in a straight line between D and A. Less than perfectly positive correlation implies an intermediate location for the risk efficient set that might resemble a curve like $DD''A$ in Fig. 13.1C. The lower is the correlation between D and A, the more the curved risk efficient set bulges out toward the return axis, and the more effective is diversification between D and A as a means of risk reduction. Perfectly negative correlation results in two straight line segments from D and A, each meeting at point D' on the expected return axis. Only the positively sloped portions of the various lines connecting D and A are considered as the risk efficient sets.

liabilities for risk averse investors. The framework can also show how an optimal portfolio responds to changes in various parameters and to corrective actions followed by private decision makers or in public policy. Changes in risk, expected returns, or wealth may shift the risk efficient set and thus trigger the portfolio adjustment process (Robison and Barry 1977).

Suppose, for example, that farmers experience greater variability in expected returns as a result of more volatile commodity prices, while the level of expected returns stays constant. This increase in business risk shifts the risk efficient set to a lower level of expected returns for the same level of risk carried earlier. The original farm portfolio becomes nonoptimal; it must change to restore optimality. The adjustment process should result in a new portfolio with lower expected returns and risk for a farmer with constant absolute risk aversion (Robison and Barry 1977). The reduction in risk and returns would be greater for decreasing absolute risk aversion. Similar patterns of response occur for changes in other parameters.

How portfolio adjustments actually occur in farm businesses and how they are evaluated are largely empirical questions. They depend on the characteristics of farmers and farming operations, on their market and legal environment, and on the responses of lenders and other financial claimants. One portfolio adjustment is to change financial leverage and thus the farm's financial risk. Similarly, changes in leasing arrangements for farm assets may counter the effects of increases in business or borrowing risks. Or, adjustments in production, marketing, and investment plans may modify the level of business risk.

Portfolio adjustments in response to changes in public policies are important too. In the early 1980s the deregulation of financial markets and curtailment of public credit programs for farmers should increase and further destabilize farmers' costs of borrowing. Risk averse farmers may respond by lowering their financial leverage; or, they may try to further stabilize expected returns. These actions could utilize other public programs. The new federal crop insurance program, for example, may affect several elements of the farm portfolio model. It should reduce the risk of losses for many farmers and thus increase their expected returns to farm assets. It may also stabilize and reduce the costs of borrowing from commercial lenders, thus affecting both assets and liabilities in farm operations.

These types of trade-offs and linkages among a firm's assets, liabilities, and risk responses are an inherent part of the portfolio adjustment process. Identifying and measuring these relationships are challenging tasks.

Capital asset pricing and portfolio analysis

The microfoundations of portfolio analysis have been aggregated to a market level in the equilibrium capital asset pricing model (CAPM). The

CAPM yields important insight about the effects of investor behavior and market characteristics on risk pricing and investment analysis (Barry 1980).

As originated by Sharpe (1964) and Lintner (1965), the CAPM shows that equilibrium rates of return on individual assets adjust to levels that reflect the risk that each asset contributes to a market portfolio. Investors holding such portfolios need only be compensated for the total market, or systematic, risk that is common to all assets in the portfolio and that cannot be diversified away. Thus, risk premiums on individual assets need only compensate for their systematic risk.

In market equilibrium, the CAPM expresses a linear relationship between an asset's expected return and its systematic risk as the sum of a risk free rate and a risk premium reflecting the product of the price and quantity of risk.

$$r_j \; = \; i_d \; + \; \left[\frac{E(r_a) - i_d}{\sigma_a^2}\right] c\sigma_a\sigma_j \qquad\qquad\qquad (13.13)$$

where r_j is the expected return of asset j, i_d is a risk free interest rate, $E(r_a)$ and σ_a^2 are the expected returns and variance, respectively, of a market portfolio, and $c\sigma_a\sigma_j$ is the covariance of returns between asset j and the market portfolio, with σ_j as the standard deviation of returns for asset j and c as the correlation coefficient.

For empirical analysis, the model is expressed as the beta approach

$$r_j \; - \; i_d \; = \; [E(r_a) \; - \; i_d]\beta_j, \; \text{where} \; \beta_j \; = \; (c\sigma_a\sigma_j)/\sigma_a^2 \qquad\qquad (13.14)$$

This equilibrium condition results from the aggregation of the linear $E-\sigma$ efficient sets (Fig. 13.1B) for all investors. The derivation is mathematically rigorous; however, an intuitive approach is followed here. Asset markets are assumed highly efficient so that expected returns quickly and fully reflect available information; no transaction costs, tax obligations, or indivisibilities exist; and lending and borrowing rates are equal for risk free assets. Investors are risk averse, well diversified, and hold homogeneous expectations that are fully characterized by means and variances over single-period horizons.

Under these conditions, the market portfolio ($\bar{A}$) contains values of all assets that contribute to wealth, and it is EV efficient. Moreover, for $\bar{A}$ to exist, the returns offered by individual assets adjust to levels that reflect the risk that each asset contributes to $\bar{A}$ (Boudreaux and Long 1978). If this were not true, either $\bar{A}$ would not lie on the aggregate capital market line (which it does) or an individual asset would be excluded from the market portfolio (which is not possible).

These relationships imply that the yields of individual assets compensate for their risk contributions to the market portfolio. Each contributes its own variance as well as its covariance with all other assets. However, in a large portfolio, an asset's own variance is swamped by the covariances with other assets and by their combined variances. Hence, much of each asset's own variance is diversified away. Compensation is only required for an asset's net contribution to total portfolio risk, which is modeled by beta (β) in (13.14).

In smaller, less diversified portfolios an asset's own variance has greater importance. In the extreme case where a firm invests in only one asset and the firm's owner(s) invests only in that firm, the risks of the asset, the firm, and the owner(s) are the same. This asset would be priced to compensate for all of its risk since none would be diversified away. An important theoretical implication is that efficiencies in risk bearing are increased as diversification increases for firms, for owners, or for both (Levy 1978). The greater diversity reduces the risk premiums on individual assets, thus lowering the cost of risk bearing.

The CAPM assumes highly efficient markets for all assets and wide diversification among investors. Thus, risk premiums are likely understated when markets and investors do not reflect these assumptions, as is likely the case for many agricultural assets. Other CAPM assumptions are restrictive too; nonetheless, empirical tests for financial assets (stocks, bonds), indicate that beta values for assets are generally consistent with their rates of return (Modigliani and Pogue 1974).

Empirical analyses of agricultural risk responses

Risk responses differ greatly among farm businesses due to numerous factors: risk aversion and other decision criteria, stage of managerial life cycles, size and type of operation, market relationships with input suppliers and product handlers, and availability of public programs for risk bearing. These factors determine the feasibility of various risk responses and thus influence the extent of their use.

Differences in risk response make it difficult to generalize about risk management in agriculture. They also make it difficult to design analytical models and empirical studies with broad applicability. Nonetheless, much progress has occurred, and in this section we review empirical studies of financial responses to risk in agriculture.

IDENTIFYING FINANCIAL RESPONSES. Financial responses to risk refer to a firm's capacity to bear risks in production and marketing, and to spread these risks among the financial claimants on the firm. In larger corporate firms, the wide dispersion of ownership spreads business risks over many stockholders who may themselves be well diversified. The smaller scale, noncorporate structure of the farm sector reduces the feasibility of this risk response. An exception occurs in leasing of farmland where extensive use of share rents allocates expected business risks between the farm operator and the landlord. These arrangements introduce perfect positive correlation between a farmer's crop returns and his rental obligations; thus, crop-share leases are highly risk efficient financing plans.

Most of farmers' financial responses to risk are expressed through the management of leverage, liquidity, and insurance. These actions affect both the firm's assets and liabilities and are interrelated with risk responses in production and marketing. Liquidity management involves methods of generating cash quickly and efficiently in order to meet cash demands. Some of the methods of providing liquidity include the following:

1. *Holding assets for sale to meet cash demands*

Asset liquidity is based on the relationships between a firm's composite value of assets and the cash proceeds expected from each asset's sale to meet liquidity needs (Barry et al. 1981). An asset is considered perfectly liquid if its sale generates cash equal to or greater than the reduction in value of the firm resulting from the sale. Assets become less liquid as their potential sale reduces the firm's value more than their expected sale value. Factors that influence an asset's liquidity include transaction costs, marketability, liquidity risk, time allowed for liquidation, and the asset's importance in generating business income.

Willingness to liquidate assets to meet financial obligations is an important financial response to risk, especially under crisis conditions. Drawing down financial reserves is the first step. Selling current business assets, like grain inventories, is also part of ordinary operations. Even then, growing crops and livestock in feedlots are illiquid due to long production periods and, for crops, attachment to land. In contrast, harvested crops held in storage are highly liquid assets; they contribute importantly to liquidity management.

Other farm assets are dominated by land, machinery, breeding livestock, and other fixed assets whose liquidation is costly and disruptive (Barry et al. 1983). Selling these capital assets is usually a last resort effort, although depleting livestock herds is a common part of their cyclical performance. Selling a tract of land often seems the most anxiety-producing response, especially in traditional family farms. But if land acquisition is part of the growth strategy, then land disposal warrants consideration in risk control as well. In general, when businesses experience heavy stress, asset sales can generate cash in larger amounts and more quickly than most other types of risk response.

2. *Managing the pace of investments and withdrawals*

Maintaining flexibility in the pace of farm investments and withdrawals is an important financial response to risk. Postponing capital expenditures, including asset replacement, is a favored financial control mechanism under adversity. It avoids large financial outlays, builds equity and reduces indebtedness, and allows productivity and profitability to strengthen in a rapidly growing operation.

Exerting control over withdrawals by family members and other business owners for consumption, taxes, and other purposes is also an important risk response. However, farmers today are more dependent on cash purchases and have much less flexibility to adjust family living to swings in income than occurred in the past. Options in meeting income tax obligations provide further opportunities for stabilization, especially in shifting taxable gains and losses among years.

3. *Holding liquid credit reserves*

Much reliance in farming is placed on establishing sound, lasting credit relationships with commercial lenders that include the capacity to carry over loans, defer payments, refinance high debt loads, or otherwise utilize credit reserves during times of financial distress (Barry et al. 1983). Holding liquid credit reserves avoids the costs of asset liquidation to meet cash demands and later reacquisition when adversity has passed. Using credit in borrowing does not directly affect a farm's asset structure or production organization; the transaction costs are relatively low; and institutional sources of loan funds generally are available in rural financial markets.

However, costs of maintaining and borrowing from credit reserves must be considered. Holding reserves restrains the returns from investment opportunities gained with financial leverage, interest is paid when loans occur, and noninterest charges like deposit balances and loan fees may occur to compensate lenders for establishing lines of credit. Moreover, financial risk must be accounted for in borrowing, including variations in the cost and availability of credit.

Using public credit programs as sources of liquidity combines the characteristics of financial and market responses to risk. Price and income support programs administered through the Commodity Credit Corporation in the USDA provide a financial control program for crop production that combines stabilization of prices for many commodities, inventory financing, added flexibility in marketing crops, and income maintenance. Longer term storage and reserve programs extend the inventory financing and shift part of the marketing control to the public sector.

Other public programs administered mainly through the Farmers Home Administration (FmHA) provide valuable credit liquidity for high risk borrowers, a category increased by natural or economic disasters. In the later 1970s the concept of emergency financing was broadened to cover various kinds of economic emergencies, including shortages of credit from commercial lenders. These public credit programs introduce added uncertainties about their continuation, as witnessed by the sharp run-up in government farm credit in the 1970s, followed by partial curtailment of these programs as the political environment changed.

4. *Using formal insurance*

Commercial insurance indemnifies an asset or flow of income against the occurrence of specified events. Examples include life, crop, loan, and household against death or accident, yield loss, default, and fire, respectively. Commercial insurance requires that insurers can sell policies at premiums exceeding actuarial cost by amounts sufficient to offset the opportunity costs of resources committed to reserves and administration. Public subsidies sometimes play an important role, as with farmers' crop insurance. Use of insurance may also build and stabilize credit reserves by reducing lending risks. However, insurance is limited in scope of insurable events, in extent of financial coverage, and sometimes in freedom of action for the insured.

FINANCIAL RESPONSES AND LIQUIDITY MANAGEMENT. Since World War II, the growing importance of credit as a means of leveraging for firm growth and as contingent sources of liquidity stimulated much study about its role in farmers' liquidity management, how credit appraisals differ among lenders, and how farmers' perceptions of these appraisals influence their business decisions. In 1966 Baker developed the concept of liquidity as an attribute of a farmer's assets and considered the implications for the structure and growth of farm firms. In 1968 he extended the concept to include credit reserves which, along with cash reserves, form a basic response to risks and a constraint on choices in production, marketing, and consumption. In 1971 Barry and Baker developed a modeling approach for estimating the levels of liquidity premiums that farmers with different risk aversion would associate with their credit reserves. Subsequent studies by Vandeputte and Baker (1977) and Baker and Bhargava (1974) provided more general specifications of functional relationships between liquidity premiums and sizes of reserves for both cash and multiple sources of credit. A major result of these studies is that the *form* of risk response for farmers with different levels of risk aversion is strongly exhibited through different holdings of credit and other financial reserves, thus implying the importance of liquidity premiums as indicators of a farmer's risk aversion.

Accompanying these studies of how farmers value various sources of liquidity was a companion set of studies that evaluated lenders' credit responses to numerous strategies in borrowing and debt management. These arise from a farmer's choice of lender, sequence and source of borrowing and repayment, financing instrument, asset structure and enterprise mix of farming operations, and interactions among lenders. Empirical measures were developed for lenders' responses to many such strategies and situations; their effects on a farm's profitability, risk, and liquidity were often evaluated using firm growth models (Baker 1968; Baker and Hopkin 1969; Barry and Baker 1977; Sonka et al. 1980).

The increased market risks of the 1970s shifted the emphasis toward the risk components of models for farm firms and for valuing farm investments. Sources of risk, measures of risk, attitudes toward risk, and their implications for financial structure came to the forefront in empirical analysis. Farm models based on risk programming and stochastic simulation were used to evaluate trade-offs between financial gains, risk, liquidity, and survival. Linkages between sources of risk and risk responses in production, marketing, and finance were evaluated in terms of their effects on a farm's credit and its capacity to support firm growth and liquidity.

We illustrate these linkages by considering a farmer's market responses to risk and their effects on credit and liquidity. Market responses should stabilize earnings and yield greater certainty in loan repayment. But they may increase financial risks as well. The farmer who provides his own storage facilities may borrow to finance the investment and to carry the inventory. Similarly, hedging with futures contracts requires a flexible credit agreement to meet margin requirements as prices of hedged commodities change through the hedging period.

In order to expand credit and reduce financing costs, a farmer may follow a forward or futures contracting strategy that accommodates the lenders' preferences for greater certainty in collateral values and loan repayment. Barry and Willmann (1976) tested these relationships between contracting and credit by using a simulated borrowing and interview approach to evaluate responses of a sample of lenders to alternative levels of forward contracting by crop farmers. They found that the most preferred level of contracting by lenders generated about 17 percent more total credit and about 53 percent more operating credit than the least preferred level. When these credit responses were evaluated in a multiperiod risk programming model, the risk efficient growth plans included contracting due to both the favorable effects on credit and the lower price risks. The model results indicated contracting even for farmers with little or no risk aversion and even though expected profits were higher for noncontracted sales.

Hedging with commodity futures contracts appears to affect credit less favorably than does forward contracting. In a mail survey of lenders in central Illinois, Harris and Baker (1981) found among respondents who loaned to hedgers that a significant percentage reported a positive credit response to hedging growing crops. However, nearly 70 percent of the respondents indicated that credit would increase by no more than the amount of expected margin calls. Hence, consistent with arguments to follow, credit uncertainty may contribute to farmers' reluctance to hedge.

A major finding of these studies has been the strong emphasis on lenders' nonprice responses in evaluating credit. Interest rates on farm loans have seldom reflected much risk or liquidity pricing among individual farmers. Instead, lenders respond to differences in farmers' credit worthiness primarily in nonprice ways: differences among borrowers in loan limits, security requirements, loan maturities, loan supervision and documentation, and other means of credit administration (Robison and Barry 1977). These nonprice responses mean that empirical analyses of lenders' credit evaluations must emphasize the relationships between the lenders' nonprice responses and the various determinants of credit.

Lenders' nonprice responses also complicate the identification and measurement of risks in farmers' costs of borrowing. Variations in borrowing costs arise both from forces in financial markets and from lenders' responses to risks in agricultural markets and changes in farmers' credit worthiness. Lenders' risk responses to differences in farmers' credit worthiness still occur primarily in nonprice ways. Thus, the impacts on farmers' costs of borrowing are subtle, focusing mainly on subjective liquidity premiums that reflect the farmers' valuation of the credit reserve.

Barry et al. (1981) demonstrated one approach, based on simulated borrowing requests, to measure the relationships between changes in farm income, the lenders' nonprice responses, and the farmers' costs of borrowing. Their results showed a positive correlation between the size of credit reserve and the level of farm income, and thus a negative correlation between farmers' costs of borrowing and farm income. Most of the lender's response involved the financing of capital expenditures rather than operating loans. The negative correlation indicates that greater variation in farmers' costs of borrowing from changes in their credit worthiness will add to farmers' total risk through both the variance and covariance effects.

The case is less clear for the borrowing risks that arise from forces in financial markets. These forces are primarily expressed through interest rates, which clearly signal farmers about changes in financial market conditions. Moreover, the growing emphasis on floating rate loans by farm lenders is speeding the transmission of interest rate changes to borrowers. Changes in interest rates and other financial market conditions are far removed from farmers' operating environment. They influence, but likely are not influenced by, farmers' financial performance. They add variance to farmers' total risk but are largely independent of farming conditions, unless aggregative farm performance contributes significantly to inflation or other national conditions. Thus, the correlation between returns to farm assets and financial market forces should be near zero.

In response to these borrowing risks, more formal methods of financial control in lender-borrower relationships appear promising. The object is to make the financial environment more stable and predictable, enabling farmers to develop more formal financial plans for countering risks in production and marketing. Numerous kinds of financial programs (variable amortization, debt reserves, loan insurance) have been evaluated and will be reviewed in Chapter 14.

Another approach to evaluating farm debt capacity is employed by Hanson and Thompson (1980) who estimated maximum feasible debt ratios under historic patterns of income variability for several types of Minnesota farms. Their approach is based on a farmer's capacity to meet the annual debt obligation in low income years under strict and lenient loan servicing conditions and under a range of credit terms. Results indicate that higher leverage is possible on more diversified farming operations, that leverage is more responsive to differences in farmers' management than to farm size or minor changes in loan terms, and that a flexible repayment agreement is essential for highly leveraged operations.

FINANCIAL RESPONSES AND PUBLIC POLICY. Financial responses to risk are closely related to public policies that influence farmers' income, wealth, price expectations, and credit under conditions of risk and inflation. A policy-oriented analysis is illustrated by Boehlje and Griffin (1979) who evaluated the effects of government price support programs on the investment and financing behavior of risk averse farmers. They reasoned that price supports, indexed to costs of farm production, should provide greater certainty in farmers' cash flows and thus reduce business risks. Bid prices for durable assets, especially land, should increase, as should farmers' credit capacity, financial leverage, and farm growth. Their simulation analysis for crop farmers differing in size, capital structure, and farmer characteristics indicated that smaller, more highly leveraged operations should receive fewer benefits from indexed price support programs than will larger operations with lower leverage. Thus farmers who respond to lower business risks with more aggressive financial practices may achieve superior performance and perhaps change the structural characteristics of the farm sector.

Gabriel and Baker (1980) demonstrate another approach to the portfolio adjustment process that emphasizes a farmer's trade-off between business risk and financial risk, subject to a maximum risk tolerance. A decline in business risk, perhaps attributed to public policy, may lead to acceptance of greater financial risk, thus offsetting the lower business risk. Their analysis of the aggregate portfolio of the farm sector yielded empirical evidence consistent with this phenomenon.

Effects of inflation on farmers' income, wealth, and liquidity also became more pronounced in the 1970s. For investments in farmland, new empirical evidence indicated that farmers' real returns to assets grew at about a 4 percent annual rate from 1960 to 1980, and that farmland prices increased to reflect this growth (Melichar 1979a). Accompanying this growth, however, were greater liquidity problems for highly leveraged investors because more of their returns occurred as capital gains relative to current income. Moreover, Melichar observed that public policies enhancing growth in farm income will exacerbate this liquidity problem. These relationships between earnings growth, inflation, and capital gains in agriculture mean that modifications of financing programs and debt repayment plans are appropriate responses to liquidity problems attributed to both inflation and variable farm income.

Concluding comments

As the review of empirical studies in this chapter has shown, financial responses to risks hold a prominent position among the methods for managing business and financial risks in agriculture. These financial responses are closely interrelated with other responses in the production and marketing organization of farm firms. Moreover, the full range of risk responses has increased in importance as new risks in financing farm businesses have emerged to combine with the traditionally high level of business risks in agriculture. In this chapter we have emphasized the development of a comprehensive framework for modeling optimal portfolios of assets and liabilities in farm businesses, where both the returns to assets and the costs of liabilities are subject to risk. This framework should contribute to greater understanding of farmers' financial responses to risk and provide a richer setting for evaluating new directions in risk management, including those associated with changes in financial markets and public policies. These latter points are treated in the following chapters.

14

Agricultural risks and lender behavior

WARREN F. LEE AND **C. B. BAKER**

IN THE PRECEDING CHAPTER it was shown that farmers' capacities to accept market and production risks depend heavily on their financial environment. Borrowing adds to total business and financial risks because debt creates a fixed claim against an uncertain future net cash flow. In addition, borrowing reduces credit reserves, which are themselves subject to variations, and increases the farmer's implicit costs of further borrowing. The predictability of the credit reserve is established by lender behavior; thus, the role of financial intermediaries and of financial markets is critically important to the farmer's capacity to manage risks. This chapter addresses the ways financial intermediaries absorb, transmit, or increase agricultural risks.

Financial intermediation and lender responses to risk

Financial intermediaries buy, sell, and transform financial instruments as they channel funds from savers to investors. They arbitrage between savers and borrowers. They evolve in response to differences between savers and borrowers in their preferences among financial instruments in terms of maturity, risk, and liquidity. At given rates of interest and transaction costs, savers' preferences relative to borrowers' are for short maturities, low risks, and a high degree of liquidity. Financial intermediaries resolve these dif-

Warren F. Lee, Ohio State University, and **C. B. Baker,** University of Illinois.

ferences with appropriate terms of exchange, while meeting their own performance objectives.

The resolution process generates a wide range of financial intermediaries, financial instruments, and constraints imposed by government regulations, managerial policies, and financing practices. Aside from leases, debt instruments dominate the financial instruments used by farmers, and commercial and cooperative lenders are the dominant source of financial services. The remainder of the chapter focuses on debt instruments and related financing programs used by these lenders.

Lenders' risks

Lenders must cope with liquidity risks and risks of loan loss. Both affect the cost of lending and cause the lenders to search for effective methods of risk management. In this section we consider both sources of risk, although we emphasize loan loss risk and related lender responses.

LIQUIDITY RISK. Liquidity risks originate with uncertainty about the demand for loans as well as with the availability and cost of loanable funds. For example, unanticipated changes in the cost of loanable funds cannot always be completely offset by adjusting interest rates on loans. Increased competition, structural changes, or major regulatory reforms may threaten lenders who have rigid cost structures that reflect the past. The last decade, and particularly 1979 through 1982, were characterized by high, unstable interest rates. This instability is unlikely to diminish in the 1980s as the U.S. financial markets undergo deregulation.

Unanticipated variations in market rates complicate the loan pricing decision. More important, however, is the inverse relationship between the value of fixed-rate loan portfolios and changes in interest rates. An increase (decrease) in market rates causes the value of any fixed-rate financial instrument to decrease (increase); moreover, the magnitude of this response varies directly with the maturity of the instrument.

Lenders could offset the potential effects of interest rate changes by matching the maturities of their assets and liabilities. In practice, however, precise matching of maturities is costly and difficult to achieve. The financial futures markets represent a promising new opportunity to hedge against interest rate variations. To date, however, few agricultural lenders have used this innovation. Thus, most agricultural lenders have opted to transfer part or all of the interest rate risk to their borrowers by means of variable rate loan contracts. In doing so, they have likely increased default risk. Variable interest rates clearly worked to the borrowers' disadvantage over the 1977–82 period when interest rates doubled while outstanding farm debt was increasing by more than 50 percent.

Many observers (e.g., Baughman 1970) have noted that rural banks were historically insulated from much of the volatility in national financial markets. This insulation has been substantially eroded as local financial markets have become more completely integrated with regional and national markets, and as interest rate ceilings are phased out. The increased use of rate sensitive liabilities such as money market certificates by banks has widened the variation over time in interest rates charged borrowers. The market share of farm loans has shifted, moreover, toward the Farm Credit System (FCS), who charge and adjust interest rates according to the rates paid on their bonds. Adjustments in FCS loan rates are more moderate because they are based on the average rate paid on all bonds outstanding. The average maturity of most commercial banks' liabilities is less than the FCS, thus causing greater rate sensitivity. In general, however, interest rate changes will likely continue to be an important source of risk for lenders and borrowers in the future.

FARM INCOME AND DEFAULT RISK. Default occurs when the borrower fails to pay all or part of principal and interest due. Excluding the borrower who willfully ignores the obligation, default occurs only when the borrower's liquidity balances are less than the payment. This situation is illustrated in Fig. 14.1 where net cash flow available for debt servicing (Y) is a random variable, while the debt-servicing commitment (A) is largely fixed. The expected cash flow available for debt servicing is $\bar{Y}$. The standard deviation of Y is a function of production and market risks and of other commitments such as personal living expenses, taxes, etc. The probability of default is represented by the area under the distribution of Y to the left of A. If A is low relative to $\bar{Y}$, the risk of default is also low. For a given

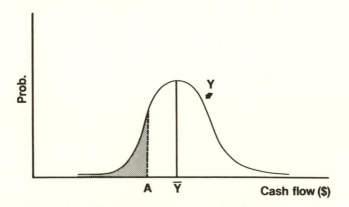

FIG. 14.1. Delinquency risk in relation to cash flow expectations.

repayment plan, the location of A relative to $\overline{Y}$ is determined by three variables: the absolute size of loan, the interest rate, and the maturity. Thus, for a given amount of loan, higher interest rates, shorter maturities, or a combination of both would increase the probability of default.

Additional liquidity problems arise from the tendency for a large proportion of farmers' total returns to occur as unrealized capital gains on land and other capital assets. Capitalization of inflation-induced growth in returns to land led to rapid appreciation in farmland values during the 1960s and 1970s. As a result capital gains have been a dominant proportion of total returns. Many buyers have financed land purchases with mortgage loans in which the payments exceed net cash flow from the purchased land early in the repayment period. Without substantial cash flows from other sources, these buyers are extremely vulnerable until inflation increases the net cash flow enough to cover loan payments. Thus, measures to reduce repayment risk must recognize inflation-induced liquidity problems, as well as cash deficits caused by random sources.

DEFAULT RISK AND LENDING COST. From the lender's standpoint, the ultimate risk is the probability of loan loss, defined as the amount uncollected on a defaulted loan. Except for equity participations, the terms of a commercial loan establish repayment only of principal and interest; thus lenders do not share outcomes from upside risk, and they must minimize any perceptible downside risk that could threaten repayment. In contrast, borrowers participate in the benefits of upside risk as well as in the penalties of downside risk. The lender's participation in downside risk is immediate and so severe that extensive protective practices are required.

To illustrate, consider lending costs, lc, given by

$$lc = f + k + r, \tag{14.1}$$

where f is the cost of acquiring loanable funds, k is the cost of administering the loan, and r is the risk premium required to induce the lender to lend, all expressed as rates with respect to principal loaned. Our main concern is with the influence of default on the risk premium, r, and thus on lending costs, lc. When a loss occurs, the lender loses the uncollected principal, the associated acquisition costs, f, and administration costs, k. Therefore, the risk premium is given by

$$r = [d/(1 - d)] (1 + f + k), \tag{14.2}$$

where d is the default rate, expressed in terms of principal loaned.

If f and k are 7 percent and 2 percent, respectively, with a default rate of 0.5 percent, the lending cost is

$$lc = 0.07 + 0.02 + 0.005/(1 - 0.005)(1 + 0.07 + 0.02) = 0.0955$$

The default rate increases lending costs by 0.05 percent of principal loaned, *in addition to* the 0.5 percent itself. With a default rate of 5 percent, *f* and *k* unchanged,

$$lc = 0.07 + 0.02 + 0.05/(1 - 0.05)(1 + 0.07 + 0.02) = 0.1474$$

Note that the increase of 4.5 percentage points in the default rate increases lending costs by 5.19 percentage points. The differential increases as the default rate increases. With *f* and *k* at 7 percent and 2 percent, respectively, lending costs become 100 percent of principal loaned when *d* reaches 45.5 percent. This break-even value of the default rate is lowered as acquisition and administrative costs increase.

The effect of default on lending costs, as suggested by (14.1), is conservative because acquisition and administration costs are assumed to be independent of the default rate. Since financial markets are sensitive to differing risks among financial instruments, higher default rates could significantly increase both the cost of funds and the administrative costs of managing delinquent loans. If, for example, the increase in default rate from 0.5 to 5 percent increases the cost of funds from 7 to 8 percent and if administrative costs increase from 2 to 3 percent, total lending costs would be 16.8 percent—an increase of 7.25 percentage points in total lending costs. Loan volume also might suffer as default increases. In sum, default risk permeates all components of lending costs and is a destructive factor for the lender if it reaches an appreciable level.

Actual default is rare in agricultural lending because potential defaults are typically managed with extensions of maturities, rescheduled payments, refinancing or other actions to avoid default; however, these actions are costly to the lender because penalties imposed on borrowers seldom offset the added administrative costs.

FEEDBACK EFFECTS. The most visible return from lending is interest paid on the loan, plus any service fees. However, rural banks frequently make loans to farmers at interest rates that appear to yield lower profits than could be earned by investing the funds in government securities. Such behavior is not explained by altruism of the rural banker; rather, lending occurs because local loans increase the bank's deposits. This increase comes from loan-induced growth in the borrower's own business activity and from loan-related stimulation of local business activity. The feedback relationship is illustrated in Fig. 14.2. Funds flow from deposits to bank profits by two channels—loans and investments. Loans to local borrowers and local investments such as municipal bonds produce further increments to deposits,

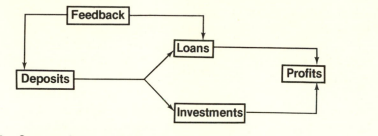

FIG. 14.2. Sources of bank profits: loans and investments.

whereas loans to nonlocal borrowers and investments in nonlocal government securities do not.

To illustrate this loan-deposit feedback process let z be the rate at which an increment of loans adds to the bank's deposits and $L(z)$ the rate at which the bank lends from this deposit increment. Then the feedback relationship adds $izL(z) - k - r$ to the bank's profits from lending, where i is the interest rate charged on loans. After accounting for lending costs, as expressed in (14.1), the bank's total profit from lending is

$$\pi = i - (f + k + r) + [izL(z) - (k + r')] \tag{14.3}$$

where $r' = [d/(1 - d)] (1 + k)$

To illustrate, let $z = 0.3$, $i = 12$ percent, $f = 7$ percent, and $k = 2$ percent and assume that 75 percent of the fedback deposit increments are loaned out. (In a survey of rural banks in Texas, Barry [1978] found z to average 0.288.) If the default rate is 0.5 percent, the bank's total profit from lending is 3.54 percent. With a default rate of 5 percent, the total profit from lending is reduced to -7.41 percent. Note the interactive effect of default and feedback. Equation (14.3) does not discount for the timing of lagged profits on loans made with fedback deposits. Accounting for this lag would diminish somewhat the magnitude of feedback effects.

The feedback mechanism provides an important incentive for depository institutions to lend; however, it also magnifies the effect of default on lending costs and hence on profits from lending. In sum, returns from lending are uncertain because many factors influence the level of local business activity. Nor is it known, in a multibank community, what fraction of the added deposits the lending bank will receive.

If lenders fully incorporated the default risk premium in the interest rate, interest rates on farm loans would vary widely at a given time. Evidence reported in Chapter 13 indicates that wide rate variations are not common. Instead, lenders respond to risk with variations in credit limits for farm borrowers and by adjusting other loan terms.

Techniques for managing default risk

As suggested earlier, commercial lenders must emphasize loan repayment and protection against default. Lenders differ in their response to default risk depending primarily on whether they are real estate or nonreal estate creditors. A mortgage lender's ultimate protection against a loan loss is the borrower's equity in the real estate security which, in most cases, can be fairly easily and accurately estimated. Since their collateral position is weaker and less certain, nonreal estate lenders tend to place relatively more emphasis on overall net worth and income-generating capacity to establish credit limits (Sonka et al. 1980). Nonreal estate lenders also tend to monitor their accounts more closely, whereas, the real estate lender may not become aware of a loan problem until the borrower actually misses a payment.

Although nonreal estate lenders are more likely to be involved in the early phase of managing loan problems, the mortgage loan obligation often plays a dominant role in default risk. It is usually large, and more importantly, it is almost totally invariant with the borrower's cash flow under traditional amortization plans. In this section we first establish these traditional amortization methods based on level or declining payment loans. Then we consider innovations in farm mortgage contracts that would reduce default risk by tailoring repayment schedules to cash flow.

TRADITIONAL LOAN AMORTIZATION METHODS. Default risk for the farm mortgage lender is associated with periodic payments established when the loan contract is written. The payment, A_t, has two components

$$A_t = iB_{t-1} + P_t \qquad t = 1, \ldots, n \qquad \textbf{(14.4)}$$

where i is the periodic interest rate applied to the unpaid balance at the end of the preceding period, B_{t-1}, and P_t is the principal payment at the end of period t.

Let p designate the proportion of the loan, B_0, that is amortized over the term of the loan. For completely amortized loans, $p = 1$. For partially amortized loans, $1 - p =$ the proportion left to be repaid as a "balloon" when the loan matures.

The two methods most commonly used to distribute the principal payments are the equal or level payment plan, where A_t is a constant, and the declining payment plan where P_t is a constant.

For the level payment plan

$$A_t = \frac{pB_0}{PVA_{i,n}} + i(1 - p)B_0 \tag{14.5}$$

where $PVA_{i,n}$ is the present value of an annuity of $1 for interest rate i and a maturity of n periods. Consider, for example, a loan of $1,000 amortized over 20 years in equal annual installments at an annual interest rate of 10 percent. If the loan is fully amortized ($p = 1$), the equal annual payment given by (14.5) is

$$A_t = \frac{(1)(1000)}{PVA_{10,20}} + (0.10)(0)(1000) = \frac{1000}{8.5135} = \$117.46$$

If half of the loan is due as a balloon, the annual payment is

$$A_t = \frac{(0.5)(1000)}{8.5135} + (0.10)(1 - 0.5)(1000) = \$108.73$$

Whenever $p < 1$, the amount of the balloon, $(1 - p)B_0$, is added to the final payment. The payments for the level payment plan are illustrated in Fig. 14.3 as LP_P, for $p = 1$, and $p = 0.5$.

For the declining payment plan,

$$A_t = \frac{pB_0}{n} + iB_{t-1} \tag{14.6}$$

Using the example of a $1,000 loan at 10 percent loan that is fully amortized over 20 years,

$$A_1 = \frac{(1.0)(1000)}{20} + (0.10)(1000) = \$150$$

The outstanding balance on this loan would decline by pB_1/n per year ($50 in our example) hence, the total payment decreases by $5 each year.

If half the loan is repaid as a balloon, the first yearly payment under the declining payment plan is

$$A = \frac{(0.5)(1000)}{20} + (0.10)(1000) = \$125$$

With $p = 0.5$, the loan balance decreases by $25 per year and the payment declines by $2.50 per year. The declining payment plan is illustrated in Fig 14.3 as DP_p, for $p = 1$ and $p = 0.5$.

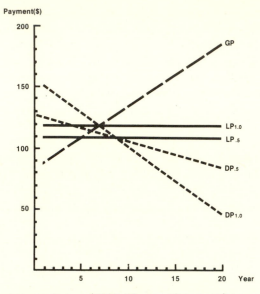

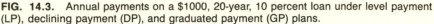

FIG. 14.3. Annual payments on a $1000, 20-year, 10 percent loan under level payment (LP), declining payment (DP), and graduated payment (GP) plans.

To meet loan payment obligations, borrowers accumulate liquidity balances from income that remains after paying for farm operating expenses, nondeferrable investments, household expenses, taxes, and nonreal estate debt commitments. Liquidity balances also include savings accumulated from preceding periods in the form of financial or physical assets and reserved credit.

For many farm real estate buyers, most sources of liquidity are at their lowest levels immediately following the land purchase. Hence the level payment plan is used more frequently by commercial lenders than is the declining payment plan. Moreover, as farm real estate prices have increased relative to expected annual net cash flow, maturities have tended to lengthen and balloon payments have returned to some degree slowing somewhat the trend toward completely amortized loans.

The problem of default management is highly visible. A farm mortgage borrower with fixed payments to be met from a variable net cash flow should have a sufficient safety margin to assure that payments can be met even when income is less than expected. If a payment cannot be met from income, then it must be met by drawing down reserves. When all reserves are depleted, default occurs, and as noted earlier, the mortgage lender may have little or no warning until the borrower misses a payment due date.

In the traditional method for managing defaults, the lender simply carries the amount of delinquency as past due. The borrower may be assessed a penalty. The borrower usually agrees to repay the arrears, hopefully restoring the loan to an acceptable schedule of installments. The traditional method leaves the borrower subject to the ad hoc policies and practices of the lender. The lender's willingness to adjust the repayment terms depends on judgments about the borrower's prospects for recovery and conditions in financial markets. An alternative approach is to formally tailor repayment schedules to the borrower's expected cash flows.

GRADUATED PAYMENTS. Graduated payment plans are appealing for a borrower whose income is expected to increase systematically over time. Setting the payment growth rate somewhere below the expected rate of increase can reduce early installments, when they are most burdensome, and increase the later installments, when they should be less burdensome. Inflation in the 1970s increased the appeal of graduated payment plans. Deflation in the early 1980s demonstrated their potential shortcomings.

Lee (1979) has proposed a graduated payment plan that amortizes all or part of the loan, subject to installments that increase at a preassigned compound growth rate, g. The first payment is given by

$$A_1 = B_0 \frac{(1 + g)}{PVA_{i'n}} \tag{14.7}$$

where $i' = (1 + i)/(1 + g) - 1$

For our example of a $1000, 10 percent, 20-year loan with $g = 4$ percent, $i' = 1.10/1.04 - 1 = 5.769$ percent. The first payment is

$$A_1 = \frac{1.04}{PVA_{5.769,20}} = (1000) \frac{1.04}{11.688} = \$88.98$$

Each successive payment is 4 percent higher than the previous one, thus $A_2 = \$92.54$, $A_3 = \$96.24$, . . ., $A_{20} = \$187.47$. The graduated payment plan is shown as GP in Fig. 14.3.

As g increases, the size of installments required to amortize a given amount of loan varies inversely with the payment growth rate, g, in early years of the repayment schedule, and directly with g in later years. This growing payment is appealing under expected systematic increases in the income available for debt servicing. It also provides both borrower and lender with a known schedule of payments.

The payment growth rate need not fully reflect the expected increase in income to generate a substantial effect. However, graduated payments are still fixed and make no formal allowance for random variations in cash flows. Moreover, should income not grow at the expected inflation rate, the use of graduated payment plans could lead to disastrous consequences in later years. These shortcomings could be resolved by using the purchasing-power mortgage where the growth rate is based on the actual rate of increase in some inflation measure. This approach provides a flexible, yet tolerable, graduated payment plan. We will suggest still another design after examining other repayment alternatives.

ALTERNATIVE PAYMENT PLANS. Numerous proposals have been made to make the repayment schedule *formally* more flexible to reduce uncertainty in the farmer's financial environment. Lenders, however, tend to resist adopting these policies because the formality would reduce their capacity for ad hoc responses to delinquency and default; thus the terms of plans offering formal flexibility must be advantageous to lenders as well as borrowers.

Lee (1979) has proposed a flexible payment plan (FPP) that would allow the borrower who experiences cash deficits to reschedule payments by reamortizing the loan balance. The flexibility provided the borrower would depend on the equity accumulated when the shortfall occurs. The FPP is reflected by shifts backward or forward in the original schedule of installments. Limits are recommended on the number of years backward and the maximum length of loan so the lender can monitor the borrower's performance and take timely, corrective action on serious default problems.

A FPP should be designed so that borrowers only use the flex provision to compensate for cash flow shortfalls. A variable interest rate is considered essential. Otherwise FPP borrowers would likely use equity reserves whenever market interest rates exceed the contracted loan rate, perhaps to avoid higher market rates on nonreal estate borrowing. These and similar abuses of FPP privileges could be minimized by levying an interest surcharge on that portion of the loan balance that exceeds the amount originally scheduled. Alternatively, interest premiums could be paid on prepaid balances.

A major advantage of a FPP for both lenders and borrowers is elimination of the administrative costs for minor default problems. Lenders would not have to investigate (and borrowers would not have to explain) underpayments that fell within the limits specified in the contract. It also reduces the need for short-term loans to meet long-term loan payments.

An alternative to the FPP is a variable amortization plan (VAP) proposed by Baker (1974) to make the loan payment responsive to changes in factors affecting net cash flow. In a VAP an index is applied to "flex" the payment. Factors that might be used in the index include crop and/or livestock yields, prices received or paid, or any combination of these and other variables that affect the borrower's net cash flow. The level of net cash flow might be used directly to flex the payment made if moral hazard is not a concern. (A contract generates a *moral hazard* if its provisions lead the contractor to behavior that alters the probability that the hazard or its consequences will occur.)

A VAP would produce a fluctuating periodic payment that could be unacceptable to commercial lenders. Hence a second feature of the VAP is a debt reserve to buffer the lender against variations in cash flow. The borrower would pay into the debt reserve when the indexed payment exceeds the contractual payment. Conversely the lender could withdraw from the debt reserve when the indexed payment fell short of the contractual payment. Thus, the debt reserve would assure the lender of a constant cash flow.

If historical trends in inflation and farm incomes continue, the debt reserve would grow over time, even if net cash flows are highly variable. After a few years the accumulated debt reserve should greatly reduce the probability of default. However, a repayment problem could arise in the early years before the debt reserve has had a chance to grow.

Three alternatives for managing shortfalls in early years are: amortization insurance, an overloan to create the initial debt reserve, or an option loan commitment that could be drawn upon. Amortization insurance would be actuarially based and would require underwriting services. It likely would involve some kind of governmental support—perhaps a role that could be played by Farmers Home Administration.

The overloan alternative could be activated with little change in existing arrangements. At the time of disbursement of loan, B_0, an amount, L ($<B_0$) would be disbursed to the borrower and the remainder, R, would be paid into the debt reserve. The larger loan would have no consequence to the borrower if interest is paid on the debt reserve at the same rate charged on the loan and if R is left unamortized in the repayment plan. This alternative bears some resemblance to the "funds held" option now provided by Federal Land banks.

The option loan commitment would obligate the lender to loan additional funds as required, within a prescribed number of installment dates, to supplement the VAP if the debt reserve does not yet provide sufficient funds to cover the payment obligation. This alternative bears some resemblance to the "open end mortgage" option now provided by Federal Land banks. However, in the VAP, the overloan or option loan would be mandatory and applied to marginal applicants.

The index and the debt reserve properties of the VAP can be designed in different ways. The flex factors could differ among farms or farmers. The index can also be changed to vary the amounts added to the debt reserve in good years or withdrawn in low income years.

The size of the debt reserve could be limited to some multiple (say, three) of the payment. The debt reserve does, after all, impound cash and thus reduces discretionary income for the borrower. This disadvantage for the borrower could be offset, in part, if interest were paid on the debt reserve. Still, the borrower would not borrow in the first instance, unless the expected rate of return on the borrowed funds exceeds the interest rate. So other incentives must be used to stimulate the borrower to maintain the debt reserve.

The most obvious gain for the borrower is the reduction in risk provided by the debt reserve and variable amortization commitment. Thus the borrower might qualify for a VAP loan, but not for a traditional repayment plan. A lower probability of default on a long-term loan might also increase the VAP borrower's nonreal estate credit reserves thus giving wider choices in production, marketing, and consumption. The flexible payment and variable amortization plans can be applied with variable or fixed rate loans, and with the level payment, decreasing payment, or graduated payment plans.

Empirical studies

Few studies have compared the effects of alternative repayment plans on either lenders or borrowers. Historical records are deficient because most farm lenders have used essentially the same repayment plans for all types of borrowers. Variation in terms between lenders is also limited; hence, a simulation approach is needed to compare traditional and alternative repayment plans.

Patrick (1979a) modelled an Indiana grain-hogs farm to compare financial performance under three mortgage repayment plans — equal principal payment (EPP), equal total payment (ETP), and ETP plus amortization insurance. For each repayment plan, 20-year simulations were made, each subject to three specifications on the maximum debt to asset ratio. Prices and yields were varied randomly over the period, and each specification was repeated 25 times.

Simulated average terminal worths, reported as the second entry in Table 14.1 for each repayment specification, are considerably larger for the higher debt maximums. The operator's net worth would have increased, over the 20 years, to $455,317 from inflation alone. Net worth accumulation differed little for debt maximums of 70 percent and 90 percent but was substantially lower for the 50 percent debt to asset ratio. With the 50 percent restriction, differences in loan payment plans had no effect on the probabilities of survival. With debt maximums of 70 percent and 90 percent, the probability of survival was lower for ETP than for the declining total payment. However, adding payment insurance to the ETP plan raised the probability of survival to a level higher than for declining payment.

Two University of Illinois studies compared farm and loan performance for fixed payment (FAP) and variable amortization payment (VAP) plans. In one study, Stone (1976) used recursive linear programming to

Table 14.1. Effects of debt levels and repayment on farm survival and growth: 20-year loan

Repayment terms and performance measures	Debt maximum as a percent of assets		
	50%	70%	90%
Equal principal payment[a]			
Probability of survival	92%	64%	72%
20-year net worth accumulation ($000)	927	1434	1412
	(6)	(9)	(12)
Equal total payment[a]			
Probability of survival	92%	56%	68%
20-year net worth accumulation ($000)	770	1470	1555
	(13)	(16)	(14)
Equal total payment and amortization insurance			
Probability of survival[b]	92%	88%	76%
20-year net worth accumulation ($000)	747	1493	1483
	(15)	(15)	(22)

Source: Patrick 1979a. Numbers in parentheses are coefficients of variation of associated net worth accumulations.

[a]If income, Y, exceeds consumption, C, draw on cash or a one-year loan to pay debt installment. Failure to survive is defined to follow three consecutive years dependent on one-year loans.

[b]If income, Y, exceeds consumption, C, set aside $1/2(Y - C)$ in a reserve, R, unit $R = 3 \times$ debt installment. If $Y < C$, draw on cash or R until $R = 0$; then draw on installment insurance. Failure to survive is defined to follow three consecutive years dependent on insurance.

compare programmed outcomes from FAP and VAP loans for cash-grain farmers in Illinois who financed land purchases with Federal Land bank loans in 1975. The VAP reduced the probability of default and increased the farmer's borrowing from nonreal estate lenders, because of compulsory payments into a debt reserve. The VAP also raised the average, and reduced the variance, of the borrower's income over the loan period. Net worth and disposable income were equal to or higher for VAP than for FAP in all cases tested. Stone found that raising the maximum ratios on debt increased the probability of survival for both the FAP and the VAP borrower.

In a second Illinois study, Aukes (1980) developed a Farm Liquidity (FL) model as an extension of Dunn's Loan Performance Simulator (LPS) (Baker and Dunn 1978; Baker et al. 1979) to compare financial outcomes for a sample of farmers with Farmers Home Administration's Farm Ownership (FO) loans. FO borrowers typically cannot qualify for loans from commercial lenders.

The farm was modelled with 432 acres, 336 crop-share rented and 96 acres owned (48 newly owned). Crops produced were corn (250 acres) and soybeans (182 acres). The operator owed $143,000 on assets valued at $241,000. The current ratio was 2.42 following the land purchase transaction. Large grain inventories constituted a large portion of the current assets but they were not liquidated to finance the land purchase. Despite this source of liquidity, limited income generating capacity caused difficult survival tests for the borrower. When financed with a VAP mortgage, $5000 were transferred from stored crops to a debt reserve, as required under the VAP.

Ten-year simulations were made with crop yields and prices drawn randomly from populations specified in terms of means, variances, and covariances. Simulations were made with a wide range of scenarios in price conditions (trend, cycle, and variance) and in beginning balance sheet liquidity, as described in the row heading of Table 14.2. The "baseline + 2%" differed from the "baseline" scenario by providing an annual increase of 2 percent for crop prices. The "cyclical" scenario subjected the operator to added stress through a reduction in prices received relative to prices paid in the first 3 to 4 years. The "larger cycle" scenario represents an initial period of greater stress, followed by a stronger recovery in crop prices. The baseline, cyclical, and large cycle scenarios then were each rerun with lower initial liquidity (see footnote c of Table 14.2). The operation was simulated under both FAP and VAP for all scenarios. For the most severe scenario ("large cycle and reduced liquidity"), a respecified VAP also was tested. (See footnote d, Table 14.2).

Table 14.2. Farm and loan performance: fixed (FAP) and variable (VAP) amortization plans, selected scenarios

	FAP				VAP			
Scenario	Failure rate (%)	Default ($00)	Growth > 8% (%)[a]	Current ratio[b]	Failure rate (%)	Default ($00)	Growth > 8% (%)[a]	Current ratio[b]
Baseline	28	31	50	.52	28	26	56	1.08
Do +2%	4	27	72	.51	4	24	74	1.43
Cyclical	62	16	10	.55	52	10	16	1.17
Large cycle	66	13	6	.51	58	8	6	1.39
Baseline and reduced liquidity	26	27	56	.48	22	24	60	.89
Cyclical & reduced liquidity	54	6	10	.53	44	5	16	1.07
Large cycle and reduced liquidity	58	10	6	.55	52	9	10	1.50
Do; alternative VAP					42	9	10	2.33

Note: both FAP and VAP are based on an ETP amortization schedule.
[a]Percent of trials producing growth rates greater than 8 percent.
[b]Current assets/current liabilities.
[c]Current assets reduced from $29,000 to $14,000; current and intermediate liabilities from $13,000 to $11,000 and $15,000 to $13,000, respectively; long term debt II, from $55,000 to $44,000. Net worth remains $98,000.
[d]Annual increments to debt reserve increased by 50 percent; debt reserve maximum doubled (to twice the annual debt service for long term debt II).

Four performance measures are reported in Table 14.2. Of these four, the failure rate is probably the most important criterion for evaluating the VAP. Comparing columns 1 and 5 reveals a rather modest reduction in the failure rate, none at all in the first two scenarios, and largest in the last scenario, especially when the VAP is respecified to include larger increments to the debt reserve and a larger debt reserve maximum. In all but the last row, the debt reserve maximum is equal to the annual debt service requirement on less than half the operator's long-term debt, so it is not surprising that improvements in loan performance are modest. For all scenarios, VAP reduces the default amount, although only slightly for the last three rows.

The farm performance measures are reported in columns 3 and 4 for FAP, and in 7 and 8 for VAP. Since the reserve is part of total liquidity, the current ratio is higher for VAP than for FAP in all scenarios. In addition, the equity growth rates under VAP are greater than those under FAP, except for the large cycle scenario. This is due to a slight reduction in the annual averages of family consumption and gross investment under the VAP. A relatively large decrease in annual variation of consumption and investment, as measured by the coefficient of variation, also occurs. These VAP effects on family consumption and gross investment are the result of contributions required for the debt reserve in years of high farm income. For gross investment, the VAP tends to reduce the effects of higher prices in years of high farm income.

At the University of Melbourne, Kent and Lloyd (1983) simulated a borrower obligated to deposit three-fourths of his disposable cash surplus in a reserve that reaches a maximum of three times the annual repayment commitment. In addition, he acquired at the time of loan disbursement an option to borrow in each of the first three years. The option loan was limited to the amount by which the annual repayment exceeded disposable cash surplus. Use of proceeds from the option loan was restricted to meet amortization payments on the farm mortgage loan. An annual fee was charged for the option loan until exercised, whereupon an interest rate was applied to the balance generated by disbursement. Simulations suggested that such a plan could reduce the probability of default by one-third.

Effects on financial intermediaries

The authors are aware of no studies to estimate the effects on lenders of the proposed modifications to manage lending risk. Some effects on lenders can be implied from the effects on borrowers. Any reduction in borrowers' risks also reduces lenders' risks. Results from studies by Patrick (1979a), Stone (1976), Aukes (1980) and by Kent and Lloyd (1983) indicate modest gains in these terms. (Research in progress at the University of Melbourne seems to show considerably greater reductions in default risk, with VAP, than was shown by Aukes [Kent and Lloyd 1983]). Thus such proposals can reduce lending risks of current loan portfolios or could enable lenders to finance higher risk loan applicants without increasing portfolio risk.

Graduated payment plans have been introduced into home mortgage loans to young urban families with expectations of increasing incomes. Insofar as inflation increases nominal incomes of farm mortgage borrowers, then graduated payment plans (GPPs) are also attractive in agriculture; however, the appeal is lessened by the diversion of inflation effects into higher land values. To adopt some form of GPP would partially substitute for ad hoc, informal management of default.

Adoption of FPP or VAP would require fundamental changes in the current practices of farm mortgage lenders. Hearings in Australia led the Industries Assistance Commission to recommend a small scale trial with VAP, despite the objections of the Australian banking community. There, as in the United States, lenders argue that informal measures suffice and that VAP (and presumably FPP) would be too costly and too complex to be feasible.

On the other hand, variable interest rates are now widely accepted in farm lending and trials are in progress with GPPs in nonfarm mortgage lending. Some variations of FPP have been applied to housing loans with variable interest rates. An increase in interest rate is reflected with an increase in length and/or amount of loan rather than an increase in the periodic payment. Similarly, a decreased interest rate shortens the length of loan.

Using FPP to respond to variable interest rates clearly is appealing to both borrower and lender. The borrower is not surprised by changes in debt payments. The lender is assured of a predictable flow of repayments, without change in lending risks. An increased use of GPP, along with variable interest rates, would likely increase the appeal of FPP. In short, FPP provides a method of stabilizing repayment flows that would otherwise be destabilized by variable interest rates.

To apply FPP to the whole amortization commitment would cause repayments to vary with variations in borrowers' net cash flow, producing new cash flow and investment problems for farm mortgage lenders. It is unlikely that this destabilization could be borne by conventional farm mortgage lenders without unacceptable increases in lending costs. It should be recognized however, that repayments also vary under traditional methods of default management.

The VAP with a debt reserve would stabilize repayment flows. Whether it increases adminstrative costs to unacceptable levels is not yet known. The complexity argument is not too plausible either. Lenders and borrowers alike already have dealt with similar complexities when the amortization concept, variable interest rates, GPP in urban home mortgages, and other innovations were adopted. Institutional farm mortgage lenders have preferred to rely on government guarantees for farm mortgage loans rather than developing their own schemes such as VAP, FPP, or GPP. And why not? The guarantee makes the loan riskless to the extent of the guarantee with *no* disturbance in lending procedures. Thus, the ultimate issue is whether to use VAP (or fully applied FPP) or to use public resources to absorb lending risks. The current retraction of government guarantees has generated renewed interest in innovations designed to reduce loan default risk.

For example, conventional repayment plans might be modified by features of a GPP and a VAP. An overloan could provide a reserve at disbursement without adding to the borrower's contractual obligation if the loan is repaid with a GPP. Increments to the reserve could be limited to amounts by which conventional payments exeed GPPs. When GPPs reach the level of conventional payments the accumulated reserves could be applied to the remaining balance, which in turn could be converted to a conventional payment plan.

15

Inflation and monetary risks for agricultural producers

JOHN R. BRAKE

INFLATION AND THE RELATED INSTABILI-
TIES in financial markets have brought new, significant sources of risks for
many types of farmers. The effects of these risks on farmers and lenders
were considered in Chapters 13 and 14. This chapter treats the sources and
relationships among these types of risks in more detail. The concepts of
inflation and its effects on farmers are identified and evaluated. Impacts on
interest rates and credit availability are also considered, along with possible
responses to these risks in public policies and financial institutions.

Concepts of inflation

Inflation is generally defined as an increase in the general level of
prices in an economy. It is measured by an indicator of aggregate prices
such as the consumer price index, the producer price index, or the gross
national product deflator. Sometimes, however, inflation is associated with
the actions that may contribute to changes in price levels. An example is an
increase in the money supply relative to the supply of goods and services.
This action is considered inflationary, even though it is not quickly reflected
in the price indexes. Nonetheless, most economists use the simpler definition of inflation as an increase in the general price level.

John R. Brake, Cornell University.

Economists may also distinguish between demand-pull and cost-push inflation, even though effects of both types of inflation may be present. Demand-pull inflation may occur from increases in demand or from shortages in resources and commodities. Cost-push inflation comes from cost increases that are passed through to consumers. Tweeten and Griffin (1976) suggest that inflation starts with demand-pull and progresses to cost-push. Deficit-financed government spending and other excess demand factors such as commodity or resource shortages could provide the initial impetus, and then inflation continues from cost-push sources. A crop failure, for example, would quickly result in higher prices. These price increases could lead the inflation and raise farm income relative to other income. Then, general inflation in input prices at a later time when crop prices return to lower levels would put farmers into a cost-price squeeze.

In a closed economy with flat-rate income taxes, a doubling of incomes with the same supply of goods and services would cause all prices to increase accordingly. Everyone could buy the same market basket as before and no one would be worse off. In practice, however, inflation brings several adverse effects. As Milton Friedman (1977) observed, inflation leads to inefficiency because prices become a less dependable signal to producers and consumers. Moreover, an unpredictable rate of inflation is itself a source of risk that may be more serious than the actual level of inflation. Inflation also distorts financial markets and investment patterns, as both nominal and real interest rates gyrate with changing economic conditions. Significant redistributions of wealth and income may occur among various economic units because the nominal prices of goods and services, investment values, and tax obligations may change at different, unpredictable rates.

Examples of the differential effects of general inflation are summarized by Starleaf (1980) as follows:

1. Inflation reduces the real incomes of those with fixed incomes and tends to increase the real before-tax incomes of those with nonfixed income
2. Unanticipated increases in inflation reallocate wealth from net monetary creditors to net monetary debtors
3. Inflation imposes a "tax" on money holders and encourages holding less cash and more earning assets
4. With a progressive income tax, inflation increases the government's real tax receipts, thus resulting in greater government spending, smaller fiscal deficits (or larger surpluses), tax rate reductions, or some combination of these events

Tweeten and Griffin (1976) give another view of these effects. They list the gainers from expansion phases of inflation as: (1) bottleneck industries with no reserve capacity or an inelastic supply; (2) industries with highly inelastic own-price demand; (3) industries with a high cross-elasticity of demand for a good with an expanding demand; (4) industries with high income elasticities of demand; (5) industries having negotiated prices or strong unions; (6) net debtors; (7) investors holding nonfinancial assets; (8) the federal government relative to state and local governments and the private sector; (9) marginal workers relative to other workers; and (10) the capitalist relative to the laborer.

Several of these effects reiterate the points made by Starleaf. Agriculture does resemble a bottleneck industry with an inelastic demand for most food products. Overcoming food shortages arising from weather events or other natural phenomena may take time because of the biological nature of production and fairly stable demand characteristics. Moreover, many farmers are net debtors and usually hold more real and durable assets than financial assets.

Price relationships for inputs and outputs

Price relationships between farm commodities and farm inputs are an important factor in evaluating the effects of inflation on agriculture. Kenneth Robinson (1979) has suggested that the price volatility associated with inflation in the 1970s gave opportunities for exceptional gains to farmers who were astute or lucky in choosing when to price their crops. He compared price changes during the 1971 to 1978 period with the inflation conditions of the 1940s and 1960s. In the 1970s, inflation in farm product prices was similar to that of industrial wholesale prices. However, in the 1940s farm product prices rose much more than industrial wholesale prices, and slightly more so in the 1960s. Farm machinery prices increased faster than industrial wholesale prices for all these time periods. Land prices rose faster than industrial prices in the 1970s and faster still in the 1960s. Increases in farm labor costs matched the increase in industrial wholesale prices in the 1970s but increased faster in both the 1940s and the 1960s.

Tweeten and Griffin (1976) also examined the historic effects of inflation on farmers' costs and income positions. They concluded that farm level demand was largely unaffected by national inflation, but farm input prices responded directly to inflation. The fastest annual price increases (6 percent or higher) during the 1964 to 1973 period involved real estate taxes; hired labor; feed, seed, livestock purchases; and machinery and equipment. Thus a 1 percent increase in inflation lowered the ratio of prices received to prices paid by farmers by about 1 percent. In the short run, these inflation effects generally decreased net farm income. In the long run, however, farmers could adjust to these conditions by reducing input purchases. The inelastic demand for farm products would then result in reduced production and higher farm income. The one exception was higher farm real estate taxes, which would depress net farm income in both the short and long run.

Tweeten and Griffin's (1976) simulation of the farm economy for 1980 to 1985 indicated that the higher the general inflation rate, the lower is aggregate net farm income. In a later analysis, Riffe and Tweeten (1977) concluded that inflation might not be a disadvantage to agriculture if exports grew sufficiently fast. If inflation were 6 percent, exports must also grow by 6 percent to maintain real net farm income.

K. R. Robinson (1979) also observed that the inflation effects may differ among commodities. In the 1970s, for example, commodity prices in general were affected by poor crops in the Soviet Union and other countries, freezing U.S. citrus crops, a soybean crop failure in Brazil, a U.S. corn crop failure, and other exogenous forces. These forces contributed to commodity price inflation, although the effects differed among commodities and farm types. Grain producers in the United States tended to gain relative to both livestock feeders and livestock producers. Within the United States, the total net income of North Dakota farmers quadrupled while the net income of New York farmers declined. Hence, the changes among product prices during the 1970s increased income inequality among regions and farm types and hampered size comparison of farms based on the levels of gross sales.

The changing relationships among and between prices of inputs and outputs under conditions of inflation has increased the volatility of farm income and thus increased farmers' risk position. With a demand-pull inflation, farm income may rise more rapidly than nonfarm income. Farmers will bid up land prices and purchase more machinery with larger, better financed farmers often having the superior bidding potential. Then, as cost-push inflation for machinery and other farm inputs follows, farm incomes fall and producers experience a cost-price squeeze. These inflation-induced risks prompt more effective risk management by farmers, as in the case of advance purchases of inputs and hedging or forward contracting. Revisions in farm programs have also mitigated some of the commodity price risks. Target prices and price support levels, for example, have increased over time as inflation increased the costs of production. Also trade embargoes used on occasion have restricted upward price movements.

Inflation, investment choices, and liquidity problems

Inflation has also brought unique effects on farmers' capital investments, especially in farmland, causing cash flow pressures and severe liquidity problems on occasion for farmer and lender alike (Robison and Brake 1980). These problems are especially important for highly leveraged farmers. One liquidity problem occurs because high rates of inflation and growth in returns to farm assets cause a higher portion of a farmer's total returns to occur as unrealized capital gains (especially on farmland) relative to current cash returns (Melichar 1979a). The other liquidity problem arises from differences in the kind of compensation required by lenders and experienced by farmers (Barry 1981b). Lenders require all of their repayment — interest and principal — in cash, of which part is a real return and part is an inflation premium needed to compensate for anticipated loss of purchasing power. The borrowing farmer, however, experiences only part of his return as a current payment; the rest is capital gain. Thus, he experiences a financing gap by having insufficient cash from the asset's early earnings to meet the debt payments (Lee and Rask 1976). This liquidity problem arises even when anticipated inflation actually occurs.

If lenders base borrowing limits on the farmer's expected income, as is typically the case, then lending limits are more restrictive with higher inflation. As a result, the firm's growth in real equity is reduced even though profitable investment opportunities may exist. Borrowers who obtain fixed rate loans when inflation is underanticipated will also benefit from inflation. The real value of their debt decreases while their net cash flows and equity increase. Results are similar for durables purchased under inflation, although cash flow limitations are less severe.

Several changes in lender policies could alleviate some of the cash flow problems and windfall gains during rising inflation. Examples include (1) the use of variable interest rate loans, which would eliminate the windfall gains for borrowers when inflation is underanticipated, and (2) developing loan repayment plans that match the debt servicing requirement with an asset's inflation-induced growth in cash flow (see Chapter 14). These financing arrangements would diminish the cash flow shortage and enable borrowers to finance an asset from its own future returns.

In general, the type of asset to hold during inflation is critical. Those investors who hold financial assets with a fixed return suffer during periods of rising inflation. Those holding inflation-sensitive assets, whose returns or capital values increase with the general price level, tend to gain. One characteristic of rapid inflation is a scramble by investors for inflation-responsive investments such as gold, silver, and, at times, land.

Inflation-driven tax increases

Inflation has also eroded farmers' wealth and income positions, increasing the rates of taxation on estate transfers and ordinary income. For U.S. federal estate taxes in particular, the tax legislation remained the same from the mid-1940s until 1976, while inflation rates were increasing substantially. Many farmers found that their estates had grown to levels that were subject to substantial tax obligations but with little capacity for generating easily the funds to pay such taxes. Subsequent legislation has eased the estate tax burden for farmers, although inflation effects are still significant for larger farming operations.

Similarly, inflation has pushed taxpayers into higher federal income tax brackets. Table 15.1 compares federal income taxes for incomes of comparable purchasing power in 1965 and 1980. For the $5,000 level of 1965 income, the total real level of federal income taxes increased by 18 percent in 1980. For $10,000 of 1965 income, the real tax obligation increased 31 percent, and for $25,000 of income, the increase was 60 percent. In 1965, a taxpayer would have paid 11.1 percent of taxable $10,000 income for federal income taxes. The same real income in 1980, $26,243, paid 14.7 percent in federal income taxes. Including social security taxes, the comparable percentages are 12.9 percent in 1965 and 20.7 percent in 1980— a 60.7 percent increase.

The combination of inflation and a progressive federal income tax structure makes it more difficult to acquire a farm unit. Suppose that in 1970 an efficient-sized farm unit for one operator was valued at $200,000. To borrow the entire amount at age 20 and repay the principal by age 60 would have required $5,000 of after-tax income per year. That amount would remain after paying for family living and income taxes from a $17,000 annual income. From 1970 to 1980, consumer prices increased by slightly over two times. Projecting a 10 percent annual rate of inflation from 1980 to 1990, the $200,000 1970 farm unit would be valued at about

Table 15.1. Comparable purchasing power incomes and federal income taxes for a 4-person family, married filing jointly, 1965 and 1980

	Dollar income level				
1965 income	5,000	10,000	15,000	20,000	25,000
"Same" 1980 inc.[a]	13,122	26,243	39,365	52,487	65,608
1965 federal income taxes	290	1114	2172	3428	4892
"Same" 1980 tax[b]	761	2923	5700	8996	12,838
Actual 1980 tax	904	3845	8233	14,037	20,546
Tax incr.	143	922	2533	5041	7708
(% tax incr.)	18.8%	31.5%	44.4%	56.0%	60.0%
	Percentages				
Marginal tax	16	19	22	28	32
Marginal tax	18	28	43	49	54
Avg. tax '65	5.8	11.1	14.5	17.1	19.6
Avg. tax '80	6.9	14.7	20.9	26.7	31.3

[a]Adjusted for change in CPI.
[b]1965 tax adjusted by CPI.

$1,050,000 in 1990. Repayment of principal in equal amounts over 40 years would require over $26,000 per year after taxes. But, to retain $26,000 after family living expenses and federal income taxes would require a before-tax annual income of $153,000 based on 1980 tax rates. The income requirement would be higher still if interest payments were included.

Tax legislation in the United States during the early 1980s has provided relief for tax obligations on smaller estates, has generally reduced the schedule of income tax rates, and has established procedures for indexing the federal income tax structure to inflation. However, the reductions in income tax rates for most taxpayers are offset in part by the increases in social security taxes required to keep the social security system solvent. Clearly, tax matters will continue to pose important sources of risk for farmers and other investors.

Inflation and interest rates

Changes in inflation create additional sources of risk for farmers due to swings in interest rates and possible loss of credit availability. In a well-functioning market, the lender and saver expect to earn a real rate of return. Thus, the nominal interest rate is expected to exceed the rate of inflation. However, for many years interest rates on various forms of savings were subject to legal rate ceilings that sometimes fell below the inflation rate. In addition, usury laws have restricted lending rates that could be charged borrowers. These restrictions led to swings in credit availability for some farmers, caused by disintermediation in depository institutions as savers sought higher returns.

The recent trend toward deregulation in financial markets has allowed interest rates on savings and borrowings to match market levels more closely. In this new environment, market rates are set by supply and demand for funds, by monetary and fiscal policies, and by the general state of the economy. While real interest rates are relatively stable over time, changes in monthly inflation rates, in monetary or fiscal policy, in loan demands, or similar factors can destabilize nominal and real interest rates within relatively short time periods. Monthly changes in inflation rates in turn change the emphasis and severity of monetary policies. Methods of implementing policies may also change, as in late 1979 when the U.S. Federal Reserve announced a change in focus from targets on interest rates to targets on the rate of growth of the money supply. Instability in financial markets sometimes results because monetary and fiscal policies are at odds.

Interest rate risk may significantly influence the costs of borrowing as well as the values of assets with fixed income streams. In the first case interest rates may change after the loan commitment occurs. If market interest rates change, one party to the loan transaction loses and the other gains depending on the direction of change.

The increasing costs of credit to borrowers were particularly severe in 1980 and 1981. The prime rates of major commercial banks and other money market rates reached new highs. As Melichar (1979b) explained, with the fixed-rate lending of the 1950s and before, borrowers were insulated from changes in interest rates on their previous debt commitments. Such rate changes were borne primarily by the financial sector where, for commercial banks, the cost of funds was constrained by rate ceilings on deposits.

In the 1980s the removal of most interest rate ceilings has contributed to higher costs of funds and much greater rate volatility. The risk that rates will change after a loan commitment has occurred is much greater due to lenders' use of variable or floating interest rates. This practice transfers interest rate risk to the borrower. In turn, depository institutions can retain loanable funds by paying market rates on savings. Lenders not using variable interest rates utilize other ways to cope with this risk. Matching maturities on selected types of assets and liabilities is one method, as is shortening maturities on loans.

The trend toward higher market interest rates, along with deregulation, has substantially increased farm loan rates. The Federal Reserve quarterly survey of bank loans to farmers showed that the modal interest rate increased from the 8 to 10 percent range in February 1977 to the 16 to 17 percent range in February 1981 and then to the 13 to 14 percent range in 1983 (Melichar and Balides 1981).

The Cooperative Farm Credit System changed completely from fixed interest rate lending to variable rate lending, thus shifting interest rate risk almost completely to farmers. For perspective, from January 1979 to January 1980 the interest cost facing farmers on Production Credit Association (PCA) loans increased almost 40 percent. From 1979 to 1980 the percentage increase in interest rates exceeded the cost increases for all other farm inputs except fuel.

The substantial increase in interest costs to farmers brought considerable concern about farmers' ability to meet debt obligations. Ruttan observed that the ratio of debt service costs to earnings on farm assets exceeded the heights that preceded the land market crash of the early 1920s. This high debt service to earnings ratio would be less serious if interest rates were in the traditional 4 to 6 percent range. But with much higher rates a modest decline in cash flow could have serious repercussions for farmers and their lenders.

The effects of interest rate changes on values of assets with fixed income streams concern investors and lenders alike. Under volatile rate conditions, investors prefer investments whose income streams are responsive to inflation so that asset values will be more stable. The volatile, higher rates of recent times have adversely affected many financial institutions too, and brought adjustments in their portfolios and pricing policies to counter the problems of disintermediation and liquidity cited above. Much more of their sources of funds are now sensitive to variations in market interest rates.

Inflation and credit availability

The relationships cited above among inflation, market interest rates, and regulations on rate ceilings have also combined in the past to destabilize the availability of credit from some lenders, especially commercial banks and life insurance companies. One indicator of fund availability from agricultural banks is their loan-to-deposit ratio. For all agricultural banks, the loan-to-deposit ratios in 1980 were substantially higher than was true 5 to 10 years before, thus indicating lower liquidity and reduced fund availability. As Melichar (1980) points out, the availability of farm loan funds depends on farm type and location and is strongly influenced by local farm income conditions. Still, Melichar (1979b) concluded that past credit crunches impacted agriculture primarily in terms of higher cost rather than curtailment of credit.

Agricultural banks mainly meet new farm loan demands through growth in deposits from their local markets. They do not, in general, have access to the national financial market. Borrowing from correspondent banks or using the seasonal borrowing privilege at the Federal Reserve banks are ways to obtain nonlocal sources of funds. However, use of correspondent banks has not been particularly helpful to rural banks; correspondents may not well understand agricultural conditions and the borrowing can be rather expensive for the rural bank. Also, the seasonal borrowing privilege appears to be underutilized.

The Depository Institutions Acts of 1980 and 1982 have brought important changes to financial markets in the United States. This legislation provided for the phase out of deposit interest rate ceilings, more liberal lending authority for thrift institutions, preemption of state usury limits, reduction in reserve requirements, as well as many other provisions. The legislation should enable commercial banks to compete more equitably for local sources of funds. Costs of these funds, however, will be higher and more volatile, which will bring continued and perhaps increased volatility to interest rates on farm loans. For agricultural producers, however, the increased rate risk should be offset in part by decreased risk of fund availability from rural banks.

Another method for rural banks to acquire nonlocal sources of funds is through loan participations with PCAs. Banks and PCAs are traditionally regarded as major competitors in farm lending; however, the Cooperative Farm Credit System (FCS) has access to funds from the nation's money markets if they are willing to pay the market price. Thus rural banks' use of FCS as a source of funds provides access to the national credit markets.

While the FCS does have access to nonlocal funds, elements of credit restraint may still occur during high interest rate periods. In 1980 during the period of credit controls implemented by the Federal Reserve System, several, if not all, of the district Federal Land banks added substantial closing costs to their farm loans. In one farm credit district the closing cost of farm real estate loans was for a time 5 percent of the loan amount. This may have had some dampening effect on the land market, as desired, but it may also have hindered some timely and appropriate purchases for farm enlargement. Further, it may have limited some young people from entering farming and prevented some farmers from retiring.

Another facet of credit availability is potential restrictions on the FCS's access to money markets. During the late 1960s, attempts to limit FCS access to money markets were based on their inclusion as an agency in the federal budget. Their net borrowing was considered to contribute to the deficit government budget. FCS borrowing is no longer considered a budget activity, but some observers and government people still believe that the agency status of their bonds and notes should be removed.

Availability of credit to agriculture will continue to be important in the future. A USDA staff report, for example, projects farm debt rising to $605 billion by 1990, with the potential under some assumptions for reaching $1 trillion. Those figures are three to five times the 1981 levels. They indicate farmers' heavy reliance on borrowed funds and their vulnerability to swings in the cost and availability of credit that are attributed in part to inflation.

Public responses to inflation and risk

Concerns about inflation tend to be time related. In the late 1970s and early 1980s, inflation was a major concern for agricultural producers. Inflation came, in part, from oil price increases that were passed through to consumers and permeated costs throughout the economy. Also, government deficits, price increases from energy shocks, and wage increases were monetized to a substantial extent by the Federal Reserve System.

The kit of policy alternatives for dealing with inflation is fairly well known. It includes: (1) slower expansion of the money supply by the Federal Reserve, (2) fiscal policy to decrease the federal deficit, (3) decreasing the power and/or ability of labor and other factor owners to obtain pay increases, and (4) diminishing the contribution to inflation arising from the structure of the tax system. While the policy alternatives are known, implementation of the policies sometimes lags because of the political nature of the decision process.

As several policy alternatives for dealing with inflation were implemented in 1981–82, inflation was reduced substantially, but at the cost of increased unemployment and a severe recession. The recession increased social expenditures for welfare and related items of the budget at the same time that tax rate reductions and decreased employment led to lower government revenues. While the inflation rate fell, the negative aspects of controlling inflation became a primary focus of concern, and pressures built to create jobs, expand the money supply, lower interest rates, and initiate an economic recovery.

The changing public responses to inflation, unemployment, budget deficits, etc., create risks for producers. This chapter has discussed risks arising from inflation and risks arising from unanticipated changes in the rate of inflation. It should be recognized, also, that courses of action taken by producers to deal with expected inflation can be very risky when the inflation rate decreases substantially from its expected level. Substantially lower inflation rates of 1982–83 and lower farm product prices contributed to lower asset values in the farm sector and resulted in increased bankruptcies and foreclosures among producers who were not financially prepared for the reversal in inflation rates.

Hence, perhaps a substantial part of the risk producers face results first from public responses to inflation and then later from the side effects of policies to control inflation. If those policies to control inflation are effective, they in turn create risks of a different nature from those implicit in inflation. The changing nature and effectiveness of public policies bring about unanticipated deviations from expected inflation rates. These are a major risk for agricultural producers.

PART 4

Policy issues and agricultural risk

16

Agricultural
policy and risk

BRUCE L. GARDNER, RICHARD E. JUST, RANDALL A. KRAMER, AND RULON D. POPE

> The rationale for public intervention in agricultural commodity markets is, and will continue to be, essentially similar to the rationale for setting rates and regulating output in the public utility and transportation industries, that is, to lend stability to an industry which technological and economic forces would render chronically unstable in the absence of such intervention. (Ruttan 1969)

AT LEAST SINCE THE BOOKS by Schultz (1945) and Johnson (1947) stabilization has been a central concept in the discussion of agricultural policy. As farm policy evolved, the concepts of stability, variability, and risk have played a significant role in rationalizing governmental intervention and in the practical realm of political action and policy formulation. But these concepts are understood somewhat differently in these two arenas (and somewhat vaguely in both). Thus, we must delineate and analyze these concepts and the different targets and instruments that comprise the stabilization umbrella.

The basic theoretical argument is that public policies that reduce societal risk can generate Pareto improvements if market participants are risk averse, where risk is associated with the expected value and dispersion

Bruce L. Gardner, University of Maryland; **Richard E. Just,** University of California-Berkeley; **Randall A. Kramer,** Virginia Polytechnic Institute and State University; and **Rulon D. Pope,** Brigham Young University.

(somehow defined) of producers' returns (Blandford and Currie 1975). Many Pareto-improving policies would be expected to function analogously to insurance, in reducing dispersion of returns at the cost of reducing farmers' expected or average returns. Viewed in terms of practical politics, however, a farm program that reduced average prices or returns would be an abject failure.

Nonetheless, all price-support programs and other government interventions in agriculture occur in a risky setting. They inevitably affect the probability distributions for farm returns and consumer prices. Since these distributions affect economic welfare, analysts must consider how policy influences economic welfare in a random world. Moreover, the economic outcomes of these policies may induce further changes in policy. Thus, feedback effects are important conceptual and empirical considerations in policy analysis.

In this chapter we consider the relationships between farm policy and risks in the markets for farm commodities and factors of production. We focus on commodity prices, output, farm income, and factor prices in an uncertain environment. We describe the relevant policies, present pertinent data, review the literature, and consider various policy impacts. International forces are considered as are the risks of unanticipated changes in policy.

Domestic U.S. commodity programs and risk

The rationale cited above for agricultural policy was not always clear. At odds were the concepts of stable prices and levels of prices that provided an appropriate return or purchasing power to farmers. The latter concept is exemplified by the quest for parity that followed the post-World War I collapse of agricultural prices. In the 1920s a series of legislative proposals under the McNary-Haugen plan were submitted to Congress. These met defeat at the urging of President Hoover who feared the plans would: (1) create uncontrolled inflation in food prices and corresponding inflationary demands for higher wages by organized labor; (2) encourage overproduction similar to wartime conditions; (3) mostly benefit the large farmers rather than the small, traditionally independent and stubborn farmers and possibly produce oligopolistic control of the industry; and (4) prompt other industries to also seek direct aid from the federal government (Wilson 1977).

However, President Hoover created a Farm Board under the Agricultural Marketing Act of 1929, which moderated the downturn in prices by purchasing farm commodities. As the Great Depression progressed, the board found itself becoming the major owner of wheat supplies.

The Roosevelt administration abolished the board, and the Agricultural Adjustment Act of 1933 (AAA) was passed within three months of Roosevelt's inauguration. Its goal was to achieve parity prices by paying farmers for voluntary acreage reductions, on-farm storage, and government purchase and disposal of some livestock. Marketing agreements between producers and handlers were supported, and a tax on processors was introduced.

An important stabilization feature of the AAA was the price band concept for managing commodity inventories. However, the initial "ever-normal granary" programs did not explicitly state a price ceiling for stock release. The Commodity Credit Corporation (CCC) was established in 1933 to provide nonrecourse loans to cotton and corn farmers. The farmer could store his crop and receive a price support loan from the CCC. When the market price was lower than the loan rate, the crop could be turned over to the CCC to meet the loan obligation. As prices rose above the loan rate, the farmer could repay the loan and sell his crop.

Distinguishing the price effects of the AAA from the effects of drought in 1934 and 1936 is difficult; nonetheless some analysts believed the AAA achieved the purpose of raising farm income (Tweeten 1979). However, the acreage controls, processing tax, and other provisions of the AAA were struck down by the U.S. Supreme Court. Acreage controls were reestablished under the Soil and Conservation Act of 1936 in which farmers received direct payments for soil conservation and building practices. Thus acreage diversion was maintained. From a risk perspective, diverted acreage provided a certain return. However, an uncertain opportunity cost of diversion placed the decision in a portfolio framework with certain returns for some activities and random returns for others. Whether the act reduced total supply is unclear (Davis 1949).

The Agricultural Adjustment Act of 1938, prompted by volatile production, established all risk crop insurance for wheat producers. Participation in the program was low, however, even though indemnities paid out exceeded the aggregate premiums. The 1938 AAA continued diversion controls and established demand expansion programs such as food stamps and school lunches. Marketing quotas and acreage controls reduced the planted acreages of corn, wheat, cotton, and tobacco.

Wartime farm policy shifted away from concern over depressed prices as demand-induced price enhancement caused by the war dominated the commodity markets. In turn, the early postwar policies responded again to the effects of reduced demand and depressed price conditions.

In the 1950s the Soil Bank concept created by the Agricultural Act of 1956 encouraged supply management and acreage diversion. Demand was expanded through Public Law 480 (1954) aid to foreign countries. However, under the Agricultural Act of 1958, mandatory price supports at 75 to 90 percent of parity along with ineffective acreage controls led to the accumulation of very large stocks. Consequently, the Kennedy administration in the 1960s encouraged demand expansion and acreage controls. Under the Wheat-Cotton Act of 1964, for example, only farmers who complied with acreage controls and voluntary diversion programs were eligible for price supports and diversion payments.

The 1970s were characterized by growing foreign demand and volatile prices of farm commodities. Marketing quotas and acreage allotments ended for cotton, feed grain, and wheat farms. Target prices became the primary means of establishing price supports. Farmers who set aside prescribed portions of their acreage were eligible for support payments limited to $55,000 per farmer for cotton, rice, wheat, and feed grains, respectively. At the same time, the real price support levels were reduced for the major commodities, except for dairy products. Disaster payments were also authorized for prevented plantings and low yields, and other types of emergency loan programs were created.

The legislation in effect in 1980 (Food and Agricultural Act of 1977) continued the target price, loan rate, and disaster payment provisions. Deficiency payments were based on the higher of the differences between the target price and the average national market price or the loan rate for farmers enrolling in the program. Higher deficiency payments occurred for farmers who voluntarily set aside additional acreage.

Commodity policy in the 1980s has put more emphasis on supply management, including the release of stocks through the CCC. All risk crop insurance has replaced the disaster payment program. But commodity prices were low in the early 1980s, and interest continued in support mechanisms, including innovative arrangements like the Payment-In-Kind (commodity) program that would reduce government stocks and eventually lower taxpayer costs. Future discussions on legislation will likely focus on the level rather than the variability of farmers' expected income. However, the Reagan administration seems committed to acreage set aside as a means of increasing price and reducing government outlays.

FARM PROGRAMS AND PRICE DISTRIBUTIONS. The impact of a government program on the distribution of market prices depends on the type of price support intervention. In the United States, farm programs have intervened in four ways: (1) production controls, (2) CCC loans and purchases with resale on the market, (3) CCC loans and purchases with noncommercial disposal through domestic or international food aid, and (4) direct payments to farmers in low price years.

Production controls through acreage set asides or allotments result in expectations of lower output and higher market prices. The effects on expected income depend on the expected elasticity of demand. If demand is stable and inelastic, then farmers' expected revenue increases. However, effects on the dispersion of the price distribution are unclear. Price variability depends on the structural components of supply and demand, which are usually measured on the basis of *ex post* conditions. In a static world, the *ex ante* and *ex post* probability distributions should be closely correlated. Over time, however, the short-run relationships between these distributions are more remote.

These effects may be reenforced when nonrestricted crops are part of the farmer's choice set. Uncontrollable crops may be more attractive because of greater income stability on controlled crops, the set aside, and other cross-supply effects. The supply effect is complicated because the controlled crop experiences reduced acreage and a price distribution with a higher mean and a reduced variance. Thus the net effects of the program on alternative crops and on general equilibrium are ambiguous a priori.

CCC loans and purchases with market resale involve a pure stabilization program; stocks removed from the market on one occasion are resold at another. Thus, ignoring dynamics, a first approximation to expected price is unchanged by the program. However, second-order effects involving a supply response to a change in price dispersion may occur for two reasons. First, unless the demand elasticity is unity, the total market revenue function is nonlinear, so that a change in price dispersion changes mean revenue. Second, risk averse farmers will increase their production when the price dispersion is reduced.

When direct (or deficiency) payments are part of the program, their effects are to increase the producers' expected returns and encourage output expansion. These factors reduce the expected market price but increase individual farmer's expected price, including the payment provision.

In summary, a price support program for wheat at, say, $3.50/bu when the expected market price is $4.00 will reduce the dispersion of farm prices and increase farmers' expected price. However, it may reduce, increase, or not change expected output and hence the market price, depending on the type of government intervention. Also, general equilibrium adjustments in nonsupported commodities further complicate the stabilization of farm prices and incomes.

Price supports via CCC loans or purchases truncate the left tail of the probability distribution of prices by putting a floor under a commodity's market price. Expected revenue per unit of production thus increases. For given cost and production, the truncated return dominates the nonsupported distribution by the first degree. Thus, all producers will prefer this program even if the support price is below the preprogram average price, or below cost of production, however measured.

The effects on market prices of CCC acquisitions with noncommercial disposal fall between the effects of production controls and direct payments. To the extent that the disposal does not displace regular commercial demand, the program increases expected market price just as if the product were not produced. When the disposal does replace commercial demand, the program creates a consumption subsidy analogous to direct payments.

FARM PRICES. This review of U.S. farm programs has identified numerous policy mechanisms, as well as variations and combinations too complex to cite here. For example, the AAA programs in which farmers received payments for agreeing to plow under crops combined the production-control and direct payment approaches. No program type has been used exclusively for enough seasons to generate a large number of output and price observations. Therefore, it is not possible to estimate with much confidence the variances or other properties of price distributions generated by these farm programs. However, taking the major periods of government intervention as a whole gives some idea of the likely effects of past policies on price variability.

The time series of the USDA index of prices received by farmers for all crops is shown in Fig. 16.1, along with an index of support prices. These data do not clearly indicate the influence of government programs on the

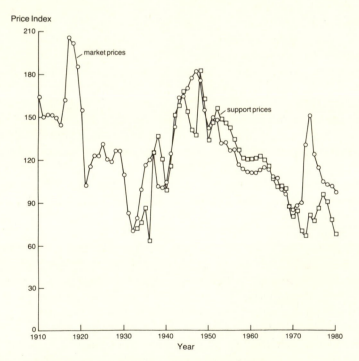

FIG. 16.1. Prices received by farmers and support price index.

level or variability of farm prices. A counterfactual data series would be needed for the prices without support policies. However, contrary to the prevailing belief, the data indicate that price movements are not dominated by random fluctuations in yearly output. Even though the year-to-year movements of prices are smoother in the 1960s than the 1920s, for example, the significant swings in prices are associated with wars, recessions, or other low frequency events. The lower frequency swings in prices appear less pronounced in the intervention era (post 1933) than prior to it, but instability for prices in aggregate and for individual commodities has by no means been eliminated. Thus, the stabilizing role of CCC loans and storage appears less important than is sometimes asserted.

Even when the effects of variability are well estimated, we are still far from having a good estimate of the policy effects on risk. One factor is the anticipation of changes in prices and returns. Risk involves random deviations from expectations, so variability around some measure of expectations is needed. Another important aspect is the distinction between *nondiversifiable* and *diversifiable* risk. Diversifiable risk is eliminated in principle by an infinitely large portfolio of production and investment activities. Thus, we cannot base a farmer's reduction in risk due to a farm program solely on the reduction in variance of expected returns, as if the farmer's only economic activity was producing the crop in question.

FARM INCOME VARIABILITY AND FARM PROGRAMS. Price supports may stabilize farm prices but be less effective in stabilizing farm income. If, for example, price variability resulted entirely from random fluctuations in domestic output, and demand was elastic, the low-price years would be the high-income years. Price support mechanisms without direct payments would increase income variability. Thus some farmers might prefer the program due to increased mean income despite the increased variance of income. Generally, the rise in prices when crops fail tends to buffer farm incomes.

A priori judgments about the influence of farm programs on farm income variability are more complex and conjectural than for the price effects. Even simple hedging has substantially different effects on income variability than on price variability (McKinnon 1967).

The impacts of farm programs on prices and total farm income are evaluated by examining market or aggregate impacts, although these impacts are complex and ever changing. More comprehensive research on these aggregate impacts is needed. A fruitful analytical approach at the farm level is to tailor national price effects to local conditions and incorporate program detail in models of farm choice (Musser and Stamoulis 1981; Richardson and Nixon 1981). Most simulation models of farm firms are normative and suggest possible microimpacts. However, if they fail to validate their predictions and ignore macroadjustments such as land rents, entry and exit pressures, and capital flows, the model results will have little significance for aggregative analysis.

We briefly consider some historical evidence on farm programs and income variability by visually appraising the variation of aggregate farm income under different policy regimes. The time series of USDA's estimate of real net farm income is shown in Fig. 16.2. The yearly as well as longer term stability of income appears to increase in the 1950s and 1960s compared to the 1920s, unlike the case of prices. Of course, this could arise from factors other than commodity programs, such as macroeconomic stabilization policy (Firch 1964) or closer integration of farm and nonfarm factor markets in the post-World War II period.

Farm programs should be better able to jointly stabilize farm incomes and prices through support payments to farmers. The payments mechanism changes the long-term balance of supply and demand in a way that price-stabilizing storage does not. Expected farm returns are increased and subjective variance decreases. Greater production on average keeps the pro-

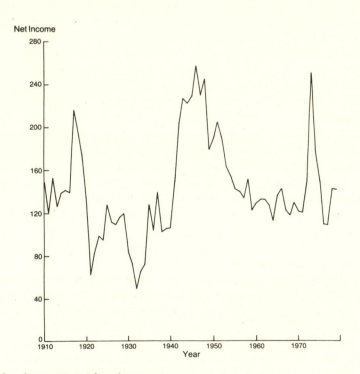

FIG. 16.2.   Aggregate net farm income.

ducer's price (including payments) at a given support level more of the time, thus stabilizing producer prices. However, prices paid by consumers are not necessarily stabilized by a program of direct payments, although consumer prices can be stabilized by CCC stock operations.

COMMODITY STORAGE AND STABILIZATION. As Fig. 16.1 shows, the real level of protection for farm commodity prices has fallen substantially in the post-World War II period. Although the political rhetoric has always emphasized stabilization as a policy goal (at least when speaking to nonfarm groups), recent evidence indicates policy has become more oriented toward stabilization than price support. The best example of this development is the Farmer-Owned-Reserve (FOR) Program, introduced in the Food and Agriculture Act of 1977, covering corn, rice, wheat, sorghum, barley, and oats.

The FOR has two notable features for price stabilization. First, the FOR uses both a support (or floor) price for covered commodities and trigger prices for stock release; the latter is a new development. The second feature is subsidy payments to farmers for storage, rather than storage by a governmental agency. The payments, as well as interest-rate subsidies on CCC loans are tied to the trigger prices. At a lower trigger price, called the *release* price (125 to 140 percent of the floor price), the storage payments cease; at a higher price, called the *call* price, the farmer must repay his CCC loan. However, the farmer need not sell his grain. Thus, the government has less control over stocks in this program compared to direct purchase and sale of the stocks at the trigger prices.

This stabilization program induces increased demand for grain when prices are low and increased market supply when prices are high. The program's cost effectiveness and stabilization capacity are interesting, difficult, and unresolved empirical issues. The main question is how much FOR-subsidized stocks would replace farmers' own intended storage.

Although the FOR program may have price-supporting effects when the initial stocks are acquired, no strong effects on long-term average market prices should occur since every bushel stored returns later to the market. This situation differs from the earlier CCC programs with noncommercial disposition of large stocks (equivalent to consumption subsidies). The traditional price-support programs truncated the lower tail of the price distribution and apparently raised long-term prices. The FOR attempts to truncate both ends of the price distribution to achieve stabilization without strong subsidies. Empirical analysis of the FOR depends crucially on distinguishing the risk response from other factors affecting production and prices. Empirical analyses of price-support programs, by contrast, have focused mainly on the mean price or revenue effects.

Models of risk considerations in
domestic agricultural policy.

Agricultural policy models and analyses have mostly ignored the risk considerations identified above. Such models were useful in determining the primary effects of many policies when government programs acted essentially as support mechanisms. For example, the primary effects of the old Cochrane and Brannan plans could be understood with a simple nonstochastic market model. But the policy shift toward stabilization, relative to support, has given emphasis to the risk components of these models.

The first market model of instability, introduced by Waugh in 1944, basically showed that consumers with a stable demand curve would favor price instability based on consumer surplus calculations. Oi (1961) showed the same result for producers using the concept of producer surplus. Massell (1969) and Samuelson (1972) then showed how these models suggest the peculiar result that both producers and consumers prefer instability. Massell showed that these results cannot hold simultaneously for both consumers and producers in a market model, and that instability causes a net reduction in welfare. Consumers tend to gain if instability originates with producers, producers tend to gain if instability originates with consumers, and the gains outweigh the losses of the other group in each case.

Massell's results are based on assumptions of linearity of supply and demand with additive disturbances in each. Turnovsky (1974) later generalized the Massell model by considering nonlinear supply and demand relationships and multiplicative disturbances. His results support the conclusion that one market group cannot gain more from instability than another market group loses. However, he shows that the group where the instability originates can gain from the instability if relationships are sufficiently nonlinear or if the multiplicative disturbances are sufficiently strong.

These concepts were applied in a number of studies to empirically evaluate the welfare effects of potential stabilization policies for agricultural prices. The basic approach is to estimate supply and demand along with their variability and then use the concepts of producer and consumer surplus to evaluate expected welfare under alternative policies. Models by Sharples et al. (1976) and Helmburger and Weaver (1977) are basically applications of the Massell framework. The model estimated by Just and Hallam (1978) applies the more general nonlinear framework of Turnovsky. These empirical studies confirm the theoretical results and show that net welfare gains can be achieved through government stabilization programs for grain prices. Some studies estimate that the potential gains are substantial.

While these models have important implications for analyzing price stabilization, they ignore some crucial risk aspects. The assumptions are equivalent to certainty, implying that any instability is perfectly anticipated, so that decision makers can react along their *ex ante* supply or demand relationships. *Thus, these are models of instability with certainty rather than models of risk.* Random prices, however, are rarely known with certainty; at best, a producer may only have some idea of the price distribution for his output when production decisions are made. When these conditions are considered, a risk averse firm will have the same expected welfare under instability as if prices are stabilized at their mean, assuming price and yield are uncorrelated.

Also, as suggested by the work of Tisdell (1963) and Hazell and Scandizzo (1975), the expected welfare benefits under uncertainty are not generally the ones realized by producers. A producer may anticipate an *ex ante* benefit from production based on his subjective distribution of prices (and yields); however, his actual *ex post* benefits from production will be associated with a particular price (yield) from that distribution. Which welfare quantity should policy makers consider in formulating agricultural policy? If each producer formulates a price distribution that is independent of the effect of his production (which is the usual competitive assumption), then producers' expected *ex ante* surplus does not reflect the likely well being of producers in an *ex post* sense. When individual producers perceive no correlation between their production and price, the aggregate of all producers, or the industry, also behaves as though the correlation of production and price is zero.

A policy maker who realizes these aggregate relationships can thus consider whether to formulate policy according to what producers say they want (*ex ante* surplus) or according to what the policy maker believes is in the producers' best interest (expected *ex post* surplus). In any case, these arguments suggest a closer examination of risk issues in agricultural policy, especially under the highly random nature of farm production and prices. The general equilibrium aspects of stabilization under risk for both consumers and producers are involved (Newbury and Stiglitz 1979).

Work has been undertaken only recently to incorporate the aggregate effects of risk aversion in empirical analyses. At present, the feasible empirical approaches are the programming approach of Hazell and Scandizzo (1975) and the econometric approaches suggested by Chavas and Pope (1981), Pope et al. (1982), and Just et al. (1982, Chap. 11, App. A, C). As argued by Just (1975b), the explicit consideration of risk effects is crucial in examining agricultural policies designed to deal with risk. For example, if producers are risk averse, then a reduction in price instability through a buffer-stock policy will increase production more than suggested by risk neutrality. Therefore, a buffer-stock policy designed to be self-liquidating under risk neutrality would lead to overaccumulation of stocks and ultimate failure of the policy.

As yet, however, these empirical approaches have been utilized in only a few studies. For example, Gray et al. (1954) considered the effects of potato price supports, concluding:

> The price-support program created an unlimited market for potatoes at approximately the average price (in relation to parity) which had prevailed for 30 years and virtually eliminated the risk of very low prices. . . . The response to the program was immediate and of such a magnitude as to be unmistakable. . . . The expansion occurred through production adjustments induced by— motivated by—the greater price certainty. (Cochrane and Ryan 1976, 375)

However, this study did not separate the effects of reduced risk from the effects of higher expected price when the price distribution was truncated by the support program.

Most econometric models of risk response have regressed acreage on variables representing the expected level and variability of price or returns per acre (Just 1974). Using this approach and the economic welfare evaluation suggested by Pope et al. (1982) and Just et al. (1982), Just and Hallam (1978) estimated that risk responses by wheat producers increased the benefits from price stabilization for consumers about fivefold compared to results for the same model without risk response. This is due to a rightward shift in supply owing to risk response and a related decline in price levels along the demand curve. Nevertheless, producers gain sufficient benefits from reduced risk to approximately offset losses from reduced prices.

Nelson (1975), Ryan (1977), and Traill (1976) used similar acreage response models. However, these models have focused on the risk responses of farmers' decisions and not on the risk effects of agricultural policy. Each of these studies attempted to relate acreage response to risks associated with price, yield, or gross revenue. Although risk was measured or estimated in various ways, each study considered a conceptual model in which *ex ante* decisions respond to risks as modified by government policies. However, alternative interpretations may also exist for the observed risk responses (Pope et al. 1982; Newbury and Stiglitz 1979). When alternative explanations arise, the appropriate methodology for modeling and analyzing policy-induced responses to risk has not been resolved.

Another policy issue is how government-induced risk reduction affects the structure of agriculture (Gardner 1978; Pope and Gardner 1978). Are small or large farms helped more, or are particular kinds of contracting, marketing, or production promoted? This problem is more difficult to model and analyze than are the policy effects discussed above. The choice of variables that influence farm size or marketing strategies is a largely unresolved issue. Although numerous authors have suggested possible relationships between farm structure (e.g., farm size) and risk, little empirical work has applied these constructs. For example, there is no econometric evidence linking commodity programs with farm growth. The microgrowth analyses are based on firm rather than market-level models that require further generalization (e.g., Richardson and Condra 1981).

Input and production assistance programs related to risk

Besides the commodity stabilization and support policies considered above, the government also uses various input and production assistance programs to influence farmers' risk and liquidity positions. In this section, we consider programs affecting farm credit, insurance, and water availability.

SUBSIDIZED CREDIT. The federal government provides subsidized loans to farmers through the Farmers Home Administration (FmHA) and the CCC. (The Small Business Administration was briefly involved in agricultural loans in the 1970s. Further, the federal government supervises the Farm Credit System [FCS]. The FCS was originally capitalized by the federal government, but it is now a member-owned cooperative. It includes [1] the Federal Land banks and Federal Land Bank associations, [2] the Federal Intermediate Credit banks and Production Credit associations, and [3] the banks for cooperatives.) These credit services are probably more extensive than those offered to any other sector of the economy; they were initiated in response to perceived gaps in credit availability for rural areas and as part of the commodity programs discussed above.

The CCC primarily provides inventory financing for crops covered by the farm commodity programs, although some financing has been available for storage facilities and equipment. Inventory financing is a liquidity feature of the more general price-stabilization goal. In contrast, FmHA loans are designed for farmers who cannot obtain credit from commercial sources or who have experienced severe distresses due to natural disasters or economic emergencies.

In principle, government lending agencies are not intended to compete with private lenders. Farmers desiring credit from the FmHA must demonstrate that they cannot obtain adequate funds on reasonable terms from private lenders. In practice, the private sector's share of farm debt appears to be inversely correlated with the government's share (Barry 1981a). Moreover, the substantial government involvement in farm lending has likely softened the impacts of volatile commodity and financial markets for many farmers.

The FmHA provides various types of loans to agriculture, including ownership loans, operating loans, disaster-emergency loans, and economic emergency loans (USDA 1981). The FmHA makes farm ownership and operating loans directly and also guarantees loans made by commercial lenders. In 1980, FmHA made $1.8 billion of direct ownership and operating loans. The FmHA disaster-emergency loans have been made at low interest rates in designated disaster counties; as a result, political pressure is often exerted to designate areas as disaster counties. In 1977, record crop production occurred in the United States, yet about two-thirds of the nation's counties were designated disaster areas and received $1.2 billion of disaster loans. The Emergency Agricultural Credit Adjustment Act of 1978 authorized the FmHA to provide or guarantee economic emergency loans. Eligibility for these loans was based on either a general tightening of agricultural credit or an unfavorable relationship between production costs and commodity prices. The FmHA loaned $2.27 billion under its emergency loan programs in 1980. This represented 55 percent of its total farm loans, up from 15 percent in 1970. As a result, during this period emergency loan borrowers became the primary FmHA farm clientele (Herr and LaDue 1981). It is likely that FmHA lending will be curtailed in the 1980s as austerity is pursued in government spending.

Emergency credit aids farmers' survival prospects and shifts the probability distribution of net farm cash flow to the right, ceteris paribus. However, if these policies encourage higher leverage and acceptance of greater business risks by farmers, they could lead to greater farm financial risk. In the short run, however, emergency loans should improve farm welfare and not increase risk since they offer a financing alternative in the firm's choice set. The government absorbs greater risk, but consumers enjoy a larger supply of agricultural commodities. Whether public credit programs improve the economic welfare of all sectors (including private lenders) remains an open question (Blandford and Currie 1975; Lee et al. 1981).

In the credit programs of the CCC, regular nonrecourse loans are generally available for the 9- to 11-month period following harvest. Longer term nonrecourse loans are available as part of the farmer-owned reserve. The CCC also offers recourse loans for grain storage and handling facilities. As of September 1980, the CCC had outstanding commodity loans of $3.7 billion and outstanding storage and facility loans of $1.5 billion. Unlike the FmHA programs, CCC loans are not restricted to farmers unable to obtain credit from commercial lenders. As the farm programs changed from high price supports to lower price supports and higher direct payments, the role of the CCC has changed. As Hottel (1981, 73) notes, "the CCC's original purpose of helping to minimize the effects of depressed commodity prices has been deemphasized as the program has shifted to the financing aspects of crop inventories."

One obvious effect of subsidized credit is lower costs of borrowing. These programs have also increased the supply of credit, particularly to limited-resource farmers. Thus, the programs have likely tended to increase output and lower expected output price.

Research on the risk effects of credit programs is lacking, but some conjectures can be made. For the direct loan programs, subsidized interest rates reduce the repayment levels for a given amount of debt. The reductions in repayment obligations in turn reduce the variability of farmers' net cash flows (Gabriel and Baker 1980). Thus, one could argue that subsidized lending reduces the financial risk of farmers.

The emergency loan programs specifically respond to the adverse impacts of production and market risk on producers by shifting risk bearing to the government. The low-cost loans are designed to help farmers recover more easily from a bad crop or price year. These programs have provided valuable liquidity to producers in adverse times. They may also have a stabilizing impact on production if the affected farmers would have curtailed production in the absence of emergency loans. However, the emergency loan programs may also discourage the development of other risk management strategies: reducing the incentives for holding financial reserves, maintaining credit reserves, diversification, hedging, forward contracting, and crop insurance.

SUBSIDIZED PRODUCTION INSURANCE: DISASTER PAYMENTS PROGRAM. The Agriculture and Consumer Protection Act of 1975 and the Rice Production Act of 1975 established the disaster payments program to compensate farmers for prevented plantings and unusually low yields due to natural disaster, adverse weather, and other conditions beyond a producer's control. The program only covered wheat, barley, corn, sorghum, rice, and cotton. The 1977 act continued this program with payment levels based on a proportion of the target price. Farmers participating in the price and income support programs were eligible for payments. Total disaster payments for 1974-79 were $2.45 billion.

Several objections to the disaster payments program have been raised. The program represents a free insurance program for farmers who comply with the price and income support programs. Hence, it was more expensive for taxpayers than crop insurance. The program also tends to encourage production in high risk areas: "A producer can collect year after year, producing in areas and by methods that would be uneconomical without the program, and remain uneconomical from the point of view of efficient use of the Nation's agricultural resources" (Miller and Walter 1977). The program may also insure against *moral hazards*, i.e., avoidable losses due to management decisions. According to the General Accounting Office, a substantial portion of 1974 payments went to Texas producers whose cotton crops were damaged by drifting chemicals aerially applied to neighboring fields. Although the farmers may have had legal recourse against the damaging party, they chose to collect disaster payments.

Several other programs compensate farmers for losses due to causes beyond their control. The dairy indemnity program authorizes the secretary of agriculture to make indemnity payments for milk or for milk-producing cows to farmers who are prohibited from marketing milk because of chemical residues, nuclear radiation, or fallout. A similar program provides indemnity payments to beekeepers who lose honey bees due to the nearby use of economic poisons. The Animal and Plant Health Inspection Service operates an indemnity program for livestock producers in severe disease situations. The emergency feed program has provided subsidies for feed purchased to preserve and maintain livestock where "because of flood, drought, fire, hurricane, earthquake, storm, or other natural disaster, the Secretary determines that an emergency exists" (PL 95–113, 91 Stat. 955, Sec. 1105).

The assorted disaster compensation programs have reduced income risk for individual producers. Through compensation for losses due to natural disasters, many farmers have more easily maintained their operations. Grain, rice, and cotton farmers have received substantial risk protection at no cost, whereas most other farmers have had to self-insure. Congress recognized the large fiscal outlays and other problems with the disaster payments program and in 1980 voted to replace it with a more comprehensive crop insurance program.

CROP INSURANCE. Some agricultural risks are better suited for an actuarially sound insurance program than others. Hail risk is frequently cited as a production risk meeting all of the requirements for insurability (Miller and Walter 1977). Losses to hail are uncorrelated across time and nearly so across farms. Hail losses are not affected by management decisions and occur frequently enough to encourage insurance purchase. Thus, hail insurance is widely available from private companies. In 1980, over $11 billion of hail insurance was written nationwide by private companies with premiums of $415 million (Crop-Hail Insurance Actuarial Association 1980).

In contrast, drought may affect many farmers simultaneously. The probability that indemnities will exceed the reserves of private companies every year is not zero. The large variability in annual losses associated with all risk or multiple-peril crop insurance makes its provision by private companies difficult. Kenneth Arrow (1974, 202), referring to medical insurance, argued "the welfare case for insurance policies of all sorts is overwhelming. It follows that the government should undertake insurance in those cases where this market, for whatever reason, has failed to emerge."

Would Arrow argue for contingent markets on all activities? The answer seems clearly no. Few economic activities are free of moral hazard and adverse selection incentives that occur when information is incomplete. Indeed, government policies have likely distorted the spatial configuration of production. Adverse selection will always occur if government policy is not carefully tailored to location specific incentives. Texas and Montana might, for example, have considerable incentive to participate in federal disaster programs due to local weather problems.

For other insurance schemes, low participation due to the above incentive problems and high premiums has led to a thin insurance market in agriculture. Early in this century, several attempts by private companies to provide multiple-peril crop insurance were unsuccessful with indemnities greatly exceeding the premiums. In some cases, the companies made the mistake of insuring price as well as yield risk. In other cases, the apparent cause of failure was inadequate geographical distribution of drought risk.

Franklin Roosevelt appointed a committee in 1936 to study the feasibility of government-sponsored crop insurance. The committee's recommendations were largely adopted in the Federal Crop Insurance Act of 1938 (Title V of the Agricultural Adjustment Act of 1938). The legislation established the Federal Crop Insurance Corporation (FCIC) to administer the progam that was initially limited to wheat.

The program's performance was disappointing during its early years. A loss ratio (indemnities divided by premiums) greater than 1.5 in each of the first three years required a subsidy from the U.S. Treasury totaling $28 million (approximately $31 per farm per year). Nearly half of the subsidy was for underwriting losses. Despite these early problems, cotton was added to the insurance program and the results were similar. Examination of data on indemnities as a percent of liabilities suggests an adverse selection problem; the FCIC was largely insuring the poorer risk farmers in early years of operation.

In 1943 Congress halted the crop insurance program due to the large underwriting losses and low participation. The program was reactivated a year later, but was reduced to an experimental basis in 1947. As a result, the FCIC cut its operation from 2500 to 375 counties.

The FCIC experimented during the 1940s and 1950s with alternative insurance plans (e.g., a yield quality plan for tobacco) and added some new crops to the program. After the program was scaled down, the FCIC did a better job of screening applicants and adjusting premiums in accordance with farmers' loss histories. In 1956, the FCIC stopped selling insurance in 14 high risk counties in Colorado, New Mexico, and Texas that had accounted for much of the total indemnities. Loss ratios declined. 1957 began a five-year period when premiums exceeded indemnities every year. The program continued to operate on a limited but satisfactory basis and experienced gradual expansion. Nonetheless, only 8 percent of U.S. acreage and 12 percent of eligible farmers were covered by federal crop insurance in 1980.

The Federal Crop Insurance Act of 1980 authorized an expansion of the federal crop insurance program to become the primary form of disaster protection for agricultural producers. The act permitted the availability of insurance in 1100 additional counties over a five-year period and enlarged the list of covered crops. The program initially expanded in counties with substantial acreages of crops formerly covered by the disaster payments programs. In addition to selling crop insurance directly, the FCIC began an extensive reinsurance program for private companies who sell multiple-peril insurance. Farmers could choose from several levels of yield and price protection on losses with different levels of subsidy available on premiums. Former Secretary of Agriculture Bob Bergland said the act "is historic because it marks a significant step toward providing farmers the opportunity to protect their large investments in crop production against uncontrollable risks. It does what our ad hoc disaster programs have not done" (USDA 1980).

A 1965 survey in Virginia and Montana found that insured farmers were in a somewhat riskier situation than their uninsured counterparts. The insured farmers were less diversified, less likely to have irrigation, and had smaller incomes, fewer savings, and larger debts. Lenders reported better loan collections from those growers with crop insurance (Jones and Larson 1965). In a simulation study, Miller and Trock (1979) found that with a 50 percent level of yield protection, crop insurance was more effective than the disaster program in stabilizing income from dry land winter wheat in Colorado. However, this analysis did not consider the relative cost of the two programs; no adjustment was made in the income calculations for crop insurance premiums. Kramer and Pope (1982) analyzed the risk reduction from the new crop insurance program in reducing risk at the farm level. Using stochastic dominance, probability distributions of net returns with and without crop insurance were compared for a representative Virginia farm. The results suggested that crop insurance can be an attractive risk response.

As with commodity programs, little progress has occurred in positive economic analysis of crop insurance and risk. Research questions include: Why do some farmers purchase subsidized crop insurance and others do not? Is crop insurance more effective in reducing risk than private schemes such as diversification? How does crop insurance influence investment decisions? What are the aggregate welfare effects of crop insurance?

SUBSIDIZED WATER PROGRAMS. Water is another agricultural input whose use has been heavily subsidized by the federal government. When the settlement of western arid lands began, small irrigation systems were established by individual farmers and groups of farmers. To speed the development of the western region, the Reclamation Act of 1902 was passed (Holmes 1972). Since then, a number of large irrigation projects have provided water at below market price to thousands of farmers. Agencies involved in providing irrigation water include the Bureau of Reclamation, the Corps of Engineers, the Soil Conservation Service, and the Agricultural Stabilization and Conservation Service. For some irrigation projects, water users repay no more than 10 percent of the construction costs attributable to irrigation (National Water Commission 1973).

Federally funded irrigation projects have reduced farmers' uncertainty about the availability of water supplies by reducing dependence on sporadic rainfall and private irrigation systems. The associated reduction in yield uncertainty has likely reduced price and income fluctuations for crops with considerable irrigated acreage. Moreover, the federal subsidies for irrigation have likely encouraged greater use of irrigation and larger production of food and fiber, thus lowering expected output price. Thus, the long-term effects of irrigation assistance for farmers have been mixed.

Risk and uncertainty in international trade

During the 1970s the United States experienced an unprecedented expansion of agricultural trade along with increased fluctuations in agricultural exports. As indicated in Fig. 16.3, the index of agricultural imports rose steadily whereas the index for exports ranged from 111 in 1970 to 225 in 1979. Thus the interrelationships between export demand and the fluctuations of agricultural prices are significant (Schuh 1974). Moreover, worldwide economic changes have impacted greatly on agriculture through floating exchange rates and the structure of world agricultural trade.

Because of these fluctuations, third world countries, as well as developed countries, are interested in stabilization policies for prices or stocks of

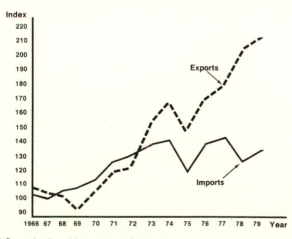

FIG. 16.3. U.S. agricultural imports and exports.

commodities. Though stabilization is important, other trade policies and institutions also affect economic outcomes. One such institution is the General Agreement on Tariffs and Trade (GATT), which attempts to negotiate multilateral reductions in trade barriers. A similar institution is the United Nations Conferences on Trade and Development (UNCTAD). Policies that expand exports to developing countries also are important. Loan policies of the CCC and PL 480 provisions have led to market expansion of U.S. agricultural exports. Other policies and institutional arrangements that affect international trade and hence prices include bilateral trade agreements, export and import marketing orders, cartels, tariffs, levies, subsidies, and quotas. Perhaps the most important factor in the long-term upward trend in U.S. agricultural exports is the opening of markets due to rising incomes in importing countries.

Research analyzing these policy instruments under uncertainty has developed on two fronts. The first involves general equilibrium models with two consumers, two products and/or two inputs. This work, begun by Brainard and Cooper (1968), basically involves adding risk generalizations to the Ricardian and Heckscher-Ohlin trade theories. The second front involves Marshallian market studies of supply and demand where risk is represented by random shifts in supplies and demands. This approach was inspired by Massell (1969) and began with the work of Hueth and Schmitz (1972). Most studies in agriculture follow this second front because empirical analysis is more difficult in a general equilibrium context.

MARKET MODELS OF INSTABILITY. The first market model of international trade under uncertainty was developed by Hueth and Schmitz (1972). They modeled trade between two countries, based on linear supply and demand curves with random additive shift terms. They considered whether producers and consumers in the importing and exporting countries gain or lose from price stabilization using the standard economic welfare concepts of producers' and consumers' surplus. They found a net positive effect of price stabilization for both countries taken together; however, the exporting country gains and the importing country loses when the instability originates in the exporting country, whereas the exporting country loses and the importing country gains when the instability originates in the importing country. Similarly, each trading group (consumers or producers in each country) tends to gain when the instability originates with other groups, but loses if the instability originates within the group. For example, consumers in the exporting country gain from international price stabilization if the instability originates in the producing group of the exporting country or from either the producing or consuming group of the importing country. In each case the gains or losses for a specific group are less if the supply or demand curve is more inelastic.

The work of Hueth and Schmitz was criticized and generalized in a number of ways (Just et al. 1982). One generalization involves the linearity assumption for supply and demand curves. Just et al. (1978) considered a similar trade model but introduced nonlinearity in the supply and demand curves. Assuming that any price-stabilizing buffer stock must be self-liquidating, they found that the gains and losses from trade may change drastically. In each case, the qualitative Hueth-Schmitz results may be reversed with sufficient nonlinearity. For example, if instability originates in the exporting country, the importing country may gain from international price stabilization rather than lose if the nonlinearity in its excess demand curve is sufficient. These results occur because the stabilized price with a self-liquidating buffer stock is dependent on linearity. If, for example, the importing country's excess demand curve is upward bending, then the stabilized price is lower than the average destabilized price; alternatively, if the excess demand curve is downward bending, then the stabilized price is above the average destabilized price (assuming variation in the excess supply curve with a fixed excess demand curve).

Just et al. (1978) also examined the implications of nonadditive disturbances in the supply and demand curves. For multiplicative disturbances they again found that the Hueth-Schmitz results can be reversed for each trading group. For example, if variation originates in the exporting country but the excess demand curve of the importing country is stable, a change from additive disturbances (parallel shifts in supply) to multiplicative disturbances can, under certain conditions, cause the importing country to gain from international price stabilization rather than to lose.

Bieri and Schmitz (1973, 1974) relaxed the assumption of competition in the Hueth-Schmitz model. They assume either that international trade by one country is conducted by a marketing board (monopoly or monopsony) or that trade between the two countries occurs through a private middleman (monopoly-monopsony). They obtain the rather peculiar result that a pure middleman will stabilize prices for the importing country but will destabilize prices for the exporting country if the disturbance originates in the exporting country and excess demand from the importing country is stable. Similarly, a pure middleman would destabilize prices for an importing country with varying demand, and stabilize prices for an exporting country with stable supply. By contrast, if variation originates in the exporting country, but demand by the importing country is stable, a producer marketing board in the exporting country benefits from storage and price stabilization in both countries. These results suggest that the Canadian Wheat Marketing Board, for example, may achieve more stable prices than do private traders for U.S. wheat producers. Thus, one approach to altering farmers' risk is to change the marketing system.

Another generalization of the Hueth-Schmitz model relaxes the assumptions of free trade and the absence of distortions. Just et al. (1977) consider nonlinearity and alternative forms of disturbances in supply and demand introduced by distortions in trading relationships. This approach is inspired by the European practice of controlling agricultural prices in order to export agricultural variation to trading partners. These policies, sometimes called price insulating policies, stabilize and regulate internal prices without buffer stocks. Any excess or deficiency in the internal market is offset by international trade. These policies increase price instability in other countries by increasing their uncertainty about the quantity of trade. These results suggest that price risk for U.S. farmers could be reduced without incurring excessive storage costs if similar price-insulating policies were developed, or if trade agreements relaxed the price-insulating policies of other countries. One should bear in mind, however, that the U.S. adoption of such price-insulating policies could bring catastrophic variability in some less developed countries.

These theoretical studies have prompted econometric analyses of supply and demand relationships between importing and exporting countries with the standard errors and estimated coefficients of the econometric equations used to assess price stabilization at an international level. Konandreas and Schmitz (1978) applied the Hueth-Schmitz framework. Reutlinger's (1976) study of international wheat price stabilization considered nonlinearity in the response function of various countries. Bigman and Reutlinger (1979) and Zwart and Meilke (1979) analyzed the effects of exporting instability through price controls and price-insulating policies. These empirical studies support the qualitative conclusions of the earlier theoretical studies. However, they add quantitative significance to the various considerations. For example, Reutlinger showed that "the storage impact on gains and losses by consumers and producers is particularly sensitive to the assumed shape of the demand function." Zwart and Meilke found that countries who relax their price-insulating policies could achieve more stability in the world wheat market than would an international buffer-stock policy.

Another important criticism of the Hueth-Schmitz model is that it ignores risk aversion by decision makers and assumes risk neutrality (Tisdell 1963; Anderson and Riley 1976). Thus, the theoretical framework developed above is characterized as instability with certainty because producers and consumers are assumed to react to price changes instantaneously along their supply and demand curves. The implications of this assumption were developed earlier in the chapter.

GENERAL EQUILIBRIUM MODELS OF RISK AND UNCERTAINTY IN INTERNATIONAL TRADE. Including the effects of risk and uncertainty in general equilibrium models of international trade is a straightforward extension of these models' formulation under conditions of certainty. However, progress along these lines is only recent and requires careful attention to specifying and measuring the risk components. These models began with the work of Brainard and Cooper (1968) and were soon followed by Bardhan (1971), Batra and Russell (1974), and Ruffin (1974a). These models are all two-country, two-good models with a random relative price representing the terms of trade. The aggregate preferences of each country are represented by a von Neuman-Morgenstern utility function defined over the quantities of the two goods consumed. Technology is represented by a general transformation curve relating the quantities of the two goods.

Early papers assume that all production and export decisions occur before the state of the world is known. In this context, Brainard and Cooper (1968) and Bardhan (1971) found that increased uncertainty results in less production of the export good and greater diversification in production. Using a mean-variance model, Brainard and Cooper also found that more uncertainty results in less exports. Batra and Russell (1974) found that more uncertainty reduces the level of welfare. This result has the disturbing implication that opening a country to international trade, and thus greater uncertainty, may imply that free trade is worse than complete autarky. On this basis, Batra and Russell recommend that government should intervene to stabilize price and maintain consumer's relative price at its expected value or offer a consumption subsidy to the import commodity to increase its consumption. Thus, international trade in a risky environment appears to call for government intervention to reduce the adverse effects of risk to the individual decision makers. Ruffin (1974a) alternatively showed that in a world having both autonomous exports and imports a country will always actively engage in international trade regardless of foreign price distributions. This result is called the *nonautarky theorem*.

These results and models (particularly those of Batra and Russell [1974]) are criticized on several grounds. The most serious criticism is their focus on *ex ante* decisions. All decisions occur before the state of the world is known. *Ex post* trade models appeared with the work of Kemp and Liviatan (1973), Ruffin (1974b) and Turnovsky (1974). These *ex post* trade models allow decisions both before and after the state of the world is known. They generally use a single productive input (labor), which is allocated between production of the two outputs at the initial stage so as to maximize expected utility. Then, once the state of the world is known (relative prices and quantities of outputs), the country can allocate each commodity between consumption and trade.

In this context, Ruffin (1974b) and Turnovsky (1974) provide conditions that assure complete specialization and, thus, complete dependence on international trade for the other commodity. Furthermore, Kemp and

Liviatan (1973) and Turnovsky show that enough risk could cause a country to specialize in producing a good in which it has a comparative disadvantage. For example, a risk averse country could specialize in food production even though it has a comparative advantage in the production of another export commodity. In a similar model, Anderson and Riley (1976) show that the introduction of risk in international trade has an ambiguous effect on the level of expected utility. In fact, the introduction of a small amount of risk around the autarky-relative price has welfare-improving effects; it enables the country to take advantage of international trade in some states of the world.

Batra (1975) focused more on technological uncertainty than on price uncertainty. Introducing a random multiplicative term in the production of one of the commodities, he showed that the standard theorem of international trade (such as the factor-price equalization, Stolper-Samuelson, and Rybczynski theorems) need not hold. However, the Stolper-Samuelson theorem holds if the utility function exhibits decreasing absolute risk aversion.

These studies of risk and uncertainty in international trade imply that the standard theorems of trade under certainty need not generalize to the case of uncertainty. Helpman and Razin (1978) argue, however, that these trade models ignore the effects of financial markets and international trade in securities. By integrating the theory of financial markets with international trade under risk, they show that the standard theorems of specialization according to comparative advantage and factor-price equalization are restored in the presence of international trade in equities and that valid versions of the Stolper-Samuelson and Rybczynski theorems do exist. These results are based on a simple model with two factors, two equities, and two commodities. However, the standard Heckscher-Ohlin theorem fails to hold whether or not securities are considered. Helpman and Razin further develop conditions under which consumers prefer restricted trade with tariffs to autarky.

Feder et al. (1977) bring these models closer to agricultural issues by considering buffer stocks. They develop a two-good trade model with a single factor of production where one good representing food is stored from period to period. Results indicate as uncertainty increases, exporters tend to reduce storage that in their case is a speculative venture. At the same time, importers increase storage that in their case is preferred to dependence on uncertain spot market conditions in the future. This result suggests, for example, that the grain-exporting countries, such as the United States and Canada, should be least interested in commodity storage just when the importing, developing countries may need it the most. Thus, from a purely economic standpoint, the United States (including individual farmers) would be better off to place the burden of emergency storage programs on the importing countries.

A brief review of the general equilibrium theory of international trade under risk shows the primitive state of the literature. Only a few general equilibrium studies of international trade have emphasized agricultural goods. For example, Chambers and Just (1982) develop a general equilibrium trade model for wheat, corn, soybeans, and the rest of the economy that illustrates the importance of monetary exchange policy for agricultural trade. Shei (1978) conducted a similar study. However, only Jabara and Thompson (1980) developed an empirically specified general equilibrium model of agricultural trade that considers risk. They found that Senegal should rely more on cereal crops than on peanuts because of trade risk considerations. This result verifies the theoretical results of Kemp and Liviatan (1973) and of Turnovsky (1974). But the relative dearth of general equilibrium analyses of agricultural trade under risk implies that much more empirical work is needed.

Policy-induced risk

To this point, we have discussed risk inherent in the agricultural economy and the effectiveness of alternative governmental policies for reducing its adverse effects. However, unanticipated change in policy is an additional source of risk that may adversely affect many farmers. Uncertainty about policy alternatives is called policy-induced risk or simply policy risk. Since different policies lead to different expectations on commodity prices, availability of credit, costs of inputs, terms of trade, and so on, the risk effects of changes in policy need to be considered.

DOMESTIC POLICY RISK. Domestic U.S. agricultural policy has undergone many changes over past decades. Some changes have involved new policy controls while others involved changes in existing controls. For example, wheat production was controlled by (1) acreage allotments with price supports and government acquisition in 1950 and 1954 to 1963, (2) price support with government acquisition from 1951 to 1953, (3) voluntary diversion requirements with price supports or certificates from 1964 to 1970, and (4) set-aside requirements with various support mechanisms (target prices, etc.) in the 1970s with a switch from government acquisition to farmer-owned reserves in 1977. Other commodities such as feed grains experienced similar changes. Each policy regime represented a substantial change in controls and, in some cases, substantially affected perceived risk in agriculture (Just 1982).

The two types of policy uncertainty include: (1) uncertainty due to legislative changes, and (2) uncertainty due to policies or rules changed or promulgated by administrative officers under legislative authority. For the latter, the secretary of agriculture has considerable discretion. For example, the 1977 act enabled the secretary to base adjustments in deficiency payments on an allocation factor. This factor was unknown to farmers when they enrolled in the program. However, legislative change likely is the more important type of uncertainty for policies that alter capital investments or disinvestments (including human capital). Moreover, it sometimes involves major and abrupt change.

The crucial issues of policy uncertainty are the costs of adjusting a farm's organization to new policy eras and farmers' costs of maintaining sufficient flexibility to respond to new, unanticipated changes in policy. In addition, once a particular set of policy controls is authorized by law, the levels of the controls often change from one production period to the next. Under 1981 legislation, price support levels, target prices, and set-aside requirements are subject to change annually, with varying degrees of lead time. The secretary of agriculture has explicit power to impose set-aside requirements in each new production period, depending on the outcome of the previous season. In contrast, farmers often have longer term decisions regarding the purchase of land, machinery, equipment, and livestock. When the future levels of various policy controls cannot be anticipated, the farmer experiences increased risk and must provide for the policy risk in his business organization.

The effects of policy risk are illustrated by two classic paradigms associated with adaptive and rational expectations. Suppose a farmer forms perceptions of price distributions adaptively in response to his experience and flows of market information. The period of policy formulation will not impose additional risk on the farmer. However, as a new policy is instituted, he will begin to observe prices from a new distribution. If he believes that these observations come from the old distribution, his perception of risk will increase initially if the new distribution has a different mean than the old one. As time passes the perception of risk will gradually diminish as information from the previous distribution decays in his adaptive process. However, once he perceives the observations to come from a new distribution, then his initial subjective risk will first be very large and then gradually fall as he builds experience and information. Thus a policy change could increase risk for the farmer until the effects of the new policy are observed. With frequent changes in policy, this may never be possible. Alternatively, risk perceptions may be reduced through a change in policy. For example, the policy may change from free market to pegged prices due to excessive risk associated with free market fluctuations.

Now suppose a farmer forms perceptions of price distributions rationally. The period of policy formulation imposes additional risk on the farmer, although risk may not be excessive once a new policy is finally instituted (if the farmer can count on the new policy for a sufficient time period). As Congress considers alternative policy controls for a new agricultural act or as the secretary of agriculture or Congress is deciding how to revise existing controls, a farmer with rational expectations (and risk) will determine a price distribution under each policy alternative and then attach probabilities to each policy choice. Thus, his subjective risk will be greater than with some or all of the individual policy alternatives. Reality likely lies between these two paradigms; thus, policy risk has adverse implications for farmers both before and immediately after policy changes.

Just (1982) examined the costs of policy risk for the adaptive expectations paradigm. He compared the effects of the farmer-owned grain reserve program on prices, quantities, and real income for grain and livestock markets relative to the case of no farmer-owned reserve. His approach utilized a 34-equation, nonlinear simultaneous equation model of the U.S. wheat/feed-grain/livestock economy. The results implied that a serious problem with the farmer-owned reserve was the sharp departure from the previous policy and the long time period required to adapt to the new policy period. The adjustment problem occurred not only for grain farmers but also for livestock producers who experienced grain prices different than in absence of the farmer-owned reserve. Initial price adjustments apparently differed from long-run equilibrium levels and caused false price signals for producers. These false price signals then caused substantial maladjustment in the livestock industry because of long lags in livestock production that fed back into the grain markets, causing maladjustment to persist for some time. In view of these results, Just concluded:

> The recent practice of changing agricultural policy substantially every four years seems to impose unnecessary costs on the agricultural sector. With policy changing every four years, the livestock industry can be continually in a state of trying to adjust to new policies because of its inability to adjust quickly.

Major developments also led to more than one major policy change during the term of some agricultural acts. A depressed grain market led to the Emergency Agricultural Act of 1978, which was soon accompanied by higher loan rates, release levels, and call levels for wheat. The Soviet embargo of 1980 was accompanied by major revisions in these and other controls. Each of these revisions apparently responded to inadequacies in the 1977 program. Thus, producers not only suffered from an inability to anticipate future set-aside requirements, but also from inability to anticipate other major policy changes. These conditions hamper business planning, shorten planning horizons, increase uncertainty about meeting financial obligations, and contribute to a lower quality of decision making. The investment inefficiency in the livestock sector can also be serious because of the long period required for herd expansion and production of feeder animals.

INTERNATIONAL POLICY RISK. The risks of change in policies of other countries and of U.S. policies toward specific countries is one reason why U.S. agricultural policies are periodically altered. This problem is underscored by the events of the 1970s. One of the largest shocks on record for U.S. grain markets occurred in the early 1970s when the Soviet Union decided to buy substantial quantities of U.S. grain rather than cut its internal standards for meat consumption. In an attempt to reduce the risks for U.S. farmers of shocks from Soviet grain policy, the United States negotiated a long-term grain trade agreement effective 1 October 1976. Nonetheless, another substantial shock occurred on 4 January 1980 when President Carter suspended delivery to the Soviet Union of any U.S. grain exceeding the minimum of 8 million metric tons specified in the agreement. This embargo occurred at a time when the Soviet Union already held contracts for delivery of 21.8 million tons of grain. The grain embargo was a response to the Soviet invasion of Afghanistan; thus, the action was based on more than economic considerations. Nevertheless, these events clearly show the importance of international policy risk to U.S. agriculture.

For farmers, it is crucial to design policy controls that dampen the adverse domestic effects of changes in international policies. If this is accomplished by revising existing policy, the farmers may suffer both from international policy risk and from policy risk associated with corrective measures. When the Soviet embargo was announced, the effects on U.S. agriculture and possible compensatory policies for U.S. farmers were uncertain. Later, the secretary of agriculture increased loan rates, release levels, and call levels for wheat and corn in order to mitigate the effects of the embargo on U.S. farmers. While this change closely followed the embargo, it illustrates the tendency for U.S. agricultural policy to respond in a piecemeal fashion to immediate needs. Thus, farmers must bear policy risk for the government's response to various situations; in addition, new risks for farmers may arise from unfamiliarity with the new policies.

REMOVING RANDOMNESS FROM THE POLITICAL PROCESS. These considerations support the need for self-adjusting policies that permit smoother, more orderly adjustments in producer prices. Policy formulation along these lines should reduce farmers' policy risks and provide for more orderly investment and growth. This section suggests some ways to reduce policy risk.

First, agricultural policies with more automatic adjustments could replace the ad hoc, piecemeal approach to policy adjustment. For example in recent history commodity loan rates have been set at a particular level and then substantially revised when market prices differ signficantly. Experience suggests that this piecemeal approach is always necessary when specific loan rates become far out of line. A potentially better approach is to specify in advance how loan rates will change in response to market conditions. In this way, farmers can better anticipate such changes through their own assessments of future market conditions. As a result, better investment conditions should occur.

Conditions that appear to strongly influence revisions of controls include farmer income levels, inflation of food prices, the size of government-related stocks, and government costs. The appropriate reaction of policy controls to each condition could be determined in advance. For example, the loan rates help to support farm incomes while the release and call levels of the farmer-owned reserve avoid rapid food price inflation. But acceptable levels of farm income and consumer prices change with inflation. Thus, loan rates and release and call levels could be keyed to inflation so that changes in their levels can be anticipated by farmers in planning decisions.

Acreage set-aside programs supposedly avoid excessive reserves and high government costs. Moreover, they may not directly distort the pricing signals for market participants as occurs with the use of price controls (Newbury and Stiglitz 1979). Perhaps the set-aside requirements could be keyed to the level of accumulated reserves. This relationship would avoid uncertainty about the use of set-asides. To illustrate, requiring a 1 percent set-aside for every 20 million bushels of wheat in government reserves would reduce farmers' policy risk compared to requiring a 20 percent set-aside, or none at all.

Alternatively, loan rate reductions could be tied to high reserve stock levels. The Food and Agriculture Act of 1977 reflected this approach by authorizing the secretary of agriculture to reduce loan rates 5 percent if he finds stocks to be excessive. Unfortunately, the discretionary nature of the decision does not promote certainty in policy.

Another example is the all or nothing applicability of loan rates and release or call levels. A more orderly application of controls is appropriate. The loan rate acts as a price floor regardless of how much grain goes under government loan at that price. Similar arguments apply to release and call levels for grain sales although the degree of enforcement is less. If farmers believe that the loan rate and release levels establish a price corridor, then the program itself alters their probability distributions by preventing low and high prices. The revised expectations may, in turn, generate an *ex ante* production response. In this context, government policy may offer reduced benefits when prices are near normal levels and costs of providing some stabilizing influence would be very cheap. On the other hand, a very high level of benefits is provided in an extreme price situation where the costs may be much greater than benefits. This type of situation sometimes causes programs to require unexpected modification.

Unexpected market developments may trigger large increases in reserve levels; consequently, government costs can increase substantially. Making the price-control levels explicitly dependent on stock levels would ease this burden interseasonally. Alternatively, the controls could operate according to a prespecified scale. Rather than the government offering to take all grain at a loan rate, it could buy, say, 1 million bu grain for every $0.01/bu the price is below the target level. Similarly, the government could sell 1 million bu from stocks for every $0.01/bu the price is above the target price. If these transactions occur at competitive market prices, then it would make no difference which farmer's grain was actually purchased by the government.

This procedure would provide a stabilizing influence when prices are near equilibrium. Furthermore, the stabilizing influence can be provided throughout a marketing season. As the price increases, the government could sell stocks to ease price increases; as price starts downward, the government could buy stocks to ease price declines. Thus, the announced policy of 1 million bu transactions for a $0.01 change in price could be applied continuously (weekly or monthly) in determining government stock transactions. Finally, to make this stabilization policy operational and self-adjusting interseasonally, a rule should be specified for modification of the target price from period to period.

Government ownership of grain reserves is viewed with considerable skepticism because it concentrates power in a few individuals who make government buy/sell decisions. Similar concerns hold, perhaps to a lesser degree, regarding other policies such as meat import quotas. The policy characteristics suggested above avoid these problems because the government buy/sell decisions are mechanically controlled by the initial terms of the policy; thus, randomness introduced through the political process is minimized.

As yet, these issues have had little theoretical or empirical study. Only recently have economists begun to consider the potential benefits and costs for society of controls with built-in responses to market conditions. The few theoretical and empirical studies in agriculture that have analyzed self-adjusting policies have concluded in their favor over the usual approach of loan rates, price bands, and so on (Danin 1975; Cochrane and Ryan 1976; Zwart and Mielke 1976; Just 1982). But these studies are short run and do not account for the longer term investment efficiency associated with reduction of policy risk.

Paul Samuelson (1972) argues that it is unrealistic to expect certainty about the role of government; policies can always be changed (Hathaway 1974). His argument is correct; but, if the policy is self-adjusting, then the incentive to intervene and change policies should result in less frequent and less substantial changes. Thus, farmers' policy risk should be less.

The changes cited here simply illustrate the issues and suggest the potential of reducing policy risk. Other self-adjusting features could also be evaluated and incorporated in agricultural policy. The development of a more orderly agricultural policy with built-in self-adjustments that can be well anticipated deserves further study.

Concluding comments

As this chapter has indicated, few studies have focused on the risk implications of agricultural policy. Those that have considered risk often lack generality as well as structural or policy detail. Many microstudies are based upon a prescribed environment and rules of behavior; their results have limited generality as well. They teach us much about potential responses and thus aid in hypothesis formulation. However, stronger validation and more analyses are needed to understand how changes in policy affect farmer behavior and the structure of the agricultural sector.

The notion that government has contributed to a riskier environment for agriculture has considerable appeal, a priori. Again, little empirical support is available for this hypothesis. Even if policy risk does occur, farmers may account for it as rational expectations are formed. Thus, the endogenizing of government behavior seems worthy of study.

The methods reviewed in this book have in most cases had widespread application in farm management-oriented research. Much less effort has been devoted to aggregate research. Also lacking is normative research on agricultural policy issues that properly and robustly models the risk components. One can only conclude that either the researcher does not believe that risk response is important, or that difficult, unresolved questions still exist about the appropriate methods of analysis. Probably both reasons govern research behavior, but we believe that the empirical applications of existing methods and the development of new methods warrant more attention. Acceptance of risk averse expected utility behavior has substantive implications for welfare measurement and concepts and, indeed, may be the raison d' être for much agricultural policy. This should be the impetus for further risk research. It is hoped the risk analysis focus of this book can contribute to society through improved social decision making.

REFERENCES

Adams, R. M., D. J. Menkhaus, and B. A. Woolery. 1980. Alternative parameter specification in E, V analysis: Implications for farm level decision making. *West. J. Agric. Econ.* 5:13–20.

Ajzen, I., and M. Fishbein. 1972. Attitudes and normative beliefs as factors influencing behavioral intentions. *J. Pers. and Soc. Psychol.* 21:1–9.

Allen, M. J., and W. M. Yen. 1979. *Introduction to measurement theory.* Monterey, Calif.: Brooks/Cole.

Anderson, J. R. 1974. Simulation: Methodology and application in agricultural economics. *Rev. Mark. Agric. Econ.* 42:3–55.

_____. 1975. Programming for efficient planning against nonnormal risk. *Aust. J. Agric. Econ.* 19:94–107.

_____. 1977. Perspectives on models of uncertain decisions. In *Risk, uncertainty and agricultural development,* eds. J. A. Roumasset, J. Boussard, and I. Singh. New York: Agric. Dev. Counc.

Anderson, J. R., and J. G. Riley. 1976. International trade with fluctuating prices. *Int. Econ. Rev.* 17:76–97.

Anderson, J. R., J. L. Dillon, and J. B. Hardaker. 1977. *Agricultural decision analysis.* Ames: Iowa State Univ. Press.

Anderson, O. D., ed. 1979. *Forecasting.* Amsterdam: North-Holland.

Arrow, K. J. 1974. *Essays in the theory of risk bearing.* Amsterdam: North-Holland.

Aukes, R. G. 1980. *Effects of variable amortization plans on borrower and lender risk: A simulation study of low equity Illinois cash grain farms.* Ph.D. diss., Univ. of Illinois.

Baker, C. B. 1966. Firm growth, liquidity management, and production choices. In *Production economics in agricultural research.* Dep. Agric. Econ. AE-4108, Univ. of Illinois.

_____. 1968. Credit in the production of the firm. *Am. J. Agric. Econ.* 49:507–21.

_____. 1974. An economic alternative to concessional farm interest rates. *Aust. J. Agric. Econ.* 18:171–92.

_____. 1976. A variable amortization plan to manage farm mortgage risk. *Agric. Financ. Rev.* 36:1–6.

_____. 1977. Instability in the capital markets of U.S. agriculture. *Am. J. Agric. Econ.* 39:170–77.

Baker, C. B., and V. Bhargava. 1974. Financing small farm development in India. *Aust. J. Agric. Econ.* 18:101–18.

Baker, C. B., and D. J. Dunn. 1978. *Measuring lending risks of the federal land banks.* AERR 44-67. Univ. of Illinois.

Baker, C. B., and J. A. Hopkin. 1969. Concepts of finance capital for a capital-using agriculture. *Am. J. Agric. Econ.* 51:1055–65.

Baker, C. B., D. J. Dunn, and W. F. Lazarus. 1979. *Risks in federal land bank lending.* 2d Int. Conf. Res. Issues Rural Financ., Calgary.

Baquet, A. E., A. N. Halter, and F. S. Conklin. 1976. The value of frost forecasting: A Bayesian appraisal. *Am. J. Agric. Econ.* 58:511–20.

Bardhan, P. K. 1971. *Uncertainty, resource allocation, and factor shares in a two-sector model.* MIT Work. Pap. 79, Cambridge.

Barnard, G. A. 1979. Do forecasts have to be framed in terms of probabilities? In *Forecasting,* ed. O. D. Anderson. Amsterdam: North-Holland.

Baron, R. A., and D. Byrne. 1981. *Social psychology: Understanding human interaction.* Boston: Allyn and Bacon.

Barry, P. J. 1978. Rural banks and farm loan participations. *Am. J. Agric. Econ.* 60:214–24.

———. 1980. Capital asset pricing and farm real estate. *Am. J. Agric. Econ.* 62:549–53.

———. 1981a. Agricultural lending by commercial banks. *Agric. Financ. Rev.* 41:28–40.

———. 1981b. What's wrong with refinancing? *Farm Money Manage.* 1st Quarter, 8, 10, 13.

———. 1983. Financing growth and adjustment of farm firms under risk and inflation. In *Modeling farm decisions for policy analysis.* Boulder, Colo.: Western Press.

Barry, P. J., and C. B. Baker. 1971. Reservation prices on credit use: A measure of response to uncertainty. *Am. J. Agric. Econ.* 53:222–28.

———. 1977. Management of financial structure: Firm level. *Agric. Financ. Rev.* 37:50–63.

Barry, P. J., and D. Fraser. 1976. Risk management in agricultural production. *Am. J. Agric. Econ.* 58:286–95.

Barry, P. J., and D. R. Willmann. 1976. A risk programming analysis of forward contracting with credit constraints. *Am. J. Agric. Econ.* 58:62–70.

Barry, P. J., C. B. Baker, and L. R. Sanint. 1981. Farmers credit risk and liquidity management. *Am. J. Agric. Econ.* 63:216–27.

Barry, P. J., J. A. Hopkin, and C. B. Baker. 1983. *Financial management in agriculture.* 3d ed. Danville, Ill.: Interstate Publishers.

Batra, R. N. 1975. Production uncertainty and the Heckscher-Ohlin theorem. *Rev. Econ. Stud.,* 259–68.

Batra, R. N., and W. R. Russell. 1974. Gains from trade under uncertainty. *Am. Econ. Rev.* 64:1040–48.

Baughman, E. T. 1970. The economic role of financial intermediaries: Challenges of a changing agriculture. In *A new look at agricultural finance research,* ed. J. Hopkin. Agric. Financ. Prog. Rep. 1, Univ. of Illinois.

Baumol, W. J. 1963. An expected gain-confidence limit criterion for portfolio selection. *Manage. Sci.* 10:174–81.

Behrman, J. R. 1968. *Supply responses in underdeveloped agriculture.* New York: North-Holland.

Benedict, M. R. 1953. *Farm policies of the United States 1790–1950.* New York: Twentieth Century Fund.

Beneke, R. R., and R. Winterboer. 1973. *Linear programming applications to agriculture.* Ames: Iowa State Univ. Press.

Berck, P. 1981. Portfolio theory and the demand for futures: The case of California cotton. *Am. J. Agric. Econ.* 63:466–74.

Bessler, D. A. 1977. *Foresight and inductive reasoning: Analysis of expectations on economic variables with California field crops.* Ph.D. diss., Univ. of California, Davis.

———. 1980. Aggregated personalistic beliefs on yields of selected crops estimated using ARIMA processes. *Am. J. Agric. Econ.* 62:666–74.

———. 1981. *Some theoretical considerations on the elicitation of subjective probability.* Purdue Univ. Agric. Exp. Stn. Bull. 332.

Bessler, D. A., and C. V. Moore. 1979. Use of probability assessments and scoring rules for agricultural forecasts. *Agric. Econ. Rev.* 31:44–47.

Betz, N. E., and D. J. Weiss. 1976. Validity of psychological measurements. In *Measurement and evaluation in rehabilitation,* ed. Brian Bolton. Baltimore: University Park Press.

Bieri, J., and A. Schmitz. 1973. Export instability, monopoly power, and welfare. *J. Int. Econ.* 3:389–96.

———. 1974. Market intermediaries and price instability: Some welfare implications. *Am. J. Agric. Econ.* 56:280–85.

Bigman, D., and S. Reutlinger. 1979. Food price and supply stabilization: National buffer stocks and trade policies. *Am. J. Agric. Econ.* 61:657–67.

Binswanger, H. 1980. Attitudes toward risk: Experimental measurement in rural India. *Am. J. Agric. Econ.* 62:395–407.

Black, J. D. 1929. *Production economics.* New York: Holt, Rhinehart and Winston.

Black, R., and M. Chaffin. 1971. Corn vs. soybeans: What mix in 1977? *Mich. Farm.,* Apr.

Blanford, D., and M. Currie. 1975. Price uncertainty: The case for government intervention. *J. Agric. Econ.* 26:37–51.

Boehlje, M. D., and S. Griffin. 1979. Financial impacts of government price support programs. *Am. J. Agric. Econ.* 61:285–96.

Boehlje, M. D., and L. D. Trede. 1977. Risk management in agriculture. *J. Am. Soc. Farm Manage. Rural Appraisers* 41:20–27.

Boehlje, M. D., and T. K. White. 1969. A production-investment decision model of farm firm growth. *Am. J. Agric. Econ.* 51:546–64.

Boisvert, R. N., and H. R. Jenson. 1973. *A method for farm planning under uncertain weather conditions with applications to corn-soybean farming in southern Minnesota.* Minn. Agric. Exp. Stn. Tech. Bull. 292.

Bolen, K. R., C. B. Baker, and R. A. Hinton. 1978. Marketing corn and soybeans under conditions of market risk. *Ill. Agric. Econ.* 18:12–19.

Bond, G., and B. Wonder. 1980. Risk attitudes amongst Australian farmers. *Aust. J. Agric. Econ.* 25:82–93.

Boudreaux, K. J., and H. W. Long. 1978. *The basic theory of corporate finance.* Englewood Cliffs, J.J.: Prentice-Hall.

Boussard, J. M. 1971a. A model of the behavior of farmers and its application to agricultural policies. *Eur. Econ. Rev.* 2:436–61.

_____. 1971b. Time horizon, objective function, and uncertainty in a multiperiod model of firm growth. *Am. J. Agric. Econ.* 53:467–77.

_____. 1979. Risk and uncertainty in programming models: A review. In *Risk, uncertainty, and agricultural development,* eds. J. A. Roumasset, J. M. Boussard, and I. Singh. New York: Agric. Dev. Counc.

Boussard, J. M., and M. Petit. 1967. Representation of farmers' behavior under uncertainty with a focus-loss constraint. *J. Farm Econ.* 49:869–80.

Box, G. E. P., and G. M. Jenkins. 1970. *Time series analysis.* San Francisco: Holden-Day.

Brainard, W. C., and R. N. Cooper. 1968. Uncertainty and diversification of international trade. *Food Res. Inst. Stud. Agric. Econ., Trade Dev.* 8:257–85.

Brake, J. R., and E. O. Melichar. 1977. Agricultural finance and capital markets. In *A survey of agricultural economics literature,* ed. L. R. Martin. Vol. 1. Minneapolis: Univ. of Minnesota Press.

Brandow, G. E. 1977. Policy for commercial agriculture, 1945–71. In *A survey of agricultural economics literature,* ed. L. R. Martin. Vol. 1. Minneapolis: Univ. of Minnesota Press.

Bravo-Ureta, B. E., and G. A. Helmers. 1980a. E,V, frontier analysis using total and random variance as measures of risk. Pap. presented West. Agric. Econ. Assoc. Annu. Meet., July 20–22.

_____. 1980b. Prices, yield, and net income variability for selected field crops and counties in Nebraska. Pap. Dep. Agric. Econ., Univ. of Nebraska.

Brigham, E. F. 1979. *Financial management theory and practice,* 2d ed. Hinsdale, Ill.: Dryden Press.

Brink, L., and B. McCarl. 1978. The trade-off between expected return and risk among Corn Belt farmers. *Am. J. Agric. Econ.* 60:259–63.

Burt, O., 1982. Dynamic programming: Has its day arrived? *West. J. Agric. Econ.* 7:381–94.

Calvin, L. 1979. *Measurement of price, yield, and gross returns risk in Washington State and Whitman County agriculture.* Master's thesis, Washington State Univ.

Candler, W., and W. Cartwright. 1969. Estimation of performance functions for budgeting and simulation studies. *Am. J. Agric. Econ.* 51:159–69.

Carlson, G. A. 1970. A decision theoretic approach to crop disease prediction and control. *Am. J. Agric. Econ.* 52:216–23.

Carter, H. O., and G. W. Dean. 1960. Income, price, and yield variability for principal California crops and cropping systems. *Hilgardia* 30:175–218.

Cassidy, P. A., J. L. Rogers, and W. O. McCarthy. 1970. A simulation approach to risk assessment in investment analysis. *Rev. Mark. Agric. Econ.* 38:3–24.

Chambers, R. G., and R. E. Just. 1982. An investigation of the effect of monetary factors on agriculture. *J. Monetary Econ.* 9:135–45.

Chapman, L. J., and J. P. Chapman. 1969. Illusory correlation as an obstacle to the use of valid psychodiagnostic signs. *J. Abnorm. Psychol.* 74:271–80.

Chavas, J-P., and R. Pope. 1981. Welfare measures of production activities under risk aversion. *South. Econ. J.* 48:187–96.

Chen, J. T. 1973. Quadratic programming for least-cost feed formulations under probabilistic protein constraints. *Am. J. Agric. Econ.* 55:175–83.

Chen, J. T., and C. B. Baker. 1974. Marginal risk constraint linear program for activity analysis. *Am. J. Agric. Econ.* 56:622–27.

Chien, Y. I., and G. L. Bradford. 1976. A sequential model of the farm firm growth process. *Am. J. Agric. Econ.* 58:456–65.

Clements, A. M., H. P. Mapp, Jr., and V. R. Eidman. 1971. *A procedure for correlating events in farm firm simulation models.* Okla. Agric. Exp. Stn. Tech. Bull. T-131.

Cochrane, W., and M. Ryan. 1976. *American farm policy, 1948–1973*. Minneapolis: Univ. of Minnesota Press.

Cocks, K. D., and H. O. Carter. 1968. Micro goal functions and economic planning. *Am. J. Agric. Econ.* 59:400–10.

Conklin, F., A. Baquet, and A. Halter. 1977. *A Bayesian simulation approach for estimating the value of information: An application to frost forecasting*. Oreg. Exp. Stn. Tech. Bull. 136, Oregon State Univ., Corvallis.

Cook, T. D., and D. T. Campbell. 1979. *Quasi-experimentation, design and analysis issues for field settings*. Chicago: Rand McNally.

Coombs, C. H. 1975. Portfolio theory and the measurement of risk. In *Human judgment and decision processes,* eds. M. F. Kaplan and S. Schwartz. New York: Academic Press.

Crop-Hail Insurance Actuarial Association. 1980. 1980 preliminary report. Chicago.

Cutler, L., and D. S. Pass. 1971. *A computer program for quadratic mathematical models to be used for aircraft design and other applications involving linear constraints*. Rand Corp. R-516-PR.

Danin, Y. 1975. Grain reserves and price stabilization, 75–80. Dep. Agric. Appl. Econ. Staff Pap., Univ. of Minnesota, Dec.

_____. 1976. *Reserve stock grain models: The world and the United States, 1975–1985*. Minn. Agric. Exp. Stn. Tech. Bull. 305.

Davis, C. 1949. The development of agricultural policy since the end of the World War. In *Readings on agricultural policy,* ed. O. B. Jesness. Philadelphia: Blackiston.

Davis, J. H., and J. R. Franzmann. 1973. Evaluation of a quantitative procedure to select among alternative marketing strategies to reduce price risks of stocker operators. *South. J. of Agric. Econ.* 5:63–71.

Dawid, A. P. 1982. The well-calibrated Bayesian. *J. Am. Stat. Assoc.* 77:605–10.

Dean, G. W. 1966. Decision theory models in range livestock research. *West. Agric. Res. Counc. Rep. 8.* San Francisco.

Dean, R., H. P. Mapp, O. L. Walker, and M. L. Hardin. 1980. *Effects of government risk management programs on farm survival and growth in the southern Great Plains*. Dep. of Agric. Econ., Okla. State Univ.

deFinetti, B. 1937. La prevision: Ses lois logiques, ses sources subjectives. *Ann. Inst. Henri Poincare* 7:1–68.

_____. 1962. Does it make good sense to speak of "good probability appraisers"? In *The scientist speculates: An anthology of partly-baked ideas,* ed. I. J. Good. New York: Basic Books.

_____. 1974. *Theory of probability.* Vol. 1. New York: Wiley.

De Groot, M. H., and S. E. Fienberg. 1981. Assessing probability assessors: Calibration and refinement. Tech. Rep. 205, Dep. Stat., Carnegie-Mellon Univ., Pittsburgh.

Dewbre, J., and L. Blakeslee. 1979. The potential for using midwest futures contracts to reduce risk and increase storage returns on Pacific Northwest wheat. Pap. presented Am. Agric. Econ. Assoc. Annu. Meet., July 29–Aug. 1, Pullman, Wash.

Dickenson, J. P. 1974. The reliability of estimation procedures in portfolio analysis. *J. Financ. Quant. Anal.* 9:447–62.

Dillon, J. L. 1971. An expository review of Bernoullian decision theory in agriculture: Is utility futility? *Rev. Mark. Agric. Econ.* 39-3-80.

_____. 1977. *The analysis of response in crop and livestock production.* 2d ed. New York: Pergamon Press.

_____. 1979. Bernoullian decision theory: Outline and problems. In *Risk, uncertainty, and agricultural development,* eds. Roumasset et al., 23-38. New York: Agric. Dev. Counc.

Dillon, J. L., and P. Scandizzo. 1978. Risk attitudes of subsistence farmers in Northeast Brazil: A sampling approach. *Am. J. Agric. Econ.* 60:425–35.

Dixon, B. L., and R. E. Howitt. 1980. Resource production under uncertainty: A stochastic control approach to timber harvest scheduling. *Am. J. Agric. Econ.* 62:499–507.

Economic growth of the agricultural firm. 1977. Coll. Agric. Res. Cen., Washington State Univ. Tech. Bull. 86. Pullman.

Eddleman, B. R., and J. E. Moya-Rodriguez. 1979. Influence of market diversification on farm income variability of soybean producers. *South. J. Agric. Econ.* 11:101–16.

Edwards, W. 1954. The theory of decison-making. *Psychol. Bull.* 51:380–417.

_____. 1961. Behavioral decision theory. *Ann. Rev. Psychol.* 12:473–98.

Edwards, W., and M. D. Boehlje. 1980. *Farm machinery selection in Iowa under variable weather conditions.* Iowa Agric. Exp. Stn. Spec. Rep. 85, Ames.

Eidman, V. R., G. W. Dean, and H. O. Carter. 1967. An application of statistical decision theory to commercial turkey production. *J. Farm Econ.* 49:852–68.

Elton, E., and M. Gruber. 1981. *Modern portfolio theory and investment analysis.* New York: Wiley.

Fama, E. F. 1976. *Foundations of finance.* New York: Basic Books.

Feder, G., R. E. Just, and A. Schmitz. 1977. Storage with price uncertainty in international trade. *Int. Econ. Rev.* 18:553–68.

Fernandez, A. 1982. *Conjoint analysis: An application to the importance of farmers' goals.* M.S. thesis, Purdue Univ.

Firch, R. S. 1964. Stability of farm income in a stabilizing economy. *J. Farm Econ.* 46:323–40.

Fishbein, M., and I. Ajzen. 1975. *Belief, attitude, intention, and behavior: An introduction to theory and research.* Reading, Mass.: Addison-Wesley.

Fishburn, P. C. 1974. Convex stochastic dominance with continuous distributions. *J. Econ. Theory* 7:143–58.

_____. 1977. Mean-risk analysis with risk associated with below-target returns. *Am. Econ. Rev.* 67:116–26.

Flood, M. 1981. *Price and yield variability in Missouri.* M.S. thesis, Univ. of Missouri-Columbia.

Francisco, E., and J. Anderson. 1972. Chance and choice west of the Darling. *Aust. J. Agric. Econ.* 16:82–93.

Frankfurter, G. M., H. E. Phillips, and J. P. Seagle. 1971. Portfolio selection: The effects of uncertain means, variances, and covariances. *J. Financ. Quant. Anal.* 6:1251–62.

Franzmann, J. 1971. Cattle cycles revisited. *South. J. Agric. Econ.* 3:69–76.

Freund, R. J. 1956. The introduction of risk into a programming model. *Econometrica* 24:253–64.

Fried, J. 1970. Forecasting and probability distributions for models of portfolio selection. *J. Financ.* 25:539–54.

Friedman, M. 1953. *Essays in positive economics.* Chicago: Univ. of Chicago Press.

_____. 1977. Nobel lecture: Inflation and unemployment. *J. Pol. Econ.* 85:466–67.

Gabriel, S. C. 1979. *Financial responses to changes in business risk in Central Illinois grain farms.* Ph.D. diss., Univ. of Illinois.

Gabriel, S. C., and C. B. Baker. 1980. Concepts of business and financial risk. *Am. J. Agric. Econ.* 62:560–64.

Gardner, B. L. 1978. Public policy and the control of agricultural production. *Am. J. Agric. Econ.* 60:836–43.

_____. 1979. The farmer's risk and financial environment under the Food and Agricultural Act of 1977. *Agric. Financ. Rev.* 39:123–41.

Gardner, B. L., and J-P. Chavas. 1979. Market equilibrium with random production. Pap. presented Am. Agric. Econ. Assoc. Annu. Meet., Pullman, Wash.

Gebremeskel, T., and C. R. Shumway. 1979. Farm planning and calf marketing strategies for risk management: An application of linear programming and statistical decision theory. *Am. J. Agric. Econ.* 61:663–70.

Goldberger, A. S. 1964. *Econometric theory.* New York: Wiley.

Good, I. J. 1952. Rational decisions. *J. Royal Stat. Soc.,* B ser., 14:107–14.

_____. 1965. *The estimation of probabilities: An essay on modern Bayesian methods.* Cambridge, Mass.: MIT Press.

Gray, R., T. Sorenson, and W. Cochrane. 1954. An economic analysis of the impact of government programs on the potato industry. Univ. Minn. Agric. Exp. Stn., Tech. Bull. 211, June.

Grether, D. M., and C. R. Plott. 1979. Economic theory of choice and the preference reversal phenomena. *Am. Econ. Rev.* 69:623–38.

Guttman, L. 1944. A basis for scaling qualitative data. *Am. Sociol. Rev.* 9:139–50.

Hadar, J., and W. R. Russell. 1969. Rules for ordering uncertain prospects. *Am. Econ. Rev.* 59:25–34.

Halter, A. M., and G. W. Dean. 1965. Use of simulation in evaluating management policies under uncertainty: An application to a large scale ranch. *J. Farm Econ.* 47:557–73.

———. 1971. *Decisions under uncertainty with research applications.* Cincinnati: South-Western Publishing.

Halter, A. M., and R. Mason. 1978. Utility measurement for those who need to know. *West. J. Agric. Econ.* 3:99–109.

Hanoch, G., and C. Levy. 1969. Efficiency analysis of choices involving risk. *Rev. Econ. Stud.* 36:335–46.

Hanson, G. D., and J. L. Thompson. 1980. A simulation study of maximum feasible farm debt burdens by farm type. *Am. J. Agric. Econ.* 62:727–33.

Hardin, M. L. 1978. *A simulation model for analyzing farm capital investment alternatives.* Ph.D. diss., Oklahoma State Univ.

Harman, W. L., R. E. Hatch, V. R. Eidman, and P. L. Claypool. 1972. *An evaluation of factors affecting the hierarchy of multiple goals.* Okla. Agric. Exp. Stn. Tech. Bull. T-134.

Harper, W. H., and C. E. Eastman. 1980. An evaluation of goal hierarchies for small farm operators. *Am. J. Agric. Econ.* 62:742–47.

Harris, D., and R. Nehring. 1976. Impact of farm size on the bidding potential for agricultural land. *Am. J. Agric. Econ.* 58:161–69.

Harris, K. S., and C. B. Baker. 1981. Does hedging increase credit for Illinois crop farmers? *North Cent. J. Agric. Econ.* 3:47–52.

Harris, T. R., and H. P. Mapp, Jr. 1980. A control theory approach to optimal irrigation scheduling in the Oklahoma Panhandle. *South. J. Agric. Econ.* 12:165–71.

———. 1981. Irrigation scheduling in the Oklahoma Panhandle using stochastic dominance theory. Prof. Pap. P-1004 Okla. Agric. Exp. Stn.

Hathaway, D. F. 1974. Food prices and inflation. *Brookings papers on economic activity* 1:63–109.

———. 1981. Government and agriculture: A review of two decades of change. *Am. J. Agric. Econ.* 63:779–87.

Hayenga, M., ed. 1981. *Applied commodity price analysis and forecasting.* Ames: Iowa State Univ.

Hazell, P. B. R. 1971. A linear alternative to quadratic and semivariance programming for farm planning under uncertainty. *Am. J. Agric. Econ.* 53:53–62.

———. 1982. Application of risk preference estimates in firm-household and agricultural sector models. *Am. J. Agric. Econ.* 64:384–90.

Hazell, P. B. R., and P. L. Scandizzo. 1975. Market intervention policies when production is risky. *Am. J. Agric. Econ.* 57:641–49.

Heady, E. O. 1949. Implications of production economics in agricultural economics methodology. *J. Farm Econ.* 31:837–50.

———. 1952. *Economics of agricultural production and resource use.* New York: Prentice-Hall.

Heifner, R. G. 1966. Determining efficient seasonal grain inventories: An application of quadratic programming. *J. Farm. Econ.* 48:648–60.

———. 1972. Optimal hedging levels and hedging effectiveness in cattle feeding. *Agric. Econ. Res.* 24:25–36.

Held, L. J., and G. A. Helmers. 1980. *Growth and survival of Nebraska Panhandle wheat farms under selected financial conditions.* Nebr. Agric. Exp. Stn. Res. Bull. 295.

———. 1981. Growth and survival in wheat farming: The impact of land expansion and borrowing restraints. *West. J. Agric. Econ.* 6:207–16.

Held, L. J., and R. A. Zink. 1982. Farm enterprise choice: Risk-return tradeoffs for cash-crop versus crop-livestock systems. *North Cent. J. Agric. Econ.* 4:11–20.

Helmberger, P., and R. Weaver. 1977. Welfare implications of commodity storage under uncertainty. *Am. J. Agric. Econ.* 59:639–51.

Helpman, E., and A. Razin. 1978. *A theory of international trade under uncertainty.* New York: Academic Press.

Herath, H., J. Hardaker, and J. Anderson. 1982. Choice of varieties of Sri Lanka rice farmers: Comparing alternative decision models. *Am. J. Agric. Econ.* 64:87–93.

Herbst, J. H. 1976. *Farm management: Principles, budgets, plans.* Champaign, Ill.: Stipes.

Herr, W. M., and E. LaDue. 1981. The Farmers Home Administration's changing role and mission. *Agric. Financ. Rev.* 41:58–72.

Hey, J. D. 1979. *Uncertainty in microeconomics.* New York: New York Univ. Press.

Hildreth, C. 1974. Ventures, bets and initial prospects. In *Decision rules and uncertainty,* eds. M. Balch and D. McFadden. Amsterdam: North-Holland.

———. 1977. What do we know about agricultural producers' behavior under price and yield instability? *Am. J. Agric. Econ.* 59:898–902.

Hillier, F. S. 1963. The derivation of probabilistic information for the evaluation of risky investments. *Manage. Sci.* 9:443–57.

Hirshleifer, J. 1958. On the theory of optimal investment. *J. Pol. Econ.* 66:329–52.

Hogan, W. W., and J. M. Warren. 1972. Compilation of the efficient boundary in the E-S portfolio selection model. *J. Financ. Quant. Anal.* 15:881–96.

Hogarth, R. M. 1975. Cognitive processes and the assessment of subjective probability distributions. *J. Am. Stat. Assoc.* 70:271–89.

Holmes, B. H. 1972. *A history of federal water resources programs, 1800–1960.* USDA Misc. Publ. 1233.

Holt, J., and K. B. Anderson. 1978. Teaching decision making under risk and uncertainty to farmers. *Am. J. Agric. Econ.* 60:249–53.

Hottel, B. 1981. The Commodity Credit Corporation and agricultural lending. *Agric. Financ. Rev.* 41:58–72.

Hueth, D. L., and A. Schmitz. 1972. International trade and intermediate and final goods: Some welfare implications of destabilized prices. *Q. J. Econ.* 86:351–65.

Hughes, D. W. 1981. An overview of farm sector capital and credit needs. *Agric. Financ. Rev.* 41:1–19.

Hughes, D. W., S. C. Gabriel, R. Meekhof, M. D. Boehlje, D. Reinders, and G. Amols. 1981. *National agricultural credit study.* Staff Pap. Rep. AGESS 810413, Econ. Res. Serv., USDA, Apr.

Ibrahim, I. B., and R. Williams. 1978. Price unpredictability and monetary standards: A comment on Klien's measure of price uncertainty. *Econ. Inq.* 26:431–37.

Illinois Cooperative Crop Report Service. *Illinois agricultural statistics.* USDA, Springfield, Ill., var. issues.

Industries Assistance Commission. 1978. *Rural income fluctuations,* Canberra, 24, 50–51, 101–13.

Jabara, C., and R. L. Thompson. 1980. Agricultural comparative advantage under international price uncertainty: The case of Senegal. *Am. J. Agric. Econ.* 62:188–98.

Jacobs, O. L. R. *Introduction to control theory.* London: Oxford Univ. Press.

Jensen, H. R. 1977. Farm management and production economics, 1946–70. In *A survey of agricultural economics literature,* ed. L. R. Martin. Vol. 1. Minneapolis: Univ. of Minnesota Press.

Jibben, D., and H. R. Allen. 1979. *Ranch management: Handling drought.* S.D. Agric. Exp. Stn., Circ. 220.

Jobson, J., and B. Korkie. 1980. Estimation for Markowitz efficient portfolios. *J. Am. Stat. Assoc.* 75:544–54.

Johnson, D. A. 1979. *Investment, production, and marketing strategies for an Iowa farmer-cattle feeder in a risky environment.* Ph.D. diss., Iowa State Univ.

Johnson, D. A., and M. D. Boehlje. 1981. Minimizing mean absolute deviations to exactly solve utility problems. *Am. J. Agric. Econ.* 63:728–29.

Johnson, E. G. 1947. *Forward prices for agriculture.* Chicago: Univ. of Chicago Press.

Johnson, L. L. 1960. The theory of hedging and speculation in commodity futures. *Rev. Econ. Stud.* 27:139–51.

Johnson, S. R., and G. C. Rausser. 1977. Systems analysis and simulation in agricultural and resource economics. In *A survey of agricultural economics literature.* Vol. 2. Minneapolis: Univ. of Minnesota Press.

———. 1982. Composite forecasting in commodity systems. In *New directions in econometric modeling and forecasting in U.S. agriculture,* ed. Gordon Rausser. Elsevier: North-Holland.

Johnston, J. 1972. *Econometric methods.* 2d ed. New York: McGraw-Hill.

Jones, B. L. 1978. *Factors affecting the borrowing potential of farmers in east-central Illinois.* M.S. thesis, Univ. of Illinois.

Jones, L. A., and D. K. Larson. 1965. *Economic impact of federal crop insurance in selected areas of Virginia and Montana.* USDA, ERS, Agric. Econ. Rep. 75, May.

Jones, R. B. 1969. Stability in farm incomes. *J. Agric. Econ.* 20:111-24.

Just, R. E. 1974. *Econometric analysis of production decisions with government intervention: The case of California field crops.* Univ. Calif. Giannini Found. Monogr. 33, Berkeley.

———. 1975a. Risk aversion under profit maximization. *Am. J. Agric. Econ.* 57:347–52.

———. 1975b. Risk response models and their use in agricultural policy evaluation. *Am. J. Agric. Econ.* 57:836-43.

Just, R. E. 1982. *Farmer-owned grain reserve program needs modification to improve effectiveness: Theoretical and empirical considerations in agricultural buffer stock policy under the Food and Agriculture Act of 1977.* Vol. 3. Rep. Congr. U.S. Gen. Account. Off., Washington, D.C., June 26.

Just, R. E., and A. Hallam. 1978. Functional flexibility and analysis of commodity price stabilization policy. In *Proc. Am. Stat. Assoc. Bus. and Econ. Stat. Sec.*

Just, R. E., and G. C. Rausser. 1981. Commodity price forecasting with large-scale econometric models and the futures market. *Am. J. Agric. Econ.* 63:197–208.

Just, R. E., E. Lutz, A. Schmitz, and S. Turnovsky. 1977. The distribution of welfare gains from international price stabilization under distortions. *Am. J. Agric. Econ.* 59:652–61.

————. 1978. The distribution of welfare gains from price stabilization: An international perspective. *J. Int. Econ.* 8:551–63.

Just, R. E., D. L. Hueth, and A. Schmitz. 1982. *Applied welfare economics and public polcy.* Englewood Cliffs, N.J.: Prentice-Hall.

Kahneman, D., and A. Tversky. 1972. Subjective probability: A judgment of representativeness. *Cognitive Psychol.* 3:430–54.

————. 1979. Prospect theory: An analysis of decision under risk. *Econometrica* 47:263–91.

Kaiser, E., and M. D. Boehlje. 1980. A multiperiod risk programming model for farm planning. *North Cent. J. Agric. Econ.* 2:47–54.

Kataoka, S. 1963. A stochastic programming model. *Econometrica* 31:181–96.

Kawaguchi, T., and Y. Maruyama. 1972. Generalized constrained games in farm planning. *Am. J. Agric. Econ.* 54:591–602.

Kemp, M. C., and N. Liviatan. 1973. Production and trade patterns under uncertainty. *Econ. Rec.* 49:215–27.

Kennedy, J. O. S., and E. M. Francisco. 1974. On the formulation of risk constraints for linear programming. *J. Agric. Econ.* 25:129–44.

Kent, M. A., and A. G. Lloyd. 1983. *Coping with rural income instability: Some estimates of probability of default under various loan repayment arrangements.* Summ. Pap. presented annu. conf. Aust. Agric. Econ. Soc., Brisbane, Queensland, 4 pp.

Kihlstrom, R. E., and L. J. Mirman. 1974. Risk aversion with many commodities. *J. Econ. Theory* 8:361–88.

King, R. P. 1979. *Operational techniques for applied decision analysis under uncertainty.* Ph.D. diss., Michigan State Univ.

King, R. P., and L. J. Robison. 1980. Implementing stochastic dominance with respect to a function. In *Risk analysis in agriculture: Research and educational developments.* Dept. Agric. Econ. AE–4492, Univ. of Illinois.

————. 1981a. An interval approach to the measurement of decision maker preference. *Am. J. Agric. Econ.* 63:510–20.

————. 1981b. Implementation of the interval approach to the measurement of decision maker preferences. Agric. Exp. Stn. Res. Rep. 418, Michigan State Univ.

Kirk, D. E. 1970. *Optimal control theory: An introduction.* Englewood Cliffs, N.J.: Prentice-Hall.

Klein, B. 1978. The measurement of long and short-term price uncertainty: A moving regression time series analysis. *Econ. Inq.* 26:438–52.

Kletke, D. D. 1979. *Operation of the enterprise budget generator.* Okla. Agric. Exp. Stn. Res. Rep. P-790, Stillwater.

Kliebenstein, J. B., D. A. Barrett, W. D. Heffernan, and C. L. Kirtley. 1980. An analysis of farmers' perceptions of benefits received from farming. *North Cent. J. Agric. Econ.* 2:131–36.

Klien, R. W., and V. S. Bawa. 1976. The effect of estimation risk on optimal portfolio choice. *J. Financ. Econ.* 3:215–31.

Klinefelter, D. A. 1979. *Optimal marketing strategies in response to uncertainty by Illinois grain farmers.* Ph.D. diss., Univ. of Illinois.

Klinefelter, D. A., S. T. Sonka, and C. B. Baker. 1980. Selection and screening of marketing options for risk evaluation. In *Risk analysis in agriculture: Research and educational developments.* Dept. Agr. Econ. AE–4492, Univ. of Illinois.

Knight, F. H. 1921. *Risk, uncertainty and profit.* Boston: Houghton Mifflin.

Knowles, G. J. 1980. Estimating utility function. In *Risk analysis in agriculture: Research and educational developments.* Dept. Agric. Econ. AE-4492, Univ. of Illinois, June.

Kogan, N., and M. A. Wallach. 1967. Risk taking as a function of the situation, the person, and the group. In *New directions in psychology III,* ed. R. Brown. New York: Holt, Rinehart and Winston.

Konandreas, P. A., and A. Schmitz. 1978. Welfare implications of grain price stabilization: Some empirical evidence for the United States. *Am. J. Agric. Econ.* 60:74–84.

Kramer, R. A. 1981. A risk analysis of the Federal Crop Insurance Act of 1980. Dep. Agric. Econ. Res. Rep. SP-81-9, Virginia Polytechnic Institute and State Univ.

Kramer, R. A., and R. D. Pope. 1981. Participation in farm commodity programs: A stochastic dominance analysis. *Am. J. Agric. Econ.* 63:119–28.

———. 1982. Crop insurance for managing risk. *J. Am. Soc. Farm Manage. Rural Appraisers* 46:34–40.

Kramer, R. A., C. McSweeney, and R. Stavros. 1983. Soil conservation with uncertainty. *Am. J. Agric. Econ.* 65:694–702.

Landon, J. 1982. *A dynamic marketing decision model for Northwest lentil producers.* M.A. thesis, Washington State Univ.

LaPiere, R. T. 1934. Attitudes and actions. *Soc. Forces* 13:230–37.

Lee, J. E., Jr., S. C. Gabriel, and M. D. Boehlje. 1981. Public policy toward agricultural credit. In *Future sources of loanable funds for agricultural banks.* Kansas City, Mo.: Federal Reserve Bank of Kansas City.

Lee, W. F. 1979. Some alternatives to conventional farm mortgage loan repayment plans. *Can. Farm Econ.* 14:12–20.

Lee, W. F., and N. Rask. 1976. Inflation and crop profitability: How much can farmers pay for land? *Am. J. Agric. Econ.* 58:984–90.

Lemieux, C. M., J. W. Richardson, and C. J. Nixon. 1982. Federal crop insurance vs. ASCS disaster assistance for Texas High Plains producers: An application of whole-farm simulation. *West. J. Agric. Econ.* 7:141–54.

Leuthold, R. M., and P. E. Peterson. 1980. Using the hog futures market effectively while hedging. *J. Am. Soc. Farm Manage. Rural Appraisers* 44:6–12

Levy, H. 1978. Equilibrium in an imperfect market: A constraint on the number of securities in the portfolio. *Am. Econ. Rev.* 68:643–58.

Levy, H., and H. M. Markowitz. 1979. Approximating expected utility by a function of mean and variance. *Am. Econ. Rev.* 69:308–17.

Levy, H., and J. Paroush. 1974. Toward multivariate efficiency criteria. *J. Econ. Theory* 7:129–42.

Levy, H., and M. Sarnat. 1972. *Investment and portfolio analysis.* New York: Wiley.

Lichtenstein, S., and P. Slovic. 1971. Reversal of preferences between bids and choices in gambling decisions. *J. Exp. Psychol.* 89:46–55.

Likert, R. 1932. A technique for the measurement of attitudes. *Arch. Psychol.* 140.

Lin, W. 1977. Measuring aggregate supply response under instability. *Am. J. Agric. Econ.* 59:903–7.

Lin, W., and H. Chang. 1978. Specification of Bernoullian utility functions in decision analysis. *Agric. Econ. Res.* 30:30–36.

Lin, W., G. Dean, and C. Moore. 1974. An empirical test of utility versus profit maximization in agricultural production. *Am. J. Agric. Econ.* 56:497–508.

Lin, W. G., G. Coffman, and J. B. Penn. 1980. *U.S. farm numbers, sizes, and related structural dimensions: Projections to year 2000.* USDA, ERS, TB-1626, July.

Lindley, D. V. 1974a. Discussion on the papers by Professor Tversky and by Professor Supes. *J. R. Stat. Soc.,* ser. B, 36:181–82.

———. 1974b. Foreword to *Theory of probability* by B. deFinetti. New York: Wiley.

Lins, D., S. Gabriel, and S. Sonka. 1981. An analysis of the risk aversion of farm operators: An asset portfolio approach. *West. J. Agric. Econ.* 6:15–30.

Lintner, J. 1965. The valuation of risky assets and the selection of risky investments in stock portfolios and capital budgets. *Rev. Econ. Stat.* 47:13–37.

Love, H. C. 1972. *Crop production risk in Alberta: Variation in yield, price, and gross income per acre for barley, oats, and wheat, 1946–66 by census division.* Univ. Alberta, Agric. Econ. Res. Bull. 5.

Luce, R., and H. Raiffa. 1957. *Games and decisions.* New York: Wiley.

Lutgen, L. H., and G. A. Helmers. 1979. Simulation of production-marketing alternatives for grain farms under uncertainty. *North Cent. J. Agric.* 1:23–30.

Machina, M. J. 1979. Expected utility analysis without the independence axiom. Discuss. Pap. 80-6, Dep. Econ., Univ. of California, San Diego.

Manley, W. T., and D. A. Reimund. 1973. Interrelations in our food system. Natl. Outlook Conf., Washington, D.C., Dec.

Mapp, H. P., M. L. Hardin, O. L. Walker, and T. Persaud. 1979. Analysis of risk management strategies for agricultural producers. *Am. J. Agric. Econ.* 61:1071–77.

Markowitz, H. M. 1959. *Portfolio selection.* New York: Wiley.

———. 1977. An algorithm for finding undominated portfolios. In *Financial decision making under uncertainty,* eds. H. Levy and M. Sarnat, 3–10. New York: Academic Press.

Maslow, A. H. 1943. A theory of human motivation. *Psychol. Rev.* 50:370–75.

Massell, B. F. 1969. Price stabilization and welfare. *Q. J. Econ.* 83:285–97.

Mathia, G. A. 1975. *Measurement of price, yield, and sales variability indexes for selected North Carolina crops.* N.C. State Univ. at Raleigh, Econ. Res. Rep. 36.

McInerney, J. P. 1967. Maximin programming: An approach to farm planning under uncertainty. *J. Agric. Econ.* 18:279–90.

———. 1969. Linear programming and game theory models: Some extensions. *J. Agric. Econ.* 20:269–78.

McKinnon, R. J. 1967. Futures markets, buffer stocks, and income stability for primary producers. *J. Pol. Econ.* 75:844–61.

Melichar, E. O. 1979a. Capital gains versus current income in the farming sector. *Am. J. Agric. Econ.* 61:1085–92.

———. 1979b. Farm risks from instability in financial markets. In *Risk management in agriculture: Behavioral, managerial, and policy issues.* AE-4478, Univ. of Illinois.

———. 1980. Rural banking conditions and farm financial trends. Wharton Agric. Forecasting Meet., Philadelphia, Mar.

Melichar, E. O., and P. T. Balides. 1981. Agricultural finance databook. Board Governors, Fed. Reserve Syst. Washington, D.C., Mon. Ser., Apr.

Meyer, J. 1977a. Choice among distributions. *J. Econ. Theory* 14:326–36.

———. 1977b. Second degree stochastic dominance with respect to a function. *Int. Econ. Rev.* 18:477–87.

Miller, T. A., and W. L. Trock. 1979. *Disaster assistance to farmers: Needs, issues, and programs.* Great Plains Agric. Counc. Publ. 88, Feb.

Miller, T. A., and A. S. Walter. 1977. An assessment of government programs that protect agricultural producers from natural risk. In *Agric. Food Policy Rev.,* USDA, ERS, AFPR-1, Jan.

Modigliani, F., and G. A. Pogue. 1974. An introduction to risk and return. *Financ. Anal. J.* 30(Mar.–Apr.):68–80, (May–June):69–86.

Moscardi, E., and A. de Janvry. 1977. Attitudes toward risk among peasants: An econometric approach. *Am. J. Agric. Econ.* 59:710–21.

Murphy, A. H., and R. L. Winkler. 1977. Reliability of subjective probability forecasts of precipitation and temperature. *Appl. Stat.* 26:41–47.

———. 1979. Probabilistic temperature forecasts: The case for an operational program. *Bull. Am. Meteorol. Soc.* 60:12–19.

Musser, W. N., and G. Stamoulis. 1981. Evaluating the Food and Agricultural Act of 1977 with firm quadratic risk programming. *Am. J. Agric. Econ.* 63:447–56.

Musser, W. N., W. D. Shurley, and F. W. Williams. 1980. An E-V analysis of beef cattle backgrounding systems in Georgia. *South. J. Agric. Econ.* 12:37–41.

Musser, W. N., B. Tew, and E. Epperson. 1981a. An economic examination of an integrated pest management production system with a contrast between E-V and stochastic dominance analysis. *South. J. Agric. Econ.* 13:119–24.

Musser, W. N., J. Ohannesian, and F. J. Benson. 1981b. A safety first model of risk management for use in extension programs. *North Cent. J. Agric. Econ.* 3:41–46.

Muth, J. 1961. Rational expectations and the theory of price movements. *Econometrica* 29:315–35.

National Water Commission. 1973. *Water policies for the future.* Washington, D.C.: GPO.

Nau, R. F. 1981. Coherent assessment of subjective probability. Oper. Res. Cent., Univ., Calif., Berkeley, Rep. ORC 81-5, Mar.

Nelson, A. G. 1980. The case for and components of a probabilistic agricultural outlook program. *West. J. Agric. Econ.* 5:185–93.

Nelson, A. G., and T. D. Harris. 1978. Designing an instructional package: The use of probabilities in farm decision making. *Am. J. Agric. Econ.* 60:993–97.

Nelson, A. G., G. Casler, and O. L. Walker. 1978. Making farm decisions in a risky world: A guidebook. Dept. Agric. Res. Econ., Oregon State Univ.

Nelson, C. R. 1973. *Applied time series analysis for managerial forecasting.* San Francisco: Holden-Day.

Nelson, F. 1975. *An economic analysis of the impact of past farm programs on livestock and crop prices, production, and resource adjustments.* Ph.D. diss., Univ. of Minnesota.

Nerlove, M. 1979. The dynamics of supply: Retrospect and prospect. *Am. J. Agric. Econ.* 61:874–88.

Newbury, D. M., and J. E. Stiglitz. 1979. The theory of commodity price stabilization rules: Welfare impacts and supply responses. *Econ. J.* 89:799–817.

Nieuwoult, W. L., J. B. Bullock, and G. A. Mathia. 1976. An economic evaluation of alternative peanut policies. *Am. J. Agric. Econ.* 56:485–95.

Nisbett, R., and L. Ross. 1980. *Human inference: Strategies and shortcomings.* Englewood Cliffs, N.J.: Prentice-Hall.

Officer, R. R., and A. N. Halter. 1968. Utility analysis in a practical setting. *Am. J. Agric. Econ.* 50:257–77.

Officer, R. R., A. N. Halter, and J. L. Dillon. 1967. Risk, utility, and the palatability of extension advice to farmer groups. *Aust. J. Agric. Econ.* 11:171–83.

Oi, W. Y. 1961. The desirability of price instability under perfect competition. *Econometrica* 27:58–64.

O'Mara, G. T. 1971. *A decision-theoretic framework of the microeconomics of technique diffusion in a developing country.* Ph.D. diss., Stanford Univ.

Paris, Q. 1979. Revenue and cost uncertainty, generalized mean-variance and linear complementarity problem. *Am. J. Agric. Econ.* 61:268–75.

Patrick, G. F. 1979a. Effects of debt levels and loan arrangements on farm firm survival and growth. In *Risk management in agriculture: Behavioral, managerial, and policy issues.* AE-4478, Univ. of Illinois.

_____. 1979b. *Risk and variability in Indiana agriculture.* Agric. Exp. Stn. Bull. 234, Purdue Univ.

Patrick, G. F., and B. F. Blake. 1981. Measurement and modeling of farmers' goals. *South. J. Agric. Econ.* 12:199–204.

Patrick, G. F., and L. M. Eisgruber. 1968. The impact of managerial ability and capital structure on farm firm growth. *Am. J. Agric. Econ.* 50:491–507.

Patrick, G. F., S. H. Whitaker, and B. F. Blake. 1980. Farmers' goals and risk aversion: Some preliminary analyses. In *Risk analysis in agriculture: Research and educational developments.* Dep. Agric. Econ. AE-4492, Univ. of Illinois.

Patrick, G. F., B. F. Blake, and S. H. Whitaker. 1981. Magnitude estimation: An application to farmers' risk-income preferences. *West. J. Agric. Econ.* 6, 2:239–48.

_____. 1983. Farmers' goals: Uni- or multi-dimensional? *Am. J. Agric. Econ.* 65:315–20.

Peck, A. E. 1975. Hedging and income stability: Concepts, implications, and an example. *Am. J. Agric. Econ.* 75:410–30.

Persaud, T. 1980. *Evaluating risk management strategies in a farm planning model.* Ph.D. diss., Oklahoma State Univ.

Persaud, T., and H. P. Mapp. 1979. Effects of alternative measures of dispersion on risk-efficient farm plans in a MOTAD framework. Pap. presented Annu. AAEA Meet., Pullman, Wash., July 29–Aug. 1.

_____. 1980. Analysis of alternative production and marketing strategies in southwestern Oklahoma: A MOTAD approach. In *Risk analysis in agriculture: Research and development.* Dep. Agric. Econ. AE-4492, Univ. of Illinois.

Peterson, P. E. 1983. *A portfolio theory-based optimal hedging technique with an application to a commercial cattle feedlot.* Ph.D. diss., Univ. of Illinois.

Pope, R. D. 1981. Supply response and the dispersion of price expectations. *Am. J. Agric. Econ.* 63:161–63.

_____. 1982. Empirical estimation and use of risk preferences. *Am. J. Agric. Econ.* 64:376–83.

Pope, R. D., and B. D. Gardner. 1978. The structure of agriculture and risk. In *Market risks in agriculture,* ed. P. Barry, Tex. Agric. Exp. Stn. DTR 78-1, July.

Pope, R. D., J-P. Chavas, and R. Just. 1982. Economic welfare evaluation for producers under uncertainty. Dep. Agric. Econ., Texas A. & M. Univ. Mimeogr.

Porter, R. B. 1974. Semivariance and stochastic dominance: A comparison. *Am. Econ. Rev.* 64:200–204.

Pratt, J. W. 1964. Risk aversion in the small and in the large. *Econometrica* 32:122–36.

Prentice, P. T., and L. P. Schertz. 1981. *Inflation: A food and agricultural perspective.* Agric. Econ. Rep. 463, Econ. Res. Serv., USDA, Feb.

Purcell, W. D., and D. A. Riffe. 1980. The impact of selected hedging strategies on the cash flow position of cattle feeders. *South. J. Agric. Econ.* 12:85–93.

Pyle, D. H., and S. J. Turnovsky. 1970. Safety-first and expected utility maximization in mean-standard deviation portfolio analysis. *Rev. Econ. Stud.* 52:75–81.

_____. 1971. Risk aversion in chance constrained portfolio selection. *Manage. Sci.* 18:218–25.

Quirk, J. P., and R. Saposnik. 1962. Admissibility and measurable utility functions. *Rev. Econ. Stud.* 29:140–46.

Raiffa, H. 1970. *Decision analysis: Introductory lectures on choice under uncertainty.* Reading, Mass.: Addison-Wesley.

Raiffa, H., with L. T. Thompson. 1974. *Analysis for decision making: An audiographic, self-instructional course.* Chicago: Encycl. Br. Educ. Corp.

Rausser, G. C., and J. W. Freebairn. 1975. Stochastic control of environment externalities. *Ann. Econ. Soc. Meas.* 4:271–92.

Reid, D. W., W. N. Musser, and N. R. Martin, Jr. 1980. Consideration of investment tax credit in a multiperiod mathematical programming model of farm growth. *Am. J. Agric. Econ.* 62:29–34.

Reimund, D., C. V. Moore, and J. R. Martin. 1977. Factors affecting structural change in agricultural subsectors. *South. J. Agric. Econ.* 9:11–20.

Rettger, M. J., and R. N. Boisvert. 1979. Flood insurance or disaster loans: An economic valuation. *Am. J. Agric. Econ.* 61:496–505.

Reutlinger, S. 1976. A simulation model for evaluating world-wide buffer stocks of wheat. *Am. J. Agric. Econ.* 58:1–12.

Richardson, J. W. 1978. *An application of optimal control theory to agricultural policy analysis.* Ph.D. diss., Oklahoma State Univ.

_____. 1980. *Generation of correlated triangularly distributed stochastic variables.* Texas A. & M. Univ., College Station. Mimeogr.

Richardson, J. W., and G. D. Condra. 1981. Farm size evaluation in the El Paso Valley: A survival success approach. *Am. J. Agric. Econ.* 63:430–47.

Richardson, J. W., and C. J. Nixon. 1981. *The farm level income and policy simulation model: FLIPSIM.* Dep. Agric. Econ., Texas A. & M. Univ. Tech. Rep. 81-2.

Richardson, J. W., D. E. Ray, and J. N. Trapp. 1979. *Illustrative applications of optimal control theory techniques to problems in agricultural economics.* Okla. Agric. Exp. Stn. Bull. B-739.

Riffe, D., and L. Tweeten. 1977. Projecting the impact of demand-supply balance and inflation on the purchasing power of farm income, 13–20. *Curr. Farm Econ.,* Okla. Agr. Exp. Stn.

Rister, E. M., and J. R. Skess. 1982. The value of outlook information in past-harvest marketing strategies. Pap. presented Am. Agric. Econ. Assoc. Meet., Logan, Utah, Aug. 1–4.

Robinson, K. R. 1979. The distributional consequences of recent inflation. *Am. J. Agric. Econ.* 61:903–8.

Robison, L. J. 1979. Farm real estate: How much is it worth—who can afford it? *Mich. Farm Econ.* 436, June, Michigan State Univ.

_____. 1982. An appraisal of expected utility hypothesis tests. *Am. J. Agric. Econ.* 64:367–75.

Robison, L. J., and P. J. Barry. 1977. Portfolio adjustments: An application to rural banking. *Am. J. Agric. Econ.* 59:311–20.

_____. 1980. Portfolio theory and asset indivisibility: Implications for analysis of risk management. *North Cent. J. Agric. Econ.* 2:41–46.

Robison, L. J., and J. R. Brake. 1979. Application of portfolio theory to farmer and lender behavior. *Am. J. Agric. Econ.* 61:158–64.

_____. 1980. Inflation, cash flows and growth: Some implications for the farm firm. *South. J. Agric. Econ.* 12:131–37.

Roumasset, J. A. 1976. *Rice and risk: Decision making among low income farmers.* Amsterdam: North-Holland.

_____. 1979. Introduction and state of the arts. In *Risk uncertainty and agricultural development,* eds. J. A. Roumasset et al. New York: Agric. Dev. Counc.

Roumasset, J. A., J. M. Boussard, and I. Singh, eds. 1979. *Risk, uncertainty and agricultural development.* New York: Agric. Dev. Counc.

Roush, C. E. 1978. *Economic evaluation of asset ownership transfer methods and family farm business arrangements after the Tax Reform Act of 1976.* Ph.D. diss., Oklahoma State Univ.

Roy, A. D. 1952. Safety first and the holding of assets. *Econometrica* 20:431–39.

Ruffin, R. J. 1974a. Comparative advantage under uncertainty. *J. Int. Econ.* 4:261–74.

_____. 1974b. International trade under uncertainty. *J. Int. Econ.* 4:243–60.

Russell, B. 1948. *Human knowledge: Its scopes and its limits.* New York: Simon and Schuster.

Ruttan, V. W. 1969. Program analysis and agricultural policy. In *The analysis and evaluation of public expenditures.* J. Econ. Comm., U.S. Congr.

_____. 1979. Inflation and productivity. *Am. J. Agric. Econ.* 61:846–902.

Ryan, D. M. 1974. Penalty and barrier functions. In *Numerical methods for constrained optimization,* eds. P. E. Gill and W. Murray. London: Academic Press.

Ryan, T. 1977. Supply response to risk: The case of U.S. pinto beans. *West. J. Agric. Econ.* 2:35–43.

Sage, A. P. 1968. *Optimum systems control.* Englewood Cliffs, N.J.: Prentice-Hall.

Samuelson, P. A. 1972. The consumer does benefit from feasible price stability. *Can. J. Econ.* 86:476–93.

Savage, L. J. 1954. *Foundations of statistics.* New York: Wiley.

_____. 1971. Elicitation of personal probabilities and expectations. *J. Am. Stat. Assoc.* 66:783–801.

Schmitz, A. 1979. The instability-storage-cost trade-off and non-optimality of price bands in stabilization policy. Univ. Calif., Berkeley, Dep. Agric. Res. Econ. Work. Pap. 15, Feb.

Schoemaker, P. J. H. 1982. The expected utility model: Its variants, responses, evidence and limitations. *J. Econ. Lit.* 20:529–63.

Schuh, E. 1974. The exchange rate and U.S. agriculture. *Am. J. Agric. Econ.* 66:1–13.

Schultz, T. W. 1945. *Agriculture in an unstable economy.* New York: McGraw-Hill.

_____. 1949. *Production and welfare of agriculture.* New York: Macmillan.

Schurle, B. W., and B. L. Erven. 1979a. Sensitivity of efficient frontiers developed for farm enterprise choice decisions. *Am. J. Agric. Econ.* 61:506–11.

_____. 1979b. The trade-off between return and risk in farm enterprise choice. *North Cent. J. Agric. Econ.* 1, no. 1.

Scott, J. T., and C. B. Baker. 1972. A practical way to select an optimum farm plan under risk. *Am. J. Agric. Econ.* 54:657–60.

Selley, R. 1980. Specification of firm level risk behavior models: Another look at the alternatives. In *Risk analysis in agriculture: Research and educational developments.* Dep. Agric. Econ. AE-4492, Univ. of Illinois, June.

Sharpe, W. F. 1964. Capital asset prices: A theory of market equilibrium under conditions of risk. *J. Financ.* 19:425–42.

Sharples, J. A., R. L. Walker, and R. W. Slaughter, Jr. 1976. Buffer stock management for wheat price stabilization. USDA, ERS, CED, Washington, D.C.

Shei, S. 1978. *The exchange rate and United States agricultural markets: General equilibrium approach.* Ph.D. diss., Purdue Univ.

Shuford, E. H., Jr., A. Albert, and H. E. Massengill. 1966. Admissible probability measurement procedures. *Psychometrika* 31:125–45.

Shurley, W. D. 1980. *Production, marketing and storage decisions under risk for cash grain and crop-hog farms in west-central Indiana.* Ph.D. diss., Purdue Univ.

Simmons, R. L., and C. Pomerada. 1975. Equilibrium quantity and timing of Mexican vegetable exports. *Am. J. Agric. Econ.* 57:472–79.

Simon, H. A. 1959a. A behavioral model of rational choice. *Q. J. Econ.* 69:99–118.

_____. 1959b. Theories of decision making in economics and behavioral science. *Am. Econ. Rev.* 49:253–83.

Simon, J. L. 1975. *Applied managerial economics.* Englewood Cliffs, N.J.: Prentice-Hall.

Sims, C. 1980. Macroeconomics and reality. *Econometrica* 48:1–48.

_____. 1981. Causality in economics: A book review. *J. Pol. Econ.* 89:578–83.

Slovic, P., B. Fischoff, and S. Lichtenstein. 1977. Behavioral decision theory. *Annu. Rev. Psychol.* 28:1–39.

Smith, A. W. 1972. The variability of net farm income. *Am. J. Agric. Econ.* 23:1957–63.

Smith, Adam. 1776/1937. *The wealth of nations,* 106, 111. New York: Modern Library.

Smith, B. A., and D. F. Capstick. 1976. *Evaluation of factors affecting the ranking of management goals by farm operators.* Arkansas Agric. Exp. Stn. Rep. 232. Nov.

Sonka, S. T. 1978. Corn yield variability since 1927. *Illinois Res.* 20:10–11.

Sonka, S. T. 1979. Risk management and risk preferences in agriculture: Discussion. *Am. J. Agric. Econ.* 61:1083–84.

Sonka, S. T., and B. L. Dixon. 1978. Determinants of lender response to short-term credit needs of small commercial farmers. *South. J. Agric. Econ.* 11:113–37.

Sonka, S. T., B. L. Dixon, and B. L. Jones. 1980. Impact of farm financial structure on the credit reserve of the farm business. *Am. J. Agric. Econ.* 62:565–70.

Stamoulis, K. G. 1979. *The impact of the Food and Agricultural Act of 1977 on optimum farm organization under risk.* M.S. thesis, Univ. of Georgia.

Starleaf, D. 1980. The impact of inflation on farmers and agriculture. Pap. presented NCR-113, Dep. Econ., Iowa State Univ.

Stein, J. L. 1961. The simultaneous determination of spot and futures prices. *Am. Econ. Rev.* 51:1012–25.

Stone, K. E. 1976. *Effects of a variable amortization payment plan on the financial organization of Illinois cash grain farms.* Ph.D. diss., Univ. of Illinios.

Structure issues of American agriculture. 1979. USDA-ERS, Agric. Econ. Rep. 438.

Swann, W. H. 1974. Constrained optimization by direct search. In *Numerical methods for constrained optimization,* eds. P. E. Gill and W. Murray. London: Academic Press.

Takayama, T., and R. L. Batterham. 1972. *Portfolio selection and resource allocation for financial and agricultural firms with the Rand QP 360 quadratic programming code.* Dep. Agric. Econ. AERR-117, Univ. of Illinois.

Telser, L. 1955–56. Safety-first and hedging. *Rev. Econ. Stud.* 23:1–6.

Thaler, R. 1980. Judgment and decision making under uncertainty: What economists can learn from psychology. In *Risk analysis in agriculture: Research and educational developments.* Dep. Agric. Econ. AE-4492, Univ. of Illinois.

Theil, H. 1965. Linear decision rules for macrodynamic policy problems. In *Quantitative planning of economics policy,* ed. B. G. Hickman, Brookings Institute.

_____. 1971. *Principles of econometrics.* New York: Wiley.

Thomas, W. E. 1971. *Economics of supplementary livestock production in the Columbia Basin of Washington.* Ph.D. diss., Washington State Univ.

Thomas, W. E., L. Blakeslee, L. Rogers, and N. Whittlesey. 1972. Separable programming for considering risk in farm planning. *Am. J. Agric. Econ.* 54:260–66.

Thomson, K. J., and P. B. R. Hazell. 1972. Reliability of using the mean absolute deviation to derive efficient EV farm plans. *Am. J. Agric. Econ.* 54:503-6.

Thurstone, L. L. 1931. The measurement of attitudes. *J. Abnorm. Soc. Psychol.* 26:249–69.

Tintner, G. 1940. *The variate difference method.* Cowles Comm. Res. Econ. Monogr. 5. Bloomington, Ind.: Principia Press.

Tisdell, C. 1963. Uncertainty, instability, and expected profit. *Econometrica* 31:243–47.

Tobin, J. L. 1958. Liquidity preference as a behavior toward risk. *Rev. Econ. Stud.* 25:65–86.

Traill, B. 1976. *Incorporation of risk variables in econometric supply response analysis.* Cornell Agric. Econ. Staff Pap. 76–27, Aug.

Tsiang, S. C. 1972. The rationale of the mean-standard deviation analysis, skewness preference, and the demand for money. *Am. Econ. Rev.* 62:354–71.

Turnovsky, S. J. 1974. Technological and price uncertainty in a Ricardian model of international trade. *Rev. Econ. Stud.* 41:201–17.

_____. 1976. The distribution of welfare gains from price stabilization: The case of multiplicative disturbances. *Int. Econ. Rev.* 17:133–48.

Tversky, A., and D. Kahneman. 1973. Availability: A heuristic for judging frequency and probability. *Cognative Psychol.* 5:207–32.

_____. 1974. Judgement under uncertainty: Heuristics and biases. *Science* 185:1124–31.

_____. 1975. Judgement under uncertainty: Heuristics and biases. In *Utility, probability and human decision making,* eds. D. Wendt and C. Vlek. Reidel: Dordrecht.

Tweeten, L. 1979. *Foundations of farm policy,* 2d ed. Lincoln: Univ. of Nebraska Press.

Tweeten, L., and S. Griffin. 1976. *General inflation and the farming economy.* Res. Rep. P-732, Agric. Exp. Stn., Oklahoma State Univ.

USDA. 1980. Bergland announces 250-county expansion of federal crop insurance program. Press release, Oct. 29.

USDA. 1981. *A brief history of Farmers Home Administration.* FmHA, Jan.

U.S. General Accounting Office. 1976. *Alleviating agricultural producer's crop losses: What should the federal role be?* Washington, D.C.: RED-76-91, May.

Vandeputte, J. M., and C. B. Baker. 1977. Specification of credit and liquidity preference schedules in linear programming models. *Overdruk uit Tijdschrift voor Economie.* Cent. Econ. Stud., Catholic Univ. of Louvain, Belg.

Van Horne, J. C. 1983. *Financial management and policy.* 6th ed. Englewood Cliffs, N.J.: Prentice-Hall.

Von Neumann, J., and O. Morgenstern. 1947. *Theory of games and economic behavior.* Princeton: Princeton Univ. Press.

Walker, O. L., and M. L. Hardin. 1979. Risk and risk control in farm growth: A simulation analysis. 1979. *Risk management and agriculture: Behavioral, managerial and policy issues.* Ill. Agric. Exp. Stn. AE-4478.

Walker, O. L., and A. G. Nelson. 1977. *Agricultural research and education related to decision making under uncertainty: An interpretative review of literature.* Okla. State Univ. Res. Rep. P-747, Mar.

———. 1980. *Dealing with risks in the management of agricultural firms: An extension/teaching viewpoint.* Dep. Agric. Econ. AE-4492, Univ. of Illinois.

Walker, O. L., M. L. Hardin, H. P. Mapp, Jr., and C. E. Roush. 1979. Farm growth and estate transfer in an uncertain environment. *South. J. Agric. Econ.* 11:33–44.

Ward, R. W., and L. B. Fletcher. 1971. From hedging to pure speculation: A micro model of optimal futures and cash market positions. *Am. J. Agric. Econ.* 53:71–78.

Waugh, F. V. 1944. Does the consumer gain from price instability? *Q. J. Econ.* 58:602–14.

———. 1966. Consumer aspects of price instability. *Econometrica* 34:504–8.

Weigel, R. H., and L. S. Newman. 1976. Increasing attitude-behavior correspondence by broadening the scope of the behavioral measure. *J. Pers. Soc. Psychol.* 33:793–802.

Weingartner, M. H. 1977. Capital rationing: N authors in search of a plot. *J. Financ.* 32:1403–32.

White, F. C., and V. R. Eidman. 1971. The Bayesian decision model with more than one predictor: An application to the stocking rate problem. *South. J. Agric. Econ.* 3:95–102.

White, F. C., and W. N. Musser. 1980. Inflation effects in farm financial management. *Am. J. Agric. Econ.* 67:1060–64.

Whitmore, G. A. 1970. Third-degree stochastic dominance. *Am. J. Econ. Rev.* 60:457–59.

Whitson, R. E., P. J. Barry, and R. D. Lacewell. 1976. Vertical integration for risk management: An application to a cattle ranch. *South. J. Agric. Econ.* 8:45–50.

Whittaker, J. K., and J. R. Winter. 1980. Risk preferences of farmers: An empirical example. In *Risk analysis in agriculture: Research and educational developments,* Ill. Agric. Exp. Stn. AE-4492, June.

Wicker, A. W. 1969. Attitudes vs. actions: The relationship of vertical and overt behavioral responses to attitude objects. *J. Soc. Issues* 25:41–78.

Wiens, T. 1976. Peasant risk aversion and allocative behavior: A quadratic programming experiment. *Am. J. Agric. Econ.* 58:629–35.

Wildermuth, J., R. Shane, and R. Gum. 1971. Risk and diversification in Arizona crop farm planning. *Prog. Agric. Ariz.* (Sept.–Oct.):8–10.

Wilson, J. H. 1977. Hoover's agricultural policies, 1921–23. *Agric. Hist.* 51:335–61.

Winkler, R. L. 1967. The assessment of prior distributions in Bayesian analysis. *J. Am. Stat. Assoc.* 62:776–800.

Wolfe, P. 1959. The simplex method of quadratic programming. *Econometrica* 27:382–98.

Wolgin, J. M. 1975. Resource allocation and risk: A case study of small-holder agriculture in Kenya. *Am. J. Agric. Econ.* 57:622–30.

Woolery, B. A., and R. M. Adams. 1980. *The trade-off between return and risk for selected Big Horn Basin crop and cattle feeding systems.* Wyo. Agric. Exp. Stn., RJ-149, Feb.

Yahya, M. T., and R. M. Adams. 1977. *Some measures of price, yield and revenue variability for Wyoming crops and cropping systems.* Univ. Wyo. Agric. Exp. Stn. Res. J. 115.

Young, D. L. 1979. Risk preferences of agricultural producers: Their use in extension and research. *Am. J. Agric. Econ.* 61:1063–70.

———. 1980. Evaluating procedures for computing objective risk from historical time series. In *Risk analysis in agriculture: Research and educational developments.* Dep. Agric. Econ. AE-4492, Univ. of Illinois.

Young, D. L., W. Lin, R. Pope, L. Robison, and R. Selley. 1979. Risk preferences of agricultural producers: Their measurement and use. In *Risk management in agriculture: Behavioral, managerial, and policy issues.* Ill. Agric. Exp. Stn., AE-4478.

Young, D. L., L. Calvin, and T. Wu. 1980. Price, yield and gross returns time series for crops in Washington State, Whitman County and the Columbia Basin. Agric. Econ. Dep. Staff Pap., AE 80–7, Washington State Univ.
Young, D. L., J. Landon, and R. Mahama. 1984. *Strategies for managing marketing risk for Palouse dry pea and lentil growers.* CARC Res. Bull., Washington State Univ.

Zadeh, L. A. 1973. Outline of a new approach to the analysis of complex decision processes. In *IEEE transactions on systems, man and cybernetics,* SMC-3.
Zwart, A. C., and K. D. Mielke. 1976. Economic implications of international wheat reserves. Sch. Agric. Econ. Ext. Educ. Discuss Pap. 1, Univ. Guelph, June.
_____. 1979. The influence of domestic pricing policies and buffer stocks on price stability in the world wheat industry. *Am. J. Agric. Econ.* 61:434–47.

INDEX